BLOGGING TOWARDS BETHLEHEM

Discovering the Eternal in the Seasons of Ordinary Time

Eugene Kennedy

Illustrations by Ronald Bailey

HiddenSpring

Jacket design by Trudi Gershenov

Book design by Celine Allen

Internal and jacket illustrations are by Ronald Bailey. Used with permission.

Library of Congress Cataloging-in-Publication Data

Kennedy, Eugene C.
    Blogging towards Bethlehem : discovering the eternal in the seasons of ordinary time / Eugene Kennedy.
        p. cm.
    ISBN 978-1-58768-042-7 (cloth : alk. paper)
    1. Catholic Church—Miscellanea. 2. Christian ethics—Catholic authors—Miscellanea. I. Title.
    BX4705.K379A5 2007
    282.09'0511—dc22

2007006276

Published by

HiddenSpring

an imprint of Paulist Press
997 Macarthur Boulevard
Mahwah, New Jersey 07430

www.hiddenspringbooks.com

Printed and bound in the
United States of America

For my Sally
who brings eternity into time

The illustrations contained
within this book
are dedicated to
Merry O'Donnell

...now I know
That twenty centuries of stony sleep
Were vexed to nightmare by a rocking cradle,
And what rough beast, its hour come round at last,
Slouches towards Bethlehem to be born?

—William Butler Yeats, *The Second Coming*

Contents

Introduction: The other side of every day

The world will never starve for wonders; but only for want of wonder.
—G. K. Chesterton

In one sense this book examines the events we witnessed together during the first years of this century. In another sense it is about everything we did not see but experienced anyway. These blogs chart the eternal we enter every day, even if we do not recognize it or cannot give it a name. These reflections open us to the timeless myths in which we all participate and to the wonder far greater than the wonders all around us.

We Americans think that there is a shot clock running on our lives. We are hard pressed to get our next play off, whether it is to find true love or our real calling, pay off our credit card bills, or just clear life's next low hurdle without getting snagged on the fencing. We are conscious of time sweeping away the seconds on our wrist watches, blinking digitally from every bank marquee and appliance, or leaving its telltale stamp on e-mails and voice messages. As we watch the sun set on a beautiful day, time seems to grasp our innards, leaving us with that poignant but profoundly human feeling that the gates are closing, that for all our hurry we are going to miss the last train anyway.

Marketing specialists tap into our common longing with "time saving" devices when, after a certain amount of experience, we know that time cannot be saved at all. Physicists discuss the possibilities of untapped dimensions of the universe. Perhaps, they suggest, time flows straight over a waterfall or it may resemble a serpentine river bending ever back on itself so that it may one day be revisited. They theorize that it may come in particles, waves, or strings. But who among us has not already experienced time in all these variations, in the grief that washes in like high tide or in the pain that unspools like an endless string or in the halo of fine particles that cling to little things so that they reinstate the past that has not passed at all.

Scientists speak of the possibilities of time travel while ordinary people embark on it regularly. That commuter supremely alone in the stopped car in the traffic jam, the student reading the paperback on the jolting subway, the shopper grazing tirelessly through the mall, those lighting candles in cathedrals or those lighting them at rock concerts: these people, just like you and I, are seeking American ecstasy, to have an experience by which they smash the constraints of time.

Others of us, of course, settle for second-hand ecstasy, delivered in movies or through television programs, such as the X-Files or its clones, that supply cut-rate fantasy and marked-down mystery. We seem never to tire of the tales of extraterrestrial visitors, of crop circles trimmed out by visitors from beyond, of a hangar in the Southwest where the government has hung the shriveled corpses of such visitors in silent and timeless exile. Some people feel that if we could break into the eternal secrets there we could break out of the temporal realities here.

Seeking ecstasy is, of course, a natural human activity, a clear signal about our nature, our transcendent possibilities, and the fact that although the poet speaks of "the measure of man" there is no measurement that adequately sums up the human person. Although a pseudo-ecstasy is for sale in various venues, real ecstasy is available free everywhere in ordinary life.

Ecstasy comes from the Latin *ex-stare,* "to stand out from." We remember those moments when we *stand out from* our everyday experience. They are as varied as falling in love, being in battle, or losing ourselves in creating something as different as a family meal or a work of art. In such everyday ecstasy, we feel our unity as persons, our harmony with the rhythms of the universe, our being free of time itself. Time's waves smooth out. It does not ooze in strings or hang heavy. Time disappears and we come upon the eternal that the mystics sought by fleeing the world and that we find every day in its very midst.

In fact, the eternal presses itself on all of us all the time. We may hear that the "kingdom of God is within you," but so bound are we by the constraints of time that we are unfamiliar or uneasy with the boundless eternal in ourselves. Ecstasy is not the smell of seasoned wood stored away in time but the fresh air of the unhidden eternal that we breathe all the time.

This book is about the eternal that we experience every day, the *mythic* dimension of our existence, that realm in which we experience our eternal depths. The great myths, such as those of the knights who seek the Grail, or the Hero's Journey, are not tales about legendary figures from a dimly lighted past. They are about us in the brightly lighted present. We keep alive the deepest human truths by telling them in story and symbolic form that insulates them from the ravages of time that invalidate encyclopedias and almanacs on the very day they are published.

These are our stories. Their meaning is not historical but spiritual, their truth is not temporal but eternal. We find ecstasy, that is, we stand out from our experience, by grasping its mythical, eternal character. The latest "re-enactment of Beauty and the Beast," as Joseph Campbell says, "is taking place right now at the corner of Fifth Avenue and 42nd Street."

This book tracks through recent events in time whose mythic elements—the great symbols of water and light and dark, for example—speak clearly of their eternal nature and of how they are not just about other people—the 9/11 victims, the single mother and the escaped killer, Terri Schiavo, or the hurricane and tsunami victims—but about us as well.

We understand myths when we open ourselves to their psychological and spiritual rather than their literal meaning. We come to understand that we are the characters in the myths, that we are tested by the great mythic challenges, that we are the knights who seek the Grail of ecstasy. The latter is not pleasure or fame but something simple, not so hidden and certainly in plain sight, that we live in the eternal as much as we do in time.

The Brink of a New Century

The millennium mystery: Y2K and the blog

Blogs, n. 1999... contain daily musings about news, dating, marriage, divorce, or politics... or millions of other things or nothing at all...
—Oxford English Dictionary

As the millennial year 2000 broke over us, computers were going to turn against us to bring an end to the world as we had known it. Y2K, a term now museum-case musty, was then a newly born force of evil that would plunge us at the stroke of midnight over the falls into a deep and silent mystery. We would be victims of what Saul Bellow called MOHA, the innate capacity of machines to resist and foil our using them effectively. All computers would reset themselves automatically to "zero zero," 00, shattering the binary code as Moses did the tablets of the commandments and scattering into the same night the digital entries by which we calculated time, measured progress, and preserved memory.

Like a hurricane changing direction at the last moment, this electronic apocalypse veered away and we did not lose our history or ourselves. Still, this non-event disappointed and to some extent depressed those who harbored, in Thomas Mann's phrase, "sympathy for the abyss." Nothing crashed, life went on, and the once impending mystery that would scramble our sense of time and place—our footing in the universe—did not occur.

It was no accident that in 1999, in the run-up to the millennium, the concept of the blog first appeared in the same computer universe that was generating fears of Y2K. Originating "in writing or maintaining a weblog," blogs "contain daily musings about news, dating, marriage, divorce, or politics... or millions of other things or nothing at all." Blogs are therefore bulletins from inside our common mystery, siftings of ordinary time for the glint of the eternal.

These essays are blogs on events that we have witnessed together and on others that I have shared with smaller groups of witnesses. Blogs are nets to capture the mystery that fills the incoming tide of this century, that mystery that infiltrates great events and those seemingly empty spaces of "nothing at all."

Allow me to begin with a personal blog about a mystery that we have all experienced at one time or another, the death out of due time of persons so filled with life that they seemed to challenge mortality. The whole nation felt it almost halfway back into the last century in the assassination of John F. Kennedy. We would feel it again in the new century in the death of thousands of good people on 9/11. With those who knew and loved Kitty Bitterman, I experienced it just as blogs were born and as we headed together on the rapids of time toward the steep drop of the year 2000.

Kitty's life and death symbolize what we have all experienced in this new century. She provides a signature note, a grace note for the great Mystery that flows from that great Deep beneath the surface of all of our lives. Kitty Bitterman was a woman in full who had known great love and great sadness. Let this blog, a blog written in the last season of the old century and delivered at Kitty's funeral, speak of her mystery and our mystery, of the eternal found in every moment of time.

The Last Season of the Old Century

Kitty Bitterman

Nearly the last words that our beloved, our dear Kitty—for none of us graced by knowing her can speak of her without such a sweet modifier —the last words our loving Kitty spoke came at the end of what we can now see was a perfect day for her—a perfect Kitty day. These were words she had spoken to all of us in one setting or another, cocking her head back, her Irish eyes twinkling, gently radiating an aura of wisdom about the world and how it can give you bad times as well as good, smiling—how easily and how often she smiled—she asked her family gathered about her, "Wasn't that fun?"

So she speaks to each of us now, as our memories cascade before our eyes, and how can we, of all those times and places we have stood with her or were touched by her, how can we not nod back at these words that sing the truth of her—for Kitty was magic for each of us— "Wasn't that fun?"

On the Sunday in 1986 after the spacecraft *Challenger* crashed into the Atlantic across the state from here, a wreath was dropped by air on the place in the ocean where it fell. Just before it hit the waters, a school of dolphins broke the surface to acknowledge that the mystery of that loss had been felt in the depths of the sea.

On that last beautiful morning, Kitty and Mike—and you cannot mention in that great love one without the other—Kitty and Mike had taken their long walk down to the shore and back. They were accompanied by a pair of dolphins—those beautiful and graceful creatures partly of the sea and partly of the broad world, and kin somehow to us, flashing in the sun as if straining for something beyond—and, as Kitty and Mike turned, so, too, did the dolphins to give them an escort, a tribute of the sea and the air and the sun gleaming on their skin—they saw Mike and Kitty all the way home as if they sensed that

Kitty Bitterman

for Kitty, whose grace and beauty rivaled theirs, the fullness of time was near.

Who can doubt that God had tuned the world and all its creatures to respond to Kitty? For the flowers turned toward her everywhere as did her Montana horses, as sleek and knowing as dolphins. Everything bright and beautiful responded to Kitty, as did everything bruised by nature or wounded by life, everything and every one of us, for we became less ordinary in her company.

Time was to Kitty as the sea is to dolphins. She was always breaking free, giving us a fleeting glance at the eternal in her and beyond us all. She was on easy terms with the eternal, for her daughter Amy was already there. So Kitty could say with peaceful confidence, "I know that when I die, Amy will be waiting for me."

"Nobody," St. John writes, "has ever seen God." Our only way of knowing what He is like is through the revelation He makes of himself in his creatures. Otherwise God would be as absent as some relative we don't hear from anymore, so busy with new persons, each with a fate as consuming as our own, that He long ago lost track of us. It is easy to be persuaded that we are wood shavings on His workshop floor and that is why our lives seem so random, so painful, so forgotten in the vast unfeeling universe.

But you cannot believe that if you know Kitty, whose whole life argues against the idea of an absent-minded God. Kitty's work on her last day—indeed, the work she did *every* day, was to extinguish such desperate thoughts by revealing to us through herself something of what God is really like.

"God," St. John writes again, "God is love." And, unsentimentally, Kitty was love, too. Kitty did nothing by halves. She loved wholeheartedly, as a mother does who knows the worst about us but loves us anyway. Kitty loved without reserve—the way she did everything—and, knowing that Kitty loved us, we glimpse how God loves us, not worrying about our frailties and faults, but whether our hearts, like Kitty's, are in the right place. For Kitty loved as God does that we might, as John writes, "have life and have it to the full."

And Kitty loved us in particular, thinking of Mike and all her family, her children and grandchildren, her nephews and nieces and the great extended family of her friends as individuals. So every one of her gifts was always special, thought out in a way that made it just for each in some secret pact of understanding that Kitty had with every one of them, and every one of us.

Kitty did all this naturally, spontaneously, enthusiastically, just the way she played golf. How could she be so free of self-consciousness? Because in that finest realization of love she did not think about herself, since she was too engaged with thinking of others. So she has made a God of love believable because in friendship with Kitty we have known something of Him, and known something of eternity.

That last perfect day was a classic Kitty day as she cared for Mike, for her beloved parents, Bill and Virginia, and, as the day moved along, she called her sister, Mary, twin to her in soul and heart, to propose a little party—and Mary and her husband George agreed. Was anything more typical of Kitty than one of her irresistible, no excuses accepted, invitations?

But first they would gather at Mike and Kitty's home, full of light and linked to sea and sky and the sweet green earth. And she asked, as the sun descended, as she had asked a thousand times since she was a little girl, if her father would recite his poem. And Kitty's mother, Virginia, mother indeed of Kitty's grace and beauty, as she had a thousand times before, said "No, not *that* again."

"Yes, daddy," Kitty said, that little girl so happy here with all those she loved best, gilded by the sunlight, and her father stood and began to recite:

> Sunset and evening star
> And one clear call for me
> And may there be no moaning of the bar
> When I set out to sea.

And Kitty stood with her father as God's creation whispered yet again in the rays that bloomed out of the sun as it was lost in the Gulf.

And so they went to dinner and Kitty changed the table to make sure that they were comfortable. And then in that time out of time that a family dinner can be, they lost themselves in stories and laughter—a delight spun out of the air by a loving wife and daughter and sister.

We can nod our heads, for we have all gathered with Kitty at just such a table for good food and good times. And now we understand what the Eucharist is like, this meal that nobody wanted to come to an end, at the center of which sat a host soon to complete his or her life's mission and to return to the Father. This time to be remembered as we remember it this afternoon, around this table, at this meal at which we recall the separation of the body and blood of the Lord, and are conscious of this great Mystery that Kitty has entered just ahead of us. "Come," she says, "you don't have to be afraid..."

And, back home, looking into this night in which nature withheld the moon, for Kitty was to reflect the light that evening, she saw her sister to her car and her parents to their room, asking, "Wasn't that fun?"

And Kitty herself lay down and the Lord came and so ready was she to meet Him, so often had she broken free of time as the dolphins do of the sea, that she entered glory without any spasm of pain, without any hint of struggle, but with that peace that God gives those who love as Kitty did. For her heart was too filled with love to bear the constraints of time any longer and she entered heaven as easily as she entered our lives or our homes.

We are not surprised to learn that newborn dolphins can keep up with their mother by remaining close and taking advantage of the aerodynamic effects of the mother's swimming. Who can doubt that God set the strings of creation so that they would make music when Kitty came by? How easy, then, for us to swim, not because of our own strength but because of the current of spiritual energy that flows from her and carries us along.

Who can say from that night without a moon to this morning when a rainbow arched across the sky, that God has not signaled us through his creation that Kitty is safely home, that we may still gain strength and direction from the wake she left in our lives and that, indeed, she is preparing for our reunion, that she is making the arrangements now, that she will be at the door, welcoming us as if we were her only guests, embracing us and ushering us into the warmth and light.

Kitty, dear Kitty, your last day, so sad for us, was perfect for you and, yes, we accept your invitation, yes, we will come as long as you are there. We know that somehow you will have gotten our sins forgiven and our records clean. As on that last perfect day for your family, you will have a good table, no drafts, where we will all fit and be comfortable.

And then, as now, we catch the deep love in that question you ask, to which we can only gratefully nod, "Wasn't that fun?"

The First Season of the New Century

Waiting for us in the past

Entering the new millennium resembled opening the gilded doors to the surprise party of history. It wasn't the last judgment but the first welcome from the people we thought we had left behind and who turned out, in myth and mystery, to have left messages of welcome everywhere for us ...

Just writing the date 2000 makes us thrill to the newness of the times. While we speculate about what waits for us in the future, however, we might also meditate on what waits in the past for every one of us, every day. Indeed, numerous flares touched off in what we call the past are just now bursting over our heads to throw light on us and on our lives.

Some of those flares were launched, of course, from the Titanic, whose story we have still not fully understood or absorbed. Its illumination comes not from movie special effects but from its passengers who remain so alive to, and so like, us: people packed for the future, each with loves and longings like our own, each whispering something to us as if death had never fully claimed them.

Their mystery is, of course, our mystery and it only deepens as we inspect their possessions, for they tell us how homely and human our things may seem to those who look at them a hundred years from now. How touching small possessions remain, how outside the grasp of time as they speak of affection and industry, of the rounds of daily life and relationship that remain now as they were then, true inventories of human hearts and souls.

So, too, the great British mountaineer, George Mallory, was waiting for us in the past, lying in the snow and ice half a mile from the peak of Mount Everest, preserved so that his discoverers could see the bruises that he might have sustained when he slipped to his death. His goggles were also found, along with the simple contents of his pockets, not so different from yours and mine. How like us this English gentleman is, speaking to us now across three quarters of a century, and how much his mystery parallels our own.

No expert can tell us if he died as he descended from conquering the peak or whether he lost his life just short of that goal. Even the team of explorers who found his body were driven away by the gales on that tallest steeple of earth. Does heroic effort survive history's passage, does it still tingle in the air around interrupted lives like Mallory's, so that we might be the discoverers of his eternal spirit as surely as the guides were of his earthly body?

So, too, waiting for us in the past, was an American town that had been abandoned for a great project that had for years submerged it in the waters of a man-made lake. As the astringent of climate slowly began to shrink the lake, the markers of that town began to emerge, each level with a new revelation about the places that had existed and the deeds that had been done, each one a jolt to the memory of the living. The town and, in a sense, their past lives, with their sins and glories, had been waiting in the past for them.

So, too, in the last spring of the century in Berlin, the bunker of Nazi propaganda chief Josef Goebbels lay waiting in the past. Like dozens of other bunkers from the Hitler period, it spoke of horrors that cannot be buried beneath a rebuilding city. As Alan Cowell wrote of it in the *New York Times* (April 8, 1998, "Underground History Surfaces Again in Berlin"), "even as [Germany] craves a future in which it can come to terms with its modern history, it is undermined by its past."

What that we have done and may have forgotten waits, like the ridges of the old town or the bunkers of Hitler's Berlin, within us ready to give testimony about us? Perhaps the greatest surprise that most people will have is that they will not be reminded of the bad things they did that they want to forget but of all the good things they did that they cannot remember.

The past even surprised that specialist of the past, the Vatican, when restoration of the facade of St. Peter's Basilica, like that of the Sistine Chapel ceiling, revealed the extraordinary colors that had been used by the original artists. A subtle straw-like color transformed the famous facade that was once bleached out by restrained white marble.

Is this an accident and no more? Or did this message wait in the past, as sacramental signs do, pulsing with an ever fresh message for those of us trapped in time?

Let those who want the Catholic Church to return to the past be prepared to discover that the past, far from being over-controlled, sings of freedom in brightly hued surprises that speak timelessly of its sympathy and support for, as well as its delight in, everything truly human.

Richard McCormick

The theologian and the cartoonist say farewell together

The new century began with good-byes to two extraordinary men whose callings seemed so different but whose goodness and integrity were so similar that coming from different directions they met, as mythical heroes do, at a final long destined moment in time. It seemed right that these men who brought such understanding to our human condition should enter eternity together...

Death took a harvest of the benevolent this past weekend, of good men whose keen eyes saw deeply into our imperfect nature, with its large and small vanities, and who loved us the more for it. The world at large knew cartoonist Charles Schulz better than it did the moral theologian Richard McCormick.

Laboring hard at different tasks into their seventies, both men tapped into a vein of the eternal so that their gifts to us can never be damaged by time. They remain forever youthful because they believed in ordinary people, concerned more about their possibilities than their liabilities.

Let me tell you a little about the great man called home on the same day with Charles Schulz by a God who understood what good companions they would be. Let me tell you about the greatest moral theologian American Catholicism has ever produced, Father Richard McCormick.

Father McCormick, son of a physician from Toledo, Ohio, became a Jesuit priest whose theological specialty extended—while not being limited—to bioethics, that vast area that encompasses all the critical questions about health care. Many of those questions are superficially debated in sound bites and headlines about our own human choices as patients, acceptable medical procedures, and the transformation of health care by economic considerations.

In his long, productive career Father McCormick produced numerous books and articles, each rooted in the Catholic tradition and each bearing his unique stamp of tight reasoning and splendid wording. Everything Dick McCormick did was right to the point, just as he was in person.

Blessed are the pure of heart, we say, but who are they anyway? We find out by meeting men like Richard McCormick. Purity is a rich concept that is diminished if we make it into a one-dimensional assessment of virtue. It is a function of how we do what we do best.

In the pure of heart, we encounter the full realization of Hemingway's often quoted but only partially developed idea of "grace under pressure." In Richard McCormick we experienced amazing grace under pressure in his readiness to draw from his deepest core and to use himself up in love and work. His pure heart is what killed him. Those of us less pure of heart cover our bets to protect ourselves, always holding something back so that we will have the cab fare home if the discussion becomes too hot.

That ungiven self betrays our fears as it shrinks our love and leeches the heart out of what could be our best efforts. The ungiven self is the scourge of a self-conscious country in which people can become so absorbed with how they look and what others will think of them that they cannot easily be themselves and lose track of what opinions they actually hold. How sad such people are, because their hearts are made impure not by lust but by fear.

In Dick McCormick we experienced the quality that Henry James identified in creative persons: that they "be all there" in whatever they do. Richard McCormick was "all there" in everything that he did, his heart and mind completely given over to the issue at hand. He was pure as great artists and athletes are, making an indelible impression because he was not out to make any impression at all. He was too unself-conscious to court a compliment, too free of affectation to make a calculation of the effects he produced in his brilliant body of work or in his equally luminous relationships with colleagues and friends.

Richard McCormick's purity of heart was clear in his great love for the church he served so wholeheartedly, in his love for the Society of Jesus, in his love for Notre Dame where he last served so well, and in his love for his family and friends, among whose great number my wife and I were blessed to find ourselves.

Meet him yourself in these words about the American obsession with "choice": "If the...exclusive emphasis is on autonomy, we will have excluded...those goods and values that make choices right or wrong...the key factors that make bioethics a moral enterprise. For they are the factors that support or undermine, promote or harm, the person. When the rightness or wrongness of choice is reduced to... this individual's choice, morality has been impoverished" (*America*, May 1, 1999).

Not as long, however, as we have the works and words of Richard McCormick to grant us light and courage.

Does the freedom to choose diminish the freedom to love?

The new millennium began with a political year that would be filled with both myth and mystery, knightly quests for the Grail of Power and, before year's end, mysteries inside mystery as we awaited the outcome of the contest. And all along the way, the professionally styled ambiguity about our freedom and our choices...

If Al Gore is the only candidate to use the phrase, he will use up everybody's quota of speaking or hearing about "a woman's right to choose," the public relations make-over of the "right to an abortion."

What, however, does this cleverly fashioned phrase really mean? Were we to decouple it from the abortion issue, what might we learn about this exaltation, if not divination, of individual choice? Even miracle drugs may have unexpected and unpleasant side-effects.

The genius of the public relations transformation of "pro-abortion" into "pro-choice" lies in its emphasis on individuals as the ultimately responsible agents of their actions—the last ones to sign off on the elections that define our moral selves. There is no morality—no possibility of goodness or badness, either—unless we "author" our lives.

The PR engineers do not have that richness of humanity in focus. They are concerned not with promoting moral authority but with choices of diminished grandeur that promote the illusion that we can control our lives. They pipe the tune of authority's ghost, posting the slogan that sells hamburgers, "Have it your way," on the walls of the soul.

Their tactic is not to qualify choice but to make it the same strength in everything so that the object of choice becomes indifferent and making the choice becomes supreme. Life then becomes a television set with two hundred mediocre programs on simultaneously. So what, the remote is under your control!

An unqualified emphasis on my right to choose what I want may actually lessen what it seems to expand, my freedom to grow as a human being. Before we build a wall, poet Robert Frost suggested, we should be sure of what we are walling in and walling out.

What do we "wall in" by so strongly emphasizing our right to choose? Ourselves, of course, as it places us firmly at the center of the universe where we can be sure that "our needs" are gratified or satisfied.

Walling ourselves in is another way of saying that we are raising our defenses, protecting ourselves from hurt but, at the same time, cutting off surprise, the charms of random discovery or chance acquaintance.

What do we wall out, if not the very things that make us ordinary people (and that is what we find, hidden, perhaps, but there beneath a bishop's forced piety, a politician's fixed smile, or a fashion model's stunned gaze), the simple gifts that make us human.

Isolating choice as the brass ring we clutch as our right to a free ride may wall out our chances for real love. It is hard to let love in if we are peeping at life over a wall, making our personality into a gated community to which we control all access.

Perhaps over-control was responsible for the muted themes on so many Valentine's cards this year. The *Wall Street Journal* reported a heavy emphasis on guarded sentiment, on highly qualified expressions of love, on a bland Bill Clinton–like double-speak about commitment, on greetings about as intimate as people waving to each other across a crowded room.

Is a generation finding that a heavy mortgage has been placed on the chance for love by a culture that makes individual choice the supreme good?

How do people who experience real and lasting love explain it? They speak not of choosing but of being chosen, not of maintaining control but of losing it, not of keeping their guard up but of happily lowering it, not of a cautious climbing but of a free fall and their balance well lost.

When people speak of love, they say that they did not find it, that love found them, that it surprised them, took them completely unaware, that, on that day, it was the last thing they expected. There is, then, an element of rapture, of being seized, of being transported rather than of being in cool control, that makes love an enthralling mystery rather than a due diligence exercise in a business takeover.

Perhaps, then, we need reflection before we blindly endorse the deliberately ambiguous phrase, "the right to choose." The cost of over-calculation in matters of our choice may rule out the magic that almost always comes to us by chance.

You can't take a stand on mid-air ethics

Nothing better reflected the carryover confusion from one century to another of making up ethics as you go along than a great newspaper's decision to institute an ethics column that resembled a musician improvising after the band had finished its last set at the country club dance...

Like the passenger sitting next to you on the airplane, American popular culture eagerly reveals its troubles to us. Just read a column entitled "The Ethicist" in the *New York Times Magazine* every Sunday.

While it is admirable that the nation's cathedral of newspapers should offer pew space for the discussion of what troubles the modern conscience, its mode and manner reflect rather than resolve the nation's ethical dilemmas.

First of all, who is able to speak as one having authority on ethics? According to the *Wall Street Journal*, Randy Cohen's credentials to write the column arise from his having been a "veteran television writer" for "David Letterman and Rosie O'Donnell."

You could not make up, as they say, the ironic triumph of having the ethics of a television culture examined by a writer of lines in the closest thing we have to invisible ink—late night lists and gags that disappear without a trace by dawn.

Don't criticize Mr. Cohen. He is just the barker for the sideshow that ensues, as it has in America, when people improvise their decisions because they are cut off from a dynamic moral tradition. In short, it is impossible to take a stand in mid-air.

Ethically impaired, we fail, as the columnist does, to distinguish between morals, law, and ethics. Morals are principles that are rooted in and wrested from human experience as the product of a long search and profound reflection on grounding and expressing intuitions about right and wrong, such as "Thou shalt not kill," that are embedded in our common human nature. America's sense of right and wrong rested on the Judeo-Christian tradition before we emptied it from the tabernacle and replaced it with the sacrament of individual choice.

The law, on the other hand, is not, of itself, either ethical or moral. It is rather that which is "set down" by a competent authority, such as the state. Good law may be in accord with fundamental moral principles but it may also be arbitrary, as in setting speed limits, and it may be immoral, as in Third Reich laws that justified the Holocaust. Law does not create basic moral insights. It may give voice to them, but only long after the moral insight has been applied to a certain situation, as, for example, the immorality of slavery.

Ethics are principles of right or good conduct, or a body of principles that codify the ideals and behavioral expectations of certain groups, such as lawyers or physicians. The word comes from the Greek *ethos*, which means "moral custom." Ethics reflect the ideals and spirit of specific entities and are, therefore, very different from morals or law.

Pause for a brief quiz. Do you think sexual harassment is wrong because it is against the law? Or because it violates professional ethics? Have we missed something here if this violation of another person's intimacy does not register on a deep level unless there is a law against it?

How does Vice President Gore's celebrated denial that "there is any governing legal authority" whitewash the solicitation of campaign funds on government property, or the general shakedown tactics of an administration that, in and of itself, parades the disasters that follow when a moral foundation is abandoned?

America's general confusion about these matters is advertised by the *Times* columnist who offers answers sometimes based on law, sometimes on tradition, and sometimes on a subjective sense of what is right and wrong.

This confounding of ethics, morals, and law is evident in other newspaper stories almost every day. A great many people expect the Supreme Court to author moral judgments when all it can do is pass on the constitutionality of laws. Legality and morality are by no means synonyms except in a country operating in the relativized space of thin air.

This problem is summed up in a *Times* story by Ethan Bronner published on June 1, 1999: "The nation's public schools, which taught the Bible routinely for generations but retreated from explicitly moral education in the individual rights boom of the 1960's, are under growing pressure to offer ethics instruction as a way to promote safe learning free of harassment" (*New York Times*, p. A17).

Further on, an official explains how muddled things have become: "...everyone is concerned about getting sued for infringing on the prerogatives of the family. No one knows where the limits are."

A return to the Judeo-Christian tradition would be a fine start.

These developments are merely the fulfillment of philosopher Daniel Callahan's observation: "If personal morality comes down to nothing more than the exercise of free choice, with no principle available for moral judgment of the quality of those choices, then law will inevitably be used to fill the resulting moral vacuum" ("Contemporary Biomedical Ethics," *New England Journal of Medicine*, May 29, 1980).

The Seinfeld Syndrome and Holy Week

The century began celebrating the "Greatest Generation" that met the demands of World War II, but one wondered at the first Easter of the new century whether the rising generation did not have challenges as daunting as those of their grandparents...

The Seinfeld Syndrome is more common than carpal tunnel and, as with the latter, it arises from the repetitive movements of modern life. Its treatment is spiritual but organized religion generally misreads it, viewing it as a cluster of moral faults rather than a muffled but anguished cry from the depths of the soul.

Afflicted with what sociologists dub the "new insecurity," young people feel hungry even though they live in a world of plenty. They cannot quite find their place or their true voice. In short, they inhabit a sit-com in which nothing seems to happen, there is no storyline, and one-liners substitute for conversations that never concern duty, honor, or any sense that dying to the self out of love or sacrifice might bring them life.

Religious leaders and other professionally righteous find them a target of opportunity for jeremiads against their attitudes and seeming self-absorption. They accuse them of not being Tom Brokaw's "Greatest Generation" whose members grew up in the Depression, fought World War II, and built American prosperity, all in a modest, dutiful, and quiet style.

These adjectives are not applied to today's young people, who might belong to chromosome generations, labeled X and Y by marketers eager to sell them an identity along with footwear, clothing, and music.

Parents wonder whether their children, some wading into and some climbing out of the Rio Grande of Thirtysomething, will ever be tested by Providence, Fate, or Bad Luck, and how they will react to such an ordeal.

These young people are, nonetheless, having a religious experience that is unnamed even though it is obviously a spiritual crisis.

Holy Week is *Everyweek* for *Everyperson* and its rhythms are *Everybody's* inheritance, including the young people who, lacking an external trial of war or want, bear within themselves a variant of the same human suffering that every generation has experienced. Its mystery has gone largely unrecognized by the religious traditions that could identify it as a challenge to their spirituality rather than evidence of their surrender to secularity.

The test faced by these young people may be likened to the uncharted preparation we find in the lives of heroes and prophets and in what are termed Jesus' "hidden years," particularly that period when He also was about to turn thirty. When nothing seems to be going on, a destiny is forming for each of today's young people. Its pain may be found in their lack of ease with all that is easeful. Their unheard question is not "How can I be born again?" but "How can I be born at all and become fully alive?"

This is the suffering of mid–Holy Week. Palm Sunday has passed while Good Friday awaits us all, including this young, mid-week generation living in a netherworld that matches that through which so many great figures, including Jesus, have passed on their way to the fulfillment of their lives.

Dante speaks of Aeneas, the first half of whose life passed before "he hardened himself to enter alone with the Sybil into hell and search for the soul of his father." What better describes this puzzled generation's quest than to find the spirit of their fathers, to learn, as Jesus did, that he had to be about the work of His Father?

So Dante, at thirty-five, felt that he had reached a high point in the arch of his life only to find himself "in the middle of the road of life ... in a dark wood alone." There, he tells us, he experienced the crucifixion, death, descent into hell and passage through Purgatory to Paradise before he found his way to serve the world. In Joyce's *Ulysses* (1922), Stephen Daedalus associates this high noon of his life with crucifixion as well. "Come," he writes, "I thirst."

This journey of descent into hell and ascension into heaven is applied in the creed to Jesus who, on the eve of His passion, found himself in the dark wood of Gethsemane, alone, His closest friends asleep with no grasp of how He would shortly complete His work and life.

Young people live in shadows as deep as those of Gethsemane. Like all men and women before them, they are headed each to a Calvary, and to the tests in which they will die a death in order to find the life they now long for.

As uncomprehending as the high priests of another time, many religious leaders call them out of this wood. They should instead meet them there and name for them its redemptive elements. Why do religious leaders so often sleep outside the Garden when their calling, as well as that of the younger generation, can be found only within it?

Long lost hearts that saved Holy Week

The Old Testament tells us that the Lord's voice is not heard in the whirlwind and the new millennium tells us the same thing.

Who could tell, despite the sweet first full moon of spring, that Holy Week would have such a surreal character that, as with the Resurrection, we would have to wait and watch for truth to emerge from a strange modern background of lies and distractions?

The week began with a *New York Times* story about what they termed the "downside" of a new drug for impotence that might help men not assisted by Viagra. The only problem, it appeared from the preparatory research, was that one in thirty men suffered such varied side-effects as getting dizzy, passing out, or driving their car off the road. In short, the earth moved for them, but not as they had expected.

Are these drug manufacturers serious or are they, as it seems from other ads, pioneering a new form of unethical ethics that is part public relations and part *Gotcha*?

The week on television displayed other direct advertising for drugs against backgrounds sunny enough to have been left over from Ronald Reagan's 1984 "It's morning again in America" campaign. Flowers bloom, children smile, fluffy clouds drift across a blue silk sky, and life is good.

Then a sweetly modulated voice quickly adds the equivalent of the fine print at the bottom of the page, the downside: "Some people have suffered dizziness, bleeding gums, nausea, or drowsiness. Do not use if you are pregnant or plan to drive a car."

This was merely a prelude, however, to the campaign unveiled in this same week by the R. J. Reynolds Tobacco Company. "The best choice for smokers who worry about their health," the ad reads, "is to quit." Jump to the next page, "Here's the next best choice."

The choice is Eclipse cigarettes, which, according to the *Wall Street Journal*, "may be less likely to cause cancer and other diseases in smokers." In short, get sick slowly. Did any of these advertising geniuses, champions of ethic-less ethics, look up the word *eclipse* in the dictionary?

Eclipse means "to obscure," "to darken," as well as "any temporary or permanent dimming or cutting off of light." Are these words that you want applied to your lungs or your life? The downside, as they say, is obvious in its signifying "a decline, a downfall," as in your health and well-being.

Then I read that, although there had been a big drop in the number of priests in the last generation, there had been a substantial increase in the number of bishops. Is this a great church, or what?

Easter Sunday would have seemed less surreal if government forces had found an empty tomb instead of a terrified Elian Gonzales in an incident that both mimicked and mocked the Resurrection. We freed him, in effect, to imprison him along with his father at the heavily armed Andrews Air Force Base. Perhaps next time the attorney general could just slay all the children under twelve years of age.

Dizziness was the week's side-effect. But there was an upside, a resurrection for us in a pair of stories about finding long lost hearts. One, in the chest cavity of a dinosaur, was grapefruit size, reddish brown, and fossilized sixty-six million years ago. Yet it had once pumped warm blood and may have been an ancestor of the warm-blooded birds who sing of new life for us every spring. What a mystery, one that was as steeped in age as the drug and tobacco ads had been in the passing moment.

The second heart, hardened into a reddish but much smaller stone, had belonged, sophisticated tests indicated, to the dauphin, the child of the last king and queen of France, whose short life was marked by illness and imprisonment, and a lingering mystery about whether he had died in the mean and darkened world of revolution.

Two lost hearts, each with a tale about time and chance, two lost hearts found with the truth still in them about the world they had known and what they had suffered, two lost hearts to buoy our own in this strangest of holy weeks when the world seemed to forget that, like the dinosaur and the dauphin, the truth—and the truth about us whose hearts can be lost at times, too—outlasts all the rewriting and distortion of this public relations age.

Remembering Cardinal O'Connor

The new millennium did not know that New York lost the very pastor it would need a year later when the Trade Towers were destroyed and thousands of people were killed. John O'Connor's successor, Edward Egan, left the smoldering and grief stricken city for Rome, claiming that he was doing so under obedience to the pope. If you knew John O'Connor you know that he would never have abandoned his city and would have been at Ground Zero on that day and throughout the weeks of searching for the lost that followed...

John O'Connor, who died as a cardinal archbishop of the Roman Catholic Church, was not yet an admiral in the United States Navy when I first met him. Fusing these titles summarizes his remarkable career and tells you something, but not quite everything, about this remarkable man.

It takes a special kind of person to achieve, in one lifetime, the highest ranks in two demanding institutions, the Navy and the church. John O'Connor's strength lay in the energy and the loyalty that he gave to these highly disciplined, by-the-book organizations. He did not, however, lose the special character of his personality or the twinkle in his pale blue eyes by investing himself completely in cultures of systems and obedience.

He was a chaplain who operated against the overwhelming and impersonal background of war by huddling in an intensely personal way over the wounded and the dying. When first we met, he was attending a workshop for chaplains at which I was a speaker.

Over the more than thirty years that have since passed, he often reminded me of a story I had told during one of the sessions, a story about bringing my father to a hospital where the receptionist gave me a tag and said, "You can forget your father's name but don't forget his number." That touched what he himself believed in.

You cannot understand John O'Connor at all unless you grasp his commitment to gaze personally at all those wearied or wounded by war or by life even after he had scaled the highest reaches of two rigid bureaucracies. In his case the uniform, whether Navy blue or Cardinala-tial crimson, did not make the man.

He was entrusted with high offices, however, because his superiors recognized that he would always support and stand by the institutions without betraying their confidences or awkwardly publicizing their mistakes. He was a stabilizer for the vessel of the Navy and a rock for the structure of the church.

John O'Connor entered the public arena as a truly counter-cultural figure in New York, a city that made little room and condemned as narrow-minded anyone bold enough to challenge its programmatic open-mindedness. As he saw his mission, it was to make clear what the Catholic Church taught on subjects, such as abortion, that power-ful and sophisticated New Yorkers had written off at sharp intellectual discount years before.

He gave voice to his institutional commitment as I rode with him one morning to visit a hospital during his first year in New York. "The Catholic Church resembles China, a sleeping giant that, when awak-ened, will be heard from."

And so, first to the city's irritation and finally, and grudgingly, to its admiration, the Catholic Church was heard from through John O'Connor. As A. M. Rosenthal, former executive editor of the *New York Times*, once told me, "I like the Cardinal. With him, as with few others, you know where he stands."

Not everybody—not even all his clergy or all New York Catholics —agreed with his positions. There was no doubt, however, that he was supporting the official views of the church and reflecting the mind of the pope who had appointed him to New York because, as the late Catholic historian Monsignor John Tracy Ellis put it, John O'Connor and the pope "were exactly alike."

He will be remembered, for good or for less than that, by many as a churchman, a man of the church who was willing to sacrifice his own feelings and to accept misunderstandings in order to stand by and with the institutional church.

He was all that, surely, but, as I sort out my memories of him, he was, first and foremost, something else as well, a pastor whose head may have been with the pope but whose heart was always with the people. He responded spontaneously to human suffering and need, going, without advance publicity, to accident scenes and fires, to hospitals and private homes, not because he had people's numbers but because he never forgot that they had names.

So I recall him as I found him one early morning in the chapel of his residence behind St. Patrick's Cathedral. Manhattan was waking up to the swelling sound of traffic. Cardinal O'Connor was kneeling upright in the first pew, his unsupported arms at his sides. He remained there, wholly concentrated, unaware that I had come and unaware when I left.

You cannot fake that, I understood, as I made my way to the great cathedral where he would say Mass half an hour later. It was part of his hidden life, of an uncompromising churchman who was, beneath his many titles and honors, what he wanted most to be, a parish priest and pastor.

Fix the airport, lose the mystery

*You may not know it, but somebody is planning to do good for you,
whether you want it done or not, right now. "Another screw-up," Saul
Bellow used to say of projects such as the following, "for the Good
Intentions Paving Company." We don't need good forced upon us as
much as we need to be freed to sense the mystery and the mythical that
whisper to us everywhere, even in airports, all the time.*

There is a move under way to make airports into destinations in themselves, according to "The Practical Traveler" in the *New York Times*,
with "innovations that make time there more bearable."

These are not the usual souvenir and magazine stands that accent
the fact that you are traveling. The makeovers are designed to make
you forget that you are traveling at all.

They include gourmet restaurants, gyms with saunas, steam rooms,
and swimming pools, a facility called "Kids on the Fly," the equivalent
of a day-care center complete with Legos and crayons, and "offices by
the minute" termed "Laptop Lane" in which you can "gather scattered
thoughts and send e-mail messages."

In short, all the discomforts of home and office. Thomas Wolfe is
famous for writing that "You can't go home again." These alarming
developments de-construct that into "You can't leave home at all."
Think of this the next time somebody's beeper or cell phone goes off at
the theater.

These so-called improvements are well-intentioned in the same way
that the recent planned burn of the dry forest near Los Alamos was. The
fire robbed thousands of people of their homes and of the large and
small mysteries that breathed and whispered from their pictures and
jewelry, from their tables and chairs, from the settings of their lives.

The transformation of airports into places indistinguishable from the places you have been and the places you are going obliterates the mysteries of travel and separation that are celebrated within them every day.

In "Mene, Mene, Tekel, Upharsin" (*The Stories of John Cheever*, 2000), John Cheever's narrator is waiting for a train in Indianapolis. "The station," he tells us, "proportioned like a cathedral and lit by a rose window—is...of that genre of architecture that means to express the mystery and drama of travel and separation. The colors of the rose windows, limpid as a kaleidoscope, dyed the marble walls and the waiting passengers..."

Train stations unconsciously acknowledged that something deeper than passing time or doing business occurred within their walls. They resembled churches right down to their pew-like benches because they were settings for the liturgy of life itself. Their soaring spaces and the shafts of pastel light that fell on their marble floors did not distract the traveler but instead provided a sacramental frame for the comings and goings, and all the waiting and expectation, too, that are aspects of the mystery of being alive.

That is why railroad stations are the setting for stories such as *Brief Encounter* that capture the excitement and heartbreak of impossible love. Why is it that we speak, as we do of few other activities, of the "romance of railroading"? Why did Monet so often paint, and why do we never tire of gazing at, the railway stations of Paris unless, with their light and shadow and curls of steam against the sky, they speak to the pilgrim soul in all of us about the spiritual nature of making or returning from a journey?

Railroad stations did not disguise their purpose but boldly immersed us in the mystery of being, as Christians are reminded, "in via," on the way, ever setting out to taste the novelty of someplace new and to feel the longing for everything familiar.

Railroad stations did not anesthetize us to the mystery of separation that is as central to our growth as it is painful to endure. In Norman Rockwell's remembered America, it is at railroad stations that people leave home for the first time to go to war or to go to college. It is to the same railroad stations that, changed utterly by their travel, they return. Railroad stations displayed the giant trains growling like dragons, reminding us that something mythical takes place whenever we travel. Railroad stations did not obscure but gave housing to the sacred moments of our lives.

Airports hold precious little of that mystery in the angled metal of their chrome sheds and bland concourses. Now, in the name of progress, they are going to extinguish any flickering of the mystery that inheres in every journey undertaken. Such special effects artists cannot see that these great places where people meet and say good-bye, where they embrace, sometimes in tears and sometimes in smiles, are sacred spaces in which all the important transactions of the soul and heart take place.

The modernizers are driving moneychangers back into the temple. They want to spare us the possibility of experiencing our own lives, of feeling their meaning as travel forces us to contemplate what we value and believe and how we are ransomed from mortality by love.

Sounds American, but it doesn't sound like progress to me.

A sense of humor, a sense of life

G. K. Chesterton once suggested that God hid his laughter from us. I am not sure whether the great British writer thought that God had good manners and did not want to embarrass us for all our foibles and misplays. He is present, I think Chesterton would agree, whenever we redeem ourselves and each other with forgiving good humor...

The vague moral climate that flowed like protoplasm over the threshold of this new century leaves the humorless but politically correct class searching for ways to bolster their sense of moral superiority. In Catholic tradition, this is known as Pharisaic scandal, named after the hypocritical religious leaders who pretended to be upset because Jesus mixed with prostitutes, tax collectors, and other sinners. In short, with people like you and me.

These tiresome zealots are back, as they say, having surfaced recently in at least two places, each group displaying differing symptoms of their impoverished souls. These groups overlap but you can easily tell them apart. One lacks a sense of humor, while the other lacks a sense of life itself.

The first group criticizes radio luminary Don Imus for allegedly allowing irreverent and prejudiced remarks to be made during his morning program. The only antidote for the plague of political correctness, of which such criticism is an example, is a sense of humor, the capacity to observe ourselves and our culture with an ironic appreciation for its fractured and uneven nature. An hour of Imus remains arguably better for the soul of America than a month of taking Pharisaic scandal at anything that may make us smile and, as a result, look more forgivingly at each other.

Worse than this is the artificial storm blown up by the special effects department of the Pharisaic Scandal Company about Saul Bellow's latest novel, *Ravelstein*, which is undeniably about the late Allan Bloom who taught with Bellow at the University of Chicago.

Nobel laureate Bellow is accused of "outing" Bloom by allowing Ravelstein, the Bloom surrogate, to die of AIDS. One had thought that the culture had become mature in being able to accept AIDS as an illness and that people, including priests, as a recent *Kansas City Star* series revealed, die from it regularly. To hold it scandalous that we can name the agent of a friend's mortality without blushing illustrates the perverted heart of political correctness.

These contemporary Pharisees have not been as interested in protecting Allan Bloom as in slamming Saul Bellow, a novelist whose works are suffused with a sympathy and support for all that is human.

I write under a handicap here because, unlike the critics, I know something about this. I am a friend to Saul Bellow and was to Allan Bloom and to both through years of good times together. It is hard to take seriously a *New York Times Magazine* article by a D. T. Max, in which his confidence in misinterpreting Mr. Bellow leads to a grotesque distortion of the man and the work. He concludes, for example, that Bellow is really writing about himself, that the great novelist can only say, "Ravelstein, c'est moi."

As to the idea that Mr. Bellow was jealous of Bloom, for example, the latter once told me of how moved he had been when, after the success of *The Closing of the American Mind*, Bellow had embraced him and said that, with his new fame, "We are now equal in everything," and gently told him of the "sleepless ecstasy" it would bring to him.

Mr. Max should have followed up on the clue Mr. Bellow offered about the art of fiction, "Very few people understand it... They try to line it up with certain knowable facts, but it doesn't always work that way."

Mr. Bloom knew that what he described as Mr. Bellow's "great dark observing eyes" saw him deeply and saw him whole. Perhaps he was anticipating the result when he told me, "I'm a schlemiel. I spend money, get spots on my tie, and am the recipient of some of Saul's best wit but there is always a tenderness to it."

Thomas Mann's grasp of the novelist's "duty" was once summarized as "...to observe and to name exactly, wounding, even possibly killing. For what a writer must name in describing are inevitably imperfections...Perfection lacks personality...What is lovable about any human being is precisely his imperfections. The writer is to find the right word for these and to send them like arrows to their mark— but with a balm, the balm of love on every point. For the mark, the imperfection, is exactly what is personal, human, natural, in the object, and the umbilical point of its life."

Saul Bellow has delivered the gloriously alive and spectacularly imperfect Mr. Bloom just as he was. Bloom died of life, lived recklessly but fully. The point is not that everyone may now know of his last illness but that they may know him exactly as he was and, to his friends, still is.

Garry Wills, John the Baptist, and passionate belief

Scholars who came to fine flower in the old century bloomed more fully in the new century. Among them was Garry Wills, and full disclosure bids me to say that we are friends. Nonetheless, I can say that he is our Chesterton as a man of profound faith, deep intelligence, and a commitment to the truth. Every century needs at least a few such observers in order to survive and bloom itself.

Garry Wills will be on the short list for the John the Baptist award, the Johnnie as modern culture might term it, for his just published book, *Papal Sin*. He joins Father Donald Cozzens, nominated earlier for his speaking the truth aloud about the gender identification problems in seminarians and priests.

John's voice boomed out of the desert the electrifying truth that the day of the Lord was at hand. His head was the price for his prophecy.

The timorous always go for the heads of the brave. They want the will, too, but never ask for the heart, perhaps because they have no interest in love and are afraid of passion.

Heresy hunters were the first advocates of political correctness. They still seek conformity, that superficial propriety so akin to superficial religion: think what we think; do what we say.

Authentic prophets have always been compelled to "recant" or "withdraw" what they have preached or written and to "submit" their wills to superiors who usually order them to bury their God-given talents in the earth, in unmarked graves if possible, never again to use them to glorify God or to serve His world and His people.

Peter Abelard was condemned for teaching the scholastic method begun by St. Albert the Great that inspired St. Thomas Aquinas and, centuries later, became the house philosophy of the Catholic Church.

He was forced to burn his work in the presence of his fellow monks and to recite in tears the creed. "And so," he later wrote, "it was burnt." How powerful the words remain these many centuries later.

Garry Wills might as well switch to the Baptist's diet of honey and locusts because in *Papal Sin* he reflects, in words cut sharp and clear as diamonds, on how poorly the richness of truth has been served by the impoverished bureaucratic maneuvers of so many high Catholic leaders, the will- and head-hunters of the official church.

Mr. Wills hands over neither, for he represents that generation of faithful Catholics whose theological sophistication and love of the church as a Mystery equals or surpasses that of most bishops who must view it as an Institution.

Mr. Wills reviews what he terms "historical" and "doctrinal dishonesties," ranging from the church's hardly perfect relationship with the Jewish people to its own often highly deceptive dealings with its own people.

These include the bureaucratic manipulations that overturned the work of the special commission established to study birth control at Vatican Council II. The overwhelming recommendations of that group, to which the testimony of human experience was brought by the laity who participated, and with which the special sub-commission of bishops, including the future Pope John Paul II, agreed, were overturned, largely on the basis of an argument extraneous to the theology of marriage and sexuality.

That political argument was championed by then head of the Holy Office, Alfredo Cardinal Ottaviani, whose unauthorized rump commission triumphed by arguing that the church could not have been wrong about birth control and that any change would be an admission of error. The church, of course, had already revisited an issue that, like birth control, it had once declared intrinsically evil, usury. It purified charging interest on money and made smooth the way for Christian capitalism.

Forcing arguments against the grain of truth continues, especially, as Wills shows, in the official refusal to examine the scriptural texts, such as "There are those who make themselves eunuchs for the kingdom of God," that, in the light of modern scholarship, do not refer to the superiority of virginity over marriage, celibacy for priests, or the exclusion of women from ordination. Pope John Paul II has so employed them and seems surprised, indeed annoyed, that Catholics don't surrender their minds or wills to him on these matters.

Mr. Wills writes from the heart as well as from his brilliant intellect. He writes with a rare quality, that passion for truth that church leaders have ignored, perhaps because they don't understand that the heart symbolizes and expresses the unity of human personality they have so long divided into flesh and spirit, intellect and emotions, in order to conquer it.

Mr. Wills is a passionate Catholic, a believer who is an expert on everything from Augustine to Chesterton. Others, unwilling to deal with his arguments, will criticize his tone, described by the generally pre–Vatican II *Wall Street Journal* as "ferocious."

That is probably what they would have said of the original John the Baptist, too. Garry Wills heralds an era in which church officials will no longer be able to demand the heads of thinkers but will be forced to examine the truth whose power frightens them because it makes them free.

Vatican irony: free hit man, throw out nun

Nobody should have been surprised, I suppose, that the new millennium began with the same condemnations of homosexuality that had echoed throughout the previous centuries. How much the world would change for the better if righteous religious leaders would look more deeply at these men and women—and they are present in every family—and realize that homosexuality is a way of being human.

The stories ran close in time but were worlds apart.

We begin at the end of the extraordinary narrative of the pope's long ago tendered forgiveness of the man who almost killed him, Mehmat Ali Agca. The pope used the Vatican's diplomatic influence to obtain a pardon for the once boyish, now silver haired former hit man. The story appeared after he was already back in Turkey.

It was a remarkable example of Christianity in action, of the "forgiving our enemies" that is so easy to talk about and so hard to do. Good for the pope.

Hidden, like her life of devoted service, on an inner page of a Saturday edition was the story of the way that the fully deployed Vatican bureaucracy had dealt with a nun who brought not death to others as did the wily Agca, but life as did the guileless Jesus. Sister Jean Gramick, whose hair had grown silver in her long years of pastoral ministry to homosexuals, was sent away from the Vatican and at its insistence out of her beloved School Sisters of Notre Dame for allegedly failing to uphold the church's teachings on homosexuality. Sad for the pope.

The cold and merciless tone of her being separated from her work alerted all the angels of the imagination. Had she worn epaulets on her habit, they would have been ripped off righteously in St. Peter's Square.

To top off her ousting, she was also asked to sign an agreement never to speak of or reveal the processes of investigation to which she and her co-worker, Father Robert Nugent, had been subjected.

Can it be true that if you shoot the pope, you can be forgiven and become a poster boy for Christian clemency, flown home to be pardoned soon for other crimes, all this in a haze of deflected papal glory? And can it be true that if you preach the gospel to homosexuals to encourage and help them, you are not only suspected of doing evil but you are tried, dismissed, silenced, and shipped home in a haze of unearned shame?

Officials will tell you that Father Nugent and Sister Gramick were not sufficiently orthodox in holding that homosexuals carry within them what the Congregation for the Doctrine of the Faith has clumsily termed an "objective disorder" and that they have not been clear enough in telling homosexuals that, in effect, the church looks down on them as it demands perpetual and perfect chastity from them. Sister Gramick's grave offense is that she has been good to those the church says are bad.

Sister Gramick has cooperated fully with the Vatican examination of her work. Just as moving as the pope's forgiving a murderer is this nun's reported patience, generosity, and unwillingness to criticize the church or her accusers during this ordeal.

Now found guilty of doing good, she honors herself and all believers by refusing to accept the judgment, the shame, or the silence that self-satisfied men want to impose on her. Following Thomas More, she refuses to sign an oath that would falsify her conscience by requiring her to accept the silence and exile ordered by Vatican officials in what they term a "clarification" of the ban placed on her work last summer.

That the would-be assassin is set free while the giver of life is forced out of the church can be so bewildering that all such Vatican announcements should carry a warning label: Contains deadly doses of unacknowledged irony and is definitely dangerous to your spiritual health.

Many Catholics would like to find a way to excuse the official church for such a blunder, but its twinning with the Agca "go now and sin no more" (see John 8:11) makes this very difficult. The pope and bishops may wonder why Catholics no longer hang on their every word. Perhaps it is because by just such flexes of power church leaders weaken their authority.

The truth is that nobody knows enough about homosexuality either spiritually or psychologically to make the unforgiving judgments that the Congregation for the Doctrine of the Faith has so confidently issued about it over the last quarter century. But everybody knows enough about the way Jesus treated sinners, harlots, and even tax collectors to reject the blanket ban on homosexual ministry that, through this case and other actions, such as denying church hospitality to meetings of the gay Catholic group, Dignity, indicate the Vatican's Unconditional Surrender policy toward homosexuals.

We wonder at the anger directed toward a good and gentle woman and at something else as well: why are Vatican officials so terrified of homosexuality? There's irony in the real answer to that question, too.

About Sir Alec Guinness

The media, reversing while taking on the role of the Inquisition, sometimes seem more interested in stamping out faith than in identifying heresy. Dissenters in any realm are applauded, but people who live by faith, like Sir Alec Guinness, are stripped of this integrating center of their lives when they are dead...

Sir Alec Guinness's death last week, like sundown in a British colony, caused the cannons to boom in glorious farewell. He was commemorated in all the media that signal first-class mourning: on the *News Hour with Jim Lehrer*, that pantheon of the distinguished dead, and with a full-page, graveyard acre of his own, in the *Times* (an honor that means you are a truly famous person and that they have been expecting you to die for some time).

Subsequent tributes, such as one by Holy Cross professor Steve Vineberg in the Sunday *New York Times* (August 13, 2000), mentioned him with Redgrave, Richardson, Olivier, and Gielgud, noting that his "self-presentation was more modest...his manner was deceptively ordinary." Vineberg suggests that we mark Guinness's passing by watching *Last Holiday*, an early film.

One may agree and yet wonder how what was central about this good man and great actor was not mentioned at all: his profound spirituality and deep Catholic faith that were seamlessly integrated into his life and work.

In this political season in which candidates are trying to show us how publicly religious they are, with the media underscoring their relationship to Jesus or to orthodox ritual, it is remarkable to have had the company of a man who was truly religious and who ended up with nobody noticing it.

But perhaps that tells us something about genuine faith and how, when it is practiced well and deeply, it does not get attention because it does not cry out for notice as it quietly informs every aspect of a person's life.

Although I never met Sir Alec, I knew him and spent a lot of time with him, but not because of his movies, which cinema savants think are all that he left behind.

I was in his company in the three memoirs he wrote, the last of which, the prophetically titled *A Positively Final Appearance* (1999), was published last year. In this and in *My Name Escapes Me* (1996) Sir Alec allows us to accompany him through the seasons of his later life as, with his wife of more than sixty years, Merula, they keep their gardens, feed their fish, visit—and are visited by—the famous, and make delightful journeys into London and beyond.

One could say, more truly than it was said of Seinfeld, that nothing happens. And yet everything happens and Guinness greets it all with a sense of wonder that would have done credit to G. K. Chesterton, that genius of everyday miracles. For Sir Alec faces every day with a vision of a redeemed world, of a universe just rolling free, like a ball of stars, from the hand of its Creator, seeing it and seeing into it with faith at the same time.

There is nothing tortured, no pious underlining, just the natural reflections of a man whose Catholic faith illuminates everything as effortlessly as he made his acting seem. How could the obituary writers miss what he wrote about with such grace on almost every page of his charming books?

It may be that, after he became a Catholic, just before making *The Bridge on the River Kwai* (1957), he felt, as many other converts have, that he had come home and that he no longer needed to search spiritually.

He writes about his conversion at length in *Blessings in Disguise* (1986), telling a story that the late Joseph Cardinal Bernardin of Chicago found of such great insight that he passed it on to priests who, in that time when charges of pedophilia were being made against their ranks, needed support for their trustworthiness.

Sir Alec was not needed on the set and so, in his cassock for his role as Chesterton's Father Brown, he started walking back to his quarters in the French town of the location shooting. He had not gone far, he writes, "when I heard scampering footsteps and a piping voice calling, 'Mon pere!' My hand was seized by a boy of seven or eight, who clutched it tightly, swung it and kept up a non-stop prattle. He was full of excitement, hop, skips, and jumps, but he never let go of me... Suddenly with a 'Bonsoir, mon pere'... he disappeared through a hole in the hedge... and I was left with an odd calm sense of elation... I reflected that a Church which could inspire such confidence in a child, making its priests, even when unknown, so easily approachable, could not be as scheming... as so often made out. I began to shake off my long-taught, long-absorbed prejudices" (*Blessings in Disguise*).

How could they miss the stream of goodness that nourished Sir Alec's soul and still nourishes our own?

Midsummer surprises for the soul

As with love, which demands falling rather than planning, wonder, sometimes dressed very simply or even out of style, brings us presents that we never expected at moments that truly surprise us...

Surprises, the dictionary tells us, may cause us "to feel wonder or astonishment." That kind of surprise is hard to come by. It's something like finding a firefly midst the fireworks, especially in a culture that has come to value sensation far more than genuine surprise.

That everything must be bigger, louder, or more vulgar just to get our attention is attested to by the summer movies that are designed for the gross-out generation. These movies feature belches and other mainstays of adolescent humor, as many commercials on television also do. A generation from now some anthropologist will get a doctorate by studying the role of the urinal in male socialization. In such low-grade humor, there are never any surprises.

On the very same passing-through-puberty-plane are films that call themselves adult entertainment. There are no surprises in any of these either. Pseudo-adults do not watch them to be surprised or to feel wonder or astonishment.

By its nature, a surprise of any kind goes against the grain of a culture that exalts personal choice as a value in itself, irrespective of what is being chosen. Anybody who makes a "right" out of every whim of their individual choice can only be upset by even a minor surprise springing at them from the side of the road to interfere with their highly private journey.

What else would explain "road rage" except the explosive conflict of individual choices about lane, speed, and right of way, powerful symbols of the isolation of self and desire that results from over-emphasis on one's own choice? The dictionary terms this kind of surprise "an unexpected encounter" in the sense that "encounter" means "to meet an enemy."

And the iron-clad act of individual choice, as I have written before, rules out experiencing surprise as "being seized," which is what its origin in Middle English, *surprysen*, signifies. Putting our choice first may harden us to being chosen, as we are whenever we are "taken" by the light in autumn woods, by the innocence that lifts off newborns, or by a book or painting that opens our lives by giving us a whole new way of seeing things.

Many good people experience pain and frustration as they try to make foolproof individual choices about the very thing that must surprise us if it is to enter our lives at all, love itself. For in love we are surprised, we are taken, we are swept away. We abandon our devotion to the gods of personal choice once love chooses us. The first lesson of real love, of course, is that we cannot choose it at all, that it chooses us in a sweet and irresistible surprise.

Once we understand that we cannot control the important experiences of living, we encounter surprises that nourish the soul and gladden the heart in the course of everyday living.

Who would expect, for example, to find it in the heart of big, anonymous cities, in the very crowds whose faces seem set against any challenge, in these fast moving groups of commuters, each of whom, the stultifying popular legend tells us, is thinking of nothing but dot coms and stock options and millions of dollars fluttering down on them.

Yet, follow these groups, as the *New York Times* did, and find people who, by "chance meetings," discover each other's love for chamber music. They gather, these people who surprise each other, to play over the scores of Mozart, Brahms, and Beethoven, transforming the soaring gray condominium buildings from within. The lonely city surprises us with the beautiful sounds of musical companions doing something that they love together.

The *Times* tells us that "the amateur classical music world... extends far beyond chamber groups. There are orchestras: the Doctors' Orchestra, the Lawyers' Orchestra, the Brooklyn Heights Orchestra and ensembles at the Bloomingdale School of Music and 92nd Street Y."

Manhattan has been seized by an unreported epidemic of fine music that does wonders for the soul and does not harm the body. Indeed, great music harmonizes and integrates the dimensions of personality. It is one of the side-effect surprises of art.

Just as surprising are the comments of one of the players. "Chamber music," he is quoted as saying, "by its very nature is a kind of analogue for community. It requires cooperation, it requires empathy, it requires listening to other people, all the things you have to do in society to make society run successfully."

Perhaps New York has become safer because of its secret musicians as much as its public police. That is a midsummer surprise that is good for everyone's soul.

Religion not as bad for politics as politics is for religion

The election season of the new century provided a political campaign and election that made one wonder if, despite all the talk, the separation of church and state that keeps Christmas displays off church grounds and the Ten Commandments out of schools is in practice something of an illusion...

The pundits and prophets have got the church/state issue backwards in this election season. Like actors relishing Shakespeare's greatest speeches, these observers lick their borrowed phrases as children do ice cream, letting them loll on the tongue, reluctant to let them disappear. They are all for maintaining a wall of separation between church and state.

But, as Robert Frost once famously asked, are they sure of what they are walling in or walling out? To which they respond in unison, unaware that they look like the monks in a choir whom they fear, that church must be kept out of the state. Don't you know how dangerous Right Wing Religion would be in the West Wing of the White House?

The readiness with which many people recite this sentiment suggests that it is a safe and politically correct position, laundered, like Mafia money, in the vats of the public relations complex so that it will pass as genuine American thinking.

The real danger, however, is, and has been for some time, just the opposite. We need to keep politics out of religion, out of churches, temples, storefront chapels, and Quaker Meeting Houses, too.

Let us start by refusing to allow any candidate to make a visit to the University of Notre Dame during this election season. The men who want to be president of the United States don't stop in South Bend, Indiana, to get the student vote. Hopeful commanders-in-chief want to use this Catholic symbol *par excellence* not to extol faith but to ravish it for their own purposes.

Is Catholicism made stronger or are its teachings better understood because some politician utters words written by someone else with the Golden Dome in the background? Or do we find here the subtraction of grandeur and mystery that is the predictable side-effect of political posturing in sacred places?

Can we possibly think that Buddhism was left untarnished by the sordid political fund-raising in a California temple and the subsequent indictments, denials, and downright lies that have followed ever since?

What has been the effect on Orthodox Judaism of Senator Joseph Lieberman's becoming the first Jew to run on a national ticket? We are all delighted that a Jew has been chosen at last for such an honor. But does it honor or does it manipulate the Jewish faith? Do we respect it more, as we hope, or less, as we fear, as a result?

Lieberman has spoken, with mixed effect and reaction, about the need for religious faith in American life, but is he championing authentic commitment to his tradition or employing it, even with a salting of sincerity, to reveal not the power of prayer but his prayer for power? Is our respect for Judaism enhanced or is it in some way diminished by our seeing its traditions and teachings interpreted and applied by politicians in conversations with people like Larry King? What can we be thinking?

Do politicians enter African-American churches to celebrate the living faith of their congregations or, in the style of vampires, to drain off their spiritual vitality for themselves? Candidates do not climb into these pulpits to *be* religious; they want to *seem* religious, for the common characteristic of politicians is to like the *idea of being religious* more than really *being religious.*

Does Protestantism seem a more lively and inspiring faith because the candidates tell us that they are born again or that they often ask themselves, "What would Jesus do?"

You want to know what Jesus would do? He would drive all these vote-seekers out of houses of worship as swiftly as he did the money-changers from the temple.

Jesus recognized that using religion is always more harmful than persecuting it. At least persecutors are not hypocritical, which is more than can be said for politicians who involve themselves in religion as they pursue high offices in a low manner.

It is even worse when political leaders actually mix their religion with political thought. If you want a reminder of the danger of a politician breaking into religion, think of former Governor Mario Cuomo, who made much of his faith but did not seem like Thomas More when the Clinton forces refused to allow speaking time to any pro-life speaker at the 1992 convention.

Common sense, as we know, is the sense of the community. And most Americans do not want church and state confounded in public life. They understand that the danger is far less that theologians will violate politics than that politicians will corrupt belief.

Save the spiritual environment: kill a pundit

Everybody talks about political pundits but nobody does anything about them. The shadow spreading across our national life falls less from the century rising before us than from the pundits hovering over history like ambulance-chasing lawyers at a traffic accident.

The great task for well-trained theologians and scripture scholars is described as hermeneutic or interpretation, that is, a fine and scholarly examination of texts to discover the depths and riches of their true meaning.

This has been appropriated in America by the pundit class that crawls and crowds the television grid as primates do the monkey bars. They are everywhere in election season, turning interpretation inside out by offering unscholarly impressions of the surface of significant events.

Real depth in this field may have died with the late Eric Sevareid, whose true learning and experience made him a man wise enough to establish some distance between himself and the personalities and events on which he commented. He not only cared about truth and falsehood but he understood attributes, such as honor, that are hardly mentioned these days.

Indeed, so fascinated with themselves are many current oracles of the media that when they run out of topics, they talk about themselves or each other. It is almost impossible to watch anything, such as a presidential debate, without pundits first telling us what we will hear and then telling us what we have heard.

This excess of explanation, often slanted one way or the other, is oppressive and removes us, by at least one degree of abstraction, from being contacted by, or making contact with, the candidates themselves. That is hard work, since we must give our full attention to what office seekers say and how they say it if we are to establish that minimum of relationship that may be termed human.

Here we are on sacred ground, because only through that real human contact can we truly say that we have faith in, or that we trust, one or the other.

This is a spiritual exchange and it not only requires the candidates to pierce their public relations engineered phoniness and reveal what they are really like but it demands that we attune ourselves to them, that we scrub, as surgeons do before an operation, so that we will not be contaminated by the preconceptions, often as subtle and invisible as bacteria, left on us by pundits.

Proof of the need to be pundit-free, whether we are Democrats or Republicans, comes from the sentiments expressed by so many people after the debates. Perhaps even you have overheard yourself saying of one candidate or the other, "I was surprised that he was different from all the things said about him or from all the impressions I had of him." By premature interpretation ("This is what he will say... This is what he said"), pundits interfere with your own ability to see and hear for yourself.

Pundit means, first of all, "a Brahminic scholar," and, second, "a learned person" (*American Heritage Dictionary*). Now we are getting somewhere in understanding and arming ourselves against pundits.

In Hinduism, Brahmin refers to "a member of the highest caste, originally composed of priests, but now occupationally diverse." Pundits functioning inside the beltway certainly see themselves as members of a higher caste or they wouldn't talk down to us so much.

It also refers to "a breed of domestic cattle... having a... pendulous dewlap." How often the pundits resemble cattle, milling amongst each other, making the same lowing sounds and, yes, some even have dewlaps.

To test this notion, ask yourself: when was the last time that you heard a contemporary pundit utter a truly original thought? America needs Pundits Anonymous. When one starts to pontificate, he or she calls another up to get talked down from it.

In the last weeks before we make choices that will shape the century, we may serve ourselves, our souls, and our country well by turning off all pundits and following the advice of St. Thomas Aquinas: "Trust the authority of your own instincts," that is, what you see and hear in and through yourself and your own experience.

That is spiritually sound and patriotic at the same time. It will also be a great relief.

The election's spiritual legacy: splitting America

America awakens after the election as a man does after falling down the stairs. He hurts all over but he is still alive, although he rises shakily and is unsure of what has happened to him and why.

The country's spirit has been tested in a way that was unpredicted by the prophets of politics, mis-measured by the exit-poll accountants, and mis-reported by the anchor men, the lesser gods of our television culture.

How can we understand an event that puzzles these outriders on whom we depend to tell us, first, what happened to us, then that it happened to us, and, finally, why it happened to us? That scores of lawyers who were dispatched to the Florida recount as if to an accident scene only underscores the feeling that something happened beyond our control, something beyond the vocabulary of our ordinary media traffic-controllers, too.

That, however, has always been the nature of spiritual crises. It is not that they hide themselves as much as that we have lost our capacity to recognize and identify them and so they surprise us by their impact on us. This can happen in a culture in which, for example, everything is interpreted for us in the lexicon of economic causes and effects.

We are told of the wisdom of market forces, that the market itself speaks, and that, if we listen to it, its cost/benefit vocabulary will explain all human activity, including sex and love. If the culture's confusion about the latter subjects is any indication, then we should be wary of economic explanations.

What occurred in Election 2000 is far better understood, as, indeed, is our confusion about sex and love as a spiritual experience, that is, one whose energies are psychological and whose determinants are moral.

This election may one day be viewed as the true legacy of a period in which the country's psyche was infected by a public ethic that reduced all behavior and decisions to a common denominator below sea level. We were persuaded not to examine our motivation too seriously by assurances that, as we had been forewarned, it was the economy, stupid, and, as long as the good times rolled, and the god Greenspan kept inflation under control, we could survive lying, manipulation, and the decay of moral standards.

That brings us to President Clinton, whose legacy we may identify at last. Nothing could reflect his personality more accurately—or better illustrate the powerful influence of character on our nation—than the agonized and agonizing division that emerged, as an unsuspected but true image does in a developing photograph, in American life on election night.

Perhaps the president had goals so high in public service that they camouflaged the low means that he settled for in setting the tone not only for his administration but also for the mood of the country during the prosperous 1990s.

Yet, everywhere one looks around this man, whose great gifts make him a tragic figure, one finds scalding and dangerous divisions. The nation has been so affected by his personality that the latter, of itself, splits electors so that many vote, not for the men running but as an expression of their like or dislike for him.

The lives and worlds of many people close to President Clinton have also been split. Think of those in prison, those forced to resign, those betrayed by his pledge that he never had sexual relations with a White House intern.

We need only remember the rancorous seasons visited on the nation by his behavior. He has stood divided before us, as faithfulness is from infidelity and honor from disgrace, so that we have had a split-screen passage that induced stress fractures in the nation. These were ignored because, in the language of economics, we were told to write it off, to take the good of prosperity and pay the price of the tolerable bad of a divided and degraded sense of morality.

President Clinton's legacy may be found in the division of the nation that bloomed from seeds long ago scattered by public relations offensives designed to scorch the earth and squelch the truth at any cost, by a fouled atmosphere in which sex and love were, in fact, roughly separated from each other on a national stage.

The evident division in America is no accident and, since it was caused by a public relations approach to honor and honesty, it cannot be treated by further applications of that strategy.

Sadly for us and the president, his legacy of divide and conquer in public and private life is now the spiritual crisis in America's public and private life. The next president must attend to this before anything else.

The moments for which we give thanks

The ongoing election uncertainty, one day this way and another that, is really an out-size version of our own lives...

This tumultuous season parallels the great American dream of completing our trek to the top of the ski slope so that we can use gravity and grace to glide smoothly down the rest of our lives. That is why we hear ourselves saying, "As soon as ..." Complete it as you will: "the kids move out," "the mortgage is paid off," "my pension is vested," "I hit the lottery..."

Life, like a gentle confessor, listens carefully and asks, "And then what?" It's the "then what?" that gets us.

We look forward to freeing ourselves from our daily emotional, financial, and physical concerns. But when people stop worrying about their kids, they start worrying about their parents. How difficult to get a sense of control of all the contingencies that tantalize us by riding the updrafts, like a paper airplane inscribed with a treasure map, that keep balance just beyond our reach.

That explains golf's popularity. Being accepted in the Golf Club is like passing the Last Judgment and the course is a re-creation of the Garden of Eden on which innocence and youth can be regained. Golf is a religion, televised on Sundays like the Mass for shut-ins. The players say more prayers than they do in church and the quiet is greater than that in a cathedral.

Golf evokes such theological concepts as "This green is forgiving," and is filled with tomorrows, second chances, favorable drops, and the answer to "And then what?" Golf is a very human game and allows us at Thanksgiving to identify what gets us by on the back nine of everyday life.

Golf is a game of moments, of those remarkable times when everything goes right, when we get ourselves together and, after multiple disappointments and as many fizzled shots, we finally are completely and truly on game, if only for an instant.

Such moments go a long way for us humans. That's all golfers talk about after the game: those few melded seconds when they played in an inspired way, when they brought the best in themselves to life. That occasional glimpse of our best possibilities keeps us all going through the long everyday of life when we often see less than the best of ourselves.

Thanksgiving allows us, against the last tawny landscape of autumn, to recall the moments in our own lives, and our relationships, in which we were one with the best that is in us.

Anne Kiley, eighty-seven years old, for fifty-eight years the wife of master landscape artist, Dan Kiley, spoke for all of us about what sustains love and life together: "... our best times together have been lived in moments. Just as the other evening we sat on the terrace gazing out over the flowers to the mountains. Bathed in the lovely light we seemed to float free of ourselves, and then it seemed we were like two leaves that drifted and touched together, a moment of homecoming, which can in that instant make up for any separation" (*New York Times*, October 5, 2000, p. B14).

A moment is an interesting concept because, like *momentum*, it comes from the Latin word for movement, that is, literally, a point in the movement of time.

Such a moment opens the mystery of time, allowing us to realize what is true and lasting about us and those we love. In moments recollected in the quiet interlude of Thanksgiving, with the world heavy in expectation of winter, we revisit those moments in which we touch and are touched by the eternal in each other.

What keeps us going if not those moments of revelation when we see that, yes, it is true, we do love each other; we have a treasure in our family that cannot be corrupted by either rust or moth; that, despite failures, we are buoyed by such memories of conquering time through love.

When fire strikes or the waters rise, why do we go back for the photographs and picture albums, if not because they are records beyond price of the moments with eternity in them that transcend loss and death and separation?

These moments of love, fidelity, and honesty give us momentum that carries us through the unfinished, indeed, never to be finished, challenge of the year. For the human and divine gifts of these moments, we give thanks this and every year.

Election mess, spiritual mystery

The twentieth century officially ends, capping the second millennium on the last day of December. It is not ending with a whimper but with a bang.

The same delusion factories that promise immediate relief for America's physical heartburn also produced post-election national spiritual distress for which they have no remedy. The public relations/advertising complex cannot cure lies and distortions by concocting more of them. As a result, the year, the century, and the national soul spiraled down together into the longest and darkest of the calendar's days.

Yet two experiences found in current dissonance carry within them the music of salvation. Waiting and being imperfect are traditional and essential mysteries in any mature spirituality. They are very simple, and they are found in every day in every life. No talking in tongues, cures, visions, or other miracles are required.

Waiting is the mystery of the season of Advent itself, not only to orchestrate the days liturgically in expectation of Christmas but as part of everything that defines and deepens us humanly.

We have been reminded of this tension in waiting for election returns. But expectation is seeded deep in our souls. Waiting remains inevitable even in the age of "Anything you can do, we can do faster" in everything from Internet connections to divorce. *Instant* is the operative word in marketing food, drink, entertainment, and that broad area of gratification-in-general.

In real life, we must wait for anything worthwhile, from growing up to growing wise, from finding our true love to finding our true calling. Waiting is our human epidemic and is found everywhere, mirroring, in its various specialized settings, the aching range of our longings and fears.

We speak of a waiting area in an airport or a railroad station as the scene of long anticipated reunions for catching first sight of a familiar face coming home again. In waiting rooms in hospitals we find the sorrows of everyone who has ever wept at the suffering of loved ones.

When will we know, we ask, as we wait, as wait we must, for the test results, the biopsy, the MRI examination, or the doctor. The measure of our belief and the depth of our love: these are revealed in the mystery of waiting.

How hard it is to wait, as sometimes we must, before we can tell the one we love that we are sorry for some injury, small or great, that we have caused. While the wound is too tender to touch, we must wait until we will not make the hurt worse by speaking, even in regret, about it.

Waiting is indeed everywhere, as part of that even larger religious mystery of being imperfect. We are learning as a nation that our voting, and our voting machines, are just like us. They make mistakes because we make mistakes. The notion of zero-defect performance in anything human, or anything really spiritual, is an illusion.

The insurance industry, service contracts, the confessional, greeting cards, the reset button, the delete key, and the eraser all depend on our most abiding and indelible characteristic, being imperfect.

The Christian is called not to icy perfection but to a kind of glorious imperfection. Were we able to be perfect, we would never have to trust anybody, hope for anything, love each other, or pray for anything. The best things about us are drawn out of us only because of the imperfect things within us.

These are the mysteries. Perhaps an election marked by waiting and imperfection is worthwhile if it reminds us that these experiences are filled with wonder and are as common as sunrise and nightfall.

Christmas, a gift of seeing

Seeing, the old saying goes, is believing. But as this year draws to a close I think that believing may be seeing...

Angels are everywhere at Christmastime, hovering brightly, lighting the cave in which Jesus is born. We see the animals' breath, the wonder in the pilgrim kings' eyes, and the glint of the treasures they lay down as gifts. This is a feast of sight, for everything draws our eyes to the child, to this mystery, not of invisible heavenly beings or their translucent wings, but of the humanity taken on by God in Jesus.

Christmas, in fact, tells us that spirituality never consists in having private visions of hidden truths but rather in seeing into the public and common mystery of God's world. Christmas comes as the light returns after its long flight and begins, little by little, to shrink winter's chill shadow.

How embedded in our religious sense is this mystery of seeing! Mystical writers say that insight into ourselves is the price and measure of spiritual growth. "Do you see what I see?" the familiar carol asks, echoing St. Paul's plangent, "I only want to show you what I have seen..."

"If your eye is healthy," Jesus says, "your whole body will be full of light" (Matthew 6:22). We have it just backward, for seeing is not believing at all. Believing is seeing, so weakness in faith is condemned because we "have eyes, and fail to see" (Mark 8:18). And false prophets are described as "blind guides of the blind. And if one blind person guides another, both will fall into a pit" (Matthew 15:14).

That is an indictment not of physical but of spiritual blindness, the effect of sinners snuffing out their own inner light. In the majestic prologue of his gospel, John the Evangelist writes that John the Baptist "himself was not the light, but he came to testify to the light. The true light, which enlightens everyone..." (John 1:8–9).

Heaven is a feast in which contemplation is linked to sight. The blessed, we are told, will experience a beatific vision. This cannot be some static condition in which we gaze, moved but unmoving, like a tour group entranced but immobilized by staring up at a Sistine Chapel ceiling for all eternity.

Seeing, like a shimmering flame or firelight, is a dynamic transaction, varying in every instant, expanding, becoming more fine and discriminating, never at rest, always going deeper and wider, never exhausted. Heaven will be a mystery but it will not be mysterious. For people who see into life, seeing their way into eternity will be as natural as breathing. We will see, we are told, even as we are seen.

Hints are found everywhere in life, signals of the divine charm of creation. Why else would we speak of one of the most profound and transforming human experiences as love "at first sight." Love, we know, comes first through the eyes. Love is not blind and, in fact, sees more, sees in the other the precious that nobody else can see.

As he was dying, Joseph Cardinal Bernardin liked to recall a pastoral visit to a man whose wife's face had been ravaged by a fatal illness. The husband explained as he cared tenderly for her, "I still see her as beautiful as the day we first met."

So the mystical poet William Blake urges us to "cleanse the doors of perception" so that we can see the "world as it is, infinite." This will enable us to extract the horror from such apocalyptic metaphors as the "end of the world."

The world ends, not in flames, but once we see into it as God's creation. The world we have known ends as its facades are burned away by our purified and purifying spiritual insight.

Creation then becomes a slowly ripening miracle. In a new book entitled *Trilobite: Eyewitness to Evolution* (2001) by paleontologist Richard Fortey, we can read about a tiny shell creature whose "most distinctive characteristic was its eyes, set atop the head...each eye was a bundle of tiny prisms, often hundreds of thousands of them, and each pointed in a slightly different direction so that the animal could scan its entire surroundings."

A tiny, ancient witness, seeded with a truth about ourselves that becomes clearer in the light of the season. The capacity to see ourselves and each other truly, the ability to see through the false images that are the false gods of our time, the power to see into the mysteries, some as transcendent as first love and some as devastating as the death of a child, that go with being human: this is the utterly human gift of God's taking on our ways that we celebrate at Christmas.

The Seasons of 2001

Pro-choice's worst nightmare: science may finish its sentence

The pro-choice/pro-life debate resembles the music of Charles Ives that reaches our ears in the natural distortions of a band parading through a shouting crowd. We hear it first from afar and tentatively, then resoundingly up close, and finally it is muffled as it turns the corner beyond us...

America lives to some extent by unfinished sentences. Everybody wants "to move on" as long as the sentence remains incomplete and the destination vague. So, too, the mantra of "a woman's right to choose" makes for powerful politics as long as the object of choice is unspecified.

"A woman's right to choose..." has been elevated to a quasi-moral principle in the national conversation on abortion. This elliptical marvel eliminates the very word *abortion*, relieving people, in classic American advertising style, of associating a possibly negative tone with the product that is being promoted.

That science might add a clear object and so fashion this fragment into a morally potent statement greatly worries pro-choice leaders. That people may add an object to the verb "to choose" not only makes pro-choice leaders uneasy, but, in a revealing reaction, strikes them as somehow cosmically unfair.

The *New York Times* (January 21, 2001) reports that "...the abortion rights position is complicated by the increasing ability to see inside the womb." In short, we might think differently if we allowed the true object of choice to take on a human shape in our imagination.

National Right to Life legislative director Douglas Johnson says that the "...new technologies create a window to the womb, which makes people much more cognizant of the humanity of the child.

Americans with sonograms of fetuses on their refrigerators," he argues, "are unlikely to think quite the same about abortion" (*New York Times*, January 2, 2001).

That the object in the partial sentence/slogan is emerging may explain why Gallup reports in the same article that "the percentage of people who consider themselves 'pro-life' rose from 33 percent to 43 percent over the past five years. The percentage who considered themselves 'pro-choice' declined from 56 to 48 percent."

Science endangers the cultural correctness generated by this amorphous, don't-hold-it-up-to-the-light "right to choose..." The greatest transformation of the abortion debate may come, not from religion, law, or ballot box but when the triumph of reason we call science allows all of us to look together at the true nature of life in the womb. This shared perception will finish that sentence and change the discussion for good.

Opus Dei's secret revealed: it takes spies in from the cold

One of the saddest and most sensational developments of this month was the arrest of Robert Hanssen, F.B.I. agent and a deeply religious member of Opus Dei, as a spy. This turned our attention to Opus Dei, meaning Work of God, founded in Spain in 1928 by Josemaria Escriva de Balaguer, who was put on the fast track to canonization by Pope John Paul II...

The trouble with this Work of God is that nobody can tell you exactly what its work is or how it is done. According to the Encyclopedia of Associations, its work is to "spread throughout society a profound awareness of the universal call to holiness and apostolate through one's professional work carried out with freedom and responsibility."

That an accused spy was accepted should move Opus Dei leaders to ask themselves: What is it about us that we attracted a man deep in disloyalty and deception to join and find support for his secret life in the depths of our own secret life?

How could a man who is a member of a Catholic group that emphasizes unquestioning loyalty to the Holy Father also be unscrupulously disloyal to his fatherland?

This intersection of secret group and secret agent, however, prompts further questions. How can any professedly Catholic group be a secret organization in the first place? There is no secret about being a Catholic. Catholicism believes in revelation, not concealment. Why else would we speak about Jesus' public life?

Indeed, Jesus always spoke of doing things "in the light," and Catholicism's richest spiritual vocabulary includes "preaching from the rooftops" and "letting your light shine before others." Jesus, John tells us, was the Light who came into the darkness and the darkness did not comprehend it.

Perhaps Opus Dei has handicapped rather than helped itself by vesting itself in darkness. That darkness may have spoken to Hanssen and may continue to attract other people to join because of the cloak it throws over their lives. It lives in the Dark Ages if, as reported on a web site devoted to it, it allows women as "assistants . . . who pledge celibacy, and are responsible for the care and cleaning of all Opus Dei residences."

Hanssen was a counterintelligence specialist, a man working in but against the bureau and the country, a man who made himself superior to his nation by finding a perch from which to spy on it. The word *spy* is instructive for, as we examine its family of meanings, we find that it is related to the Latin *spex*, "one who sees." This, in turn, is the core of *despicari*, "to look down on," "to despise." The word *secret* leads us back to roots that mean "to set apart," "to be separate."

Here, then, the spy who separates himself from and looks down on his fellow Americans pledges himself to an organization in which he separates himself from and looks down on his fellow Catholics.

The secret spy and the hidden organization were made for each other. The biggest flaw in this self-styled diamond of an organization is basic: it misunderstands the church. Catholicism is a mystery, but it can never be a secret.

A time to embrace

Detained Air Force crew members were recently returned home from China. Their arrival illustrated the deepest meaning of the famous proclamation in Ecclesiastes: There is "a time for embracing..."

How interesting that, in the age of big screens, tiny phones, and noisy restaurants, the return of these wonderfully varied Americans occurred in silence. We could see but not hear the words exchanged. Still, there was no missing the language of homecoming.

This was the time for embracing, for hugging, for making that physical contact with each other that bears the direct current of love. The scene was moving because it was unrehearsed, was not preceded, as often previously, by each returned service person reciting some pat lines prepared by a Pentagon public relations consultant.

Nor was the president there, as has also happened in the past, to drain off the concentrated energies of the moment. After each man saluted and ran a brief gauntlet of greeters, they all broke free of their drill field discipline to hurry, shedding self-consciousness, toward those they loved. In the spontaneous moments that followed, there was no hiding what was human in them, for they found it in each other's arms.

In that instant, impossible to plan, we glimpsed a mystery, *the* mystery, as we might say, that lies at the heart of all authentic religion. This mystery centers on our becoming human through our relationships with each other. Organized religion, often mistaken for the mysteries in its keeping, is meant to celebrate and protect the revelation of our nature and destiny that was on display on that landing field last weekend.

We are not surprised to read that Jesus embraced his friends, and that he was conscious, in another moment, of desperate human need communicated to him by the hand of a person in a crowd. "Someone *touched* me," he said, aware that his spiritual strength had been tapped by the simple, sure means of someone making physical contact with him.

Jesus knew that a spiritual transaction had taken place. How did he know, except through what the touch told him? The language of touch is subtle, for we know, as Jesus did, that a hand placed on us to take something away from us can be a violation of love, a betrayal of the trust that makes intimacy a warm and well lighted place against the dark and isolating cold of confiscated pleasure.

Did Jesus know that Judas would betray him through some divine enlightenment? Or could he feel every aspect—every ambivalent flutter of this apostle's false heart, his life story even to his terrible fate—in the arms that embraced him, in the body that touched his, in the unmistakable messages that they delivered? Do what you do quickly, Jesus said, knowing that in a lying embrace Judas had done it already.

When babies were first born in hospitals, many developed a wasting illness, marasmus, losing rather than gaining weight each day. It was attributed finally to the rules for an antiseptic environment that forbade any touching of the newborns by nurses. Picking up infants and hugging them then became a routine part of infant care, ending the illness.

Babies need human touch as much as milk if they are to flourish. We, too, waste away without the touch of those who love us. We say it to each other, often not realizing what a deep truth we are expressing, "Let's keep in *touch*," "Let's not lose *contact*."

The same revelation occurs, in a minor but true key, during Mass at what, out of misplaced embarrassment at the human, is often called the *greeting*, rather than the *kiss*, of peace. It is a display as unrehearsed and yet as transcendent as the embraces of the returned American crew.

Watch them. People who look stolid and preoccupied and about as receptive as they would be to a dinnertime call from a mortgage broker suddenly brighten. Their features relax and they smile as a stranger clasps their hand or embraces them and wishes them peace. It is as sacramental as striking fire in the darkness of Holy Saturday night to light the Easter candle. By it, we see how human we are.

Like the Lord, we also feel the message in every embrace. Some try to possess us, some make a check mark and no more, and some affirm us humanly and, therefore, spiritually so that we wonder what need we have of angels when our hugs are as simple and true as those we saw on television last weekend.

Physicists and the sacraments of little things

Baby Boomers, marketers say, glory in big houses, big deals, and big bucks. Like every generation, however, they store their greatest human treasures in the smallest of events and moments and the shortest of words...

Song writers and poets have long understood that trifling objects—a ticket stub, a lock of hair, a sled named Rosebud—are big enough to hold the world of our lives and our loves and keep them fresh and free of the ravages of passing time. Ask Marcel Proust. He can tell you how eating a madeleine set him to recapturing his past.

Should we be surprised that scientists who have been preoccupied with the Big Bang are now turning to what the *New York Times* (April 24, 2001) calls "life's little mysteries" to understand the development of life?

Enter what they term the "elusive realm" of the *mesocosm*, "containing matter... bigger than a simple molecule but smaller than a living cell." Here, physicists say, "the constituents of cells interact with one another." In short, this is where the magic takes place. On this tiniest of landscapes an enormous mystery of life is initiated.

At this level, the *Times* informs us, "things do not act according to well-described theories of chemistry and physics... Systems this size seem to obey a unique set of rules that cannot be deduced from studying their individual components."

This mystery-laden field of nanotechnology sounds like the mystery-laden field of human life. Scientists had thought that "the same linear sequence of amino acids always led to the same protein... [and] that proteins followed more or less the same course when they folded."

Instead, they find that "a huge variety of amino acid sequences can fold up to form the same protein... These findings have turned protein folding into one of the most intractable problems in biology."

Lovers, however, are not surprised to learn about what Lao Tzu called "the long littleness of life" or that its important elements are not subject to the laws of physics and cannot be measured at all. What is now recognized as an infinitely mysterious code of protein development merely reflects the profoundly mysterious code of love's development.

Ask people about finding a friend or falling in love and they will tell you an unpredictable tale every time. They are always "surprised," they weren't "looking for that," and it often began not with a big thing but with something too small to measure and too powerful to explain: a smile, a look in the eyes, even an imperfection, a tiny scar turned by laughter into a dimple.

The list is endless and, while there are similarities, these footings for the great structures of love and friendship remain, like fingerprints and snowflakes, one different from the other. Every love is a mosaic of little moments of recognition and response.

Examine what people leave behind, not in their wills but in their wallets or desk drawers. Where did they get this, or why did they keep that, we ask, feeling love's still pulsing mystery in a sealed flower petal or a few words on a worn and folded slip of paper?

What scientists now examine and what lovers know, each in a unique way, is the sacramental nature of existence, that what is so profoundly natural is also profoundly religious, that the mysteries of life and faith are one Mystery and that faith is less about keeping rules than about entering the mysteries of our relationships with each other.

That is why Pierre Teilhard de Chardin wrote: "Love alone is capable of uniting living beings... to complete and fulfill them, for it alone takes them and joins them by what is deepest in themselves... Does not love every instant achieve all around us... the magic feat of 'personalizing' by totalizing? And if that is what it can achieve daily on a small scale, why should it not repeat this one day on world-wide dimensions?" (*The Phenomenon of Man*, 1959).

Dear Jack, Dear Rosemary

Before my oldest friend died in the last week of this month, he asked me to speak at his funeral Mass. This was offered in a small church on the south shore of Long Island where many of those in the great crowd had grown up with the sound of the sea in their ears...

Dear Jack—and how can any of us blessed by your friendship speak, except in this way, about you? Dear Jack, yes, and dear Rosemary, too, for you are as linked in our thoughts and affection as you were in life and remain still, for it is of just such a bond that the apostle writes that "love is stronger than death."

Dear Jack and dear Rosemary, showing us with such easy grace what it means to be a man and woman, what it means to fall in love once and for all, what it means that one never spoke of the other without saying, effortlessly and un-self-consciously, "My darling..."

And dear to them, and so to all of us, their children and grandchildren, their riches and their treasures, who, in their eyes and glances, in the turn of a head and the way they laugh, in the goodness of their hearts and the purpose in their lives, reflect their father and mother, their grandfather and grandmother.

Many of us gathered today grew up together here in Point Lookout, playing long ago in something like the innocence of Eden, on the sands and in the sea, and share memories, as the poet says, "of barefoot beaches and limbs of brown when hoops were rolling round the town and London bridges were falling down." How Jack loved the shore and the sea, how they seemed to speak to him and now, of him, to all of us. How right that he was so at home where the great elements of life itself—the water and the earth—intermingled beneath the endless sky.

This was not an accidental affinity for the sea but a treasure, as Jack was, ever renewing, as Jack was, and deep at its heart, as he was, too, and buoyant enough to bear us up, as Jack did for so many of us in so many different ways, yet seasoned with enough salt so that the good he did avoided the sickly sweet of sentimentality. Scoop up the sea in a shell and behold the riches and mysteries of God's creation, the elements necessary for life. And dear Jack, as clear and unclouded as the water brimming in that shell, a vessel himself overflowing with life.

For there was nothing occluded about Jack, no facade and no pretense. He was like his house. You could walk right in and meet the truth of him. It was as easy to meet him as it was hard to forget him. You learned that, as Nobel Laureate Saul Bellow said to me of him, "Jack's a man, an up-front guy." He made friendship a delight, an adventure, a way, against encroaching age, to go on being Tom Sawyer and Huck Finn together, riding whatever brightly lighted paddlewheeler came along—a new book, an innovation in business, an opera, Verdi and Shakespeare, the Sopranos, too, a political context, a religious question, a word.

How he loved words! And how, for example, in a way that defined his passion for what he hoped the law could deliver, and for what he strove for as a lawyer himself, he would quote one of the Beatitudes: "Blessed are they who hunger and thirst after justice for they shall be *sated.*" *Sated*, he would say, that is what the word is, *sated*. They shall not have a portion of justice; they shall be *satisfied to the full*.

What, then, as I count the years we all shared with him in friendship, does the word *friend* mean? Like our scoop of the sea, we find Jack in the handful of this word. The word for friend in almost every language but English comes from that for love—*amor* as in *amigo*, *amici, mon ami*. And friend's root is *pri* and means "beloved." In the family of language, it rests in the very middle of *sapphire*, meaning "dear" or "precious." It is found in *Friday*, the day of love. And it means "a place of safety." A friend—a friend like Jack—welcomes us into a place of *safety*, where we know that we will not be hurt, where we can, therefore, be free, where we can be ourselves.

How safe he made other people feel, how at ease, valued for themselves, true subjects of his concern and interest. Social science speaks of "unobtrusive measures," occasions or incidents that give us a measure of something that we did not plan to get. Following Jack across an office and down a corridor at King Kullen's headquarters recently, I collected just such a measure. What I could see, like a panning camera, was how everyone turned from their desks toward him, how their faces lighted up and they smiled spontaneously, how people took his hand and exchanged a few whispered words, how they seemed touched by something invisible that came from him as he passed among them, an alabaster lamp made translucent by illness, its gentle light touching and transforming others.

One of the challenges of being a friend of Jack's, however, was that you had to be good, perhaps better than you felt like being, reformed when you may not have been ready for reform. Only the truth, unshaded, would do. Ethics and morals were to be lived by, as good food was to be eaten, fine wine to be quaffed, life to be lived seriously but never solemnly. How could one think otherwise after spending time with Jack?

There were not many times when dear Jack was at a loss for words. Perhaps the only time in my memory was on the day that he and Rosemary wed each other and I was the church's official witness. How radiantly beautiful she looked, how handsome and proud was he, this man who was so different from other men, as Rosemary thought when they first met, that wonderful moment when they fell in love and when, after midnight, he saw her all the way to the northern reaches of the subway line and counted himself reborn.

I asked her the familiar question: "Will you take this man . . . to love him, to honor him . . . for richer for poorer . . . as long as you both shall live?"

There was a slight pause. Jack glanced over, disconcerted.

"Would you please repeat that again?" she asked. A flash of discomfort on the groom's face quickly faded when she said, at last, "I will."

Jack told the story often, a little uneasily, as if the whole thing, after all these children and houses, might still be reconsidered and called off by his beloved Rosemary.

But I thought then and know better now that Rosemary—although I know that she reads labels, fine print, and even computer instructions written by Japanese very carefully—did not want to hear the words repeated for purposes of re-evaluation. No, she did it then to savor them and the sweet prospect of the life with Jack just opening up. She wanted to absorb them, to make them, in their ideals and their demands, the coda for their great love for each other. She wanted to hear them again so that, as in everything, she could put them into her heart as she put her whole heart into them.

And so, with a tenderness beyond any singing of it, she has kept her pledge as Jack kept his, in good times and bad, in sickness and in health until death parted them—but only in a way and only for a while.

And now I think of my last visit with them on an afternoon a few weeks ago. They were sitting in front of their house, so at ease, so comfortable, as married as flavors are said to be when they can no longer be distinguished from one another. Jack looked over his half glasses, raised the new book he was reading, *The Founding Brothers*, and recommended it highly. For a man supposedly looking into the darkness, he was filled with light and, as had been true of him these long months and years, he did not complain. He was, in fact, cheerful, optimistic, without illusion, and without self-pity. A man of faith. A man in full.

I watched them, as I had watched them at the wedding ceremony forty and more years ago, and I realized that I was a witness again, a witness to everything they had pledged that day, to the happily ever after, to the rounding out in time of an eternal story. For, if they had said yes to their vows then, they were keeping them now as they had always. And life, their life, and the life they had given, came by to testify—daughters and granddaughters, sweet and safe in the presence of their grandparents, hugging and being hugged, and slipping away into their own lives. And neighbors and friends, representing all of us, smiled and waved and said hello.

And the yellow school bus stopped and a tousle-haired grandson stepped down and came, as his mother did, to spend a few moments, under that same endless sky and not far from that border where earth and sea mingled, in the safe place made for them by the love of dear Jack and dear Rosemary. Life, I thought, the life that began in that long-ago wedding, was parading by, paying court, paying tribute, singing a hymn to them in the breath of these tiny children.

No wonder dear Rosemary savored those words, their glories and their trials, all before them then, their keeping their promises so lovingly that it had become second nature, so that, sitting side by side in the sun, they were an unobtrusive measure of love itself.

It is that love, as fresh as the sea, as renewing as the sun, as firm as the earth, that is stronger than death. It is your love we remember, dear Jack, and all that your love has given to all of us. We know that you are waiting to see us again, standing by that open front door, perhaps standing by the stove, to be sure we will have a meal when we arrive. How blessed are we who have been your friends. The whole point was to witness your love, yours and Rosemary's for each other, for your children and grandchildren, for life itself. Blessed are we, for we are sated on this love, satisfied to the full, by this love that conquers death and gives life to us all.

Blasphemy or prophecy?

The Ninth Hour *was auctioned this week after a few days of viewing at Christie's Rockefeller Center showrooms. Sculpted by Italian artist Maurizio Cattelan, it is, according to the* New York Times, *"a wax effigy of Pope John Paul II lying beneath a meteorite that has presumably crashed through a shattered skylight overhead." What are we to think of this?*

After the exhibition of this sculpture in Poland last December, two Parliament members entered the gallery, removed the rock, and tried to place the figure of the pope in a standing position. They left a copy of a letter sent to government officials demanding the dismissal of the gallery's director, charging, according to the *New York Times* (May 13, 2001), "that 'a civil servant of Jewish origin' should not be spending the Roman Catholic majority's money on disgusting works of art..."

The woman director eventually did resign in circumstances rich in post-modern irony. Anti-Catholicism was overcome under banners emblazoned with anti-Semitism. How, in other words, to lose everything through a victory that mocked the Catholic values in whose name it was won.

Yet this saga yields a grace note that, like a sunset slashed across the end of a stormy day, radiates hope by lighting up what otherwise would be a total loss. Before the Jewish museum director was forced out, the president of Poland, Aleksander Kwasniewski, and two local priests made a remarkable intervention.

They "stated publicly," the *Times* informs us, "that 'The Ninth Hour' served as an allegory for the pope's heavenly burden." This reaction celebrates the best in Catholicism by inviting people to view the

work as a statement made in the language of art rather than of theological politics. Before demolishing the artwork, these brave men suggested, let us see if there is some wholeness in it, something healing
rather than wounding.

In this particular case, we may turn to an aesthetic of art appreciation that the church itself has often fostered. It is altogether Catholic to
stand back from the dulling flack so that we may attune ourselves to
the work itself. Can we pick up the message, which even the artist cannot tell us, that signals to us from the work?

The notion of an allegory for his heavy burdens is sweet but shallow because the art is deeper and fundamentally sympathetic to the
pope. The sculptor presents the pope in a cosmic historical and spiritual perspective.

First, he understands the centrality of the pope as a symbol for
faith and for the institutions of faith. This work is about the pope in a
literal sense but, in a larger metaphorical sense, it is about institutional
authority in general.

This speaks to us not as a newspaper or a history book do, but as a
poem does, evoking forces at work, not just on the Holy Father, but on
all of us.

The work speaks mysteriously about the impact of the Space/
Information Age on our sense of where we are—whether we stand on
the same earth that we once distinguished from the heavens.

The Space Age has sent an earthquake tremor under all the institutions rooted in previous ages when we imagined the heavens as
above and the earth as below. Now, as space exploration allows us literally to see the unity of the universe, there is no up or down. That
makes it difficult to speak of firm moral principles or certain conclu-
sions about right and wrong. We have lost not right and wrong but an
exhausted vocabulary, out of the age of hierarchies, that no longer
expresses them well.

It is as if a meteorite had crashed through the old ceiling we had
imagined as the dome of heaven to knock us to the ground, where we
remain surrounded by the shattered glass of a covering that was never
there.

The pope symbolizes our institutions and us, dazed by the blow of the disordering new age. That we lie here with him does not mean that we, he, or authority have been slain but that we can lift the weight of the fallen heavens from us and find a new language for perennial faith and morals.

This sculpture may be disturbing but, let protestors take heed, it is pro-Catholic, and pro-pope.

Let us now praise not so famous women

When more than a thousand people came to Chicago's Holy Name Cathedral for the funeral of Monsignor Jack Egan, referred to by the Chicago Tribune *(May 25, 2001) as the "conscience of the city," they expected a feast of memory and celebration for a greatly loved priest. What was delivered, however, was an unexpected footnote, as in one of the discourses reference was made to Peggy Roach, Egan's secretary for thirty and more years...*

The crowd in the cathedral recognized this unplanned moment and, like a rapidly cresting wave, surged from their seats and broke into applause to salute this remarkable woman who had never sought acclaim and had hardly ever gotten her name in the papers.

The standing ovation recognized a treasure overlooked, carrying out a ministry of service always just outside the light that fell so rightly on Monsignor Egan and his public struggles for justice and peace. The applause was for Peggy Roach, whose supportive presence in the shadow of his great work, like that of so many women in the church, had been something everyone counted on even when her name did not roll in the credits.

The salute was sacramental, as the community, thinking it had come to say farewell to Monsignor Egan, found that it wanted to say well done to Peggy Roach, too. These are moments in which the community is wiser than its members, moments when the community, gathered together, gives spontaneous witness to a truth that the members could never voice as well, or perhaps at all, as individuals.

The sense of the Catholic community is its common sense about how much Peggy Roach, and legions of other unsung women, contribute without title, recognition, and often not much pay, to the pastoral work of the church. This truth has been here waiting for us to rediscover beneath the group photos of men caparisoned in crimson —no women need apply—who exercise power in the institutional church.

The truth, however, is that the everyday work of the church, including its multiple pastoral ministries and its educational activities, has been and is still carried out mostly by women. A fair case can be made that the Catholic Church in the United States owes its success not so much to its greatly heralded churchmen but to its almost unheralded churchwomen.

The members of the Catholic community at Monsignor Egan's funeral were hailing these women who had gladly sacrificed their lives to establish schools whose standards, practices, and good order have survived the disasters that have gutted so much public education of its promise, schools that stand now as models for others and tributes to themselves.

What do these women get, beyond being told that, no matter that they have proved the opposite, they are unworthy for ordination because they are not men? They make *Time*'s cover, not as teachers, but as subjects in a study of Alzheimer's disease. They are lampooned in theatrical revues as petty and pitiful classroom tyrants, and, since the institution made no financial planning for them, Catholics pass the hat annually to fund their later years.

In saluting Peggy Roach, the people acclaimed all women standing in the shadows with her. These include many laywomen who, without the minimal recognition granted to nuns, have contributed significantly to Catholicism as a faith and as leaven in the dough of society.

They are everywhere, but start in Chicago. Patty Crowley, with her late husband, Pat, worked with Monsignor Egan in the Cana (premarriage) Movement and would work for gospel values tirelessly until her own death.

"Tanchie" Misomann followed Cardinal Bernardin from his South Carolina days to Chicago, ever invisible but ever key in handling the details of his great life.

Mary Louise Schniedwind resigned from a travel agency when barred from booking a black couple on a train. She sought work in the church, laboring with Egan for many years, later at the National Federation of Priests' Councils, and still does for me, while helping her eighty-something age-mate, Sister Monica, tutor black teenagers.

We leave thousands more out to get these few in. How blessed that moment when Catholics, gathered for one good thing, did another, honoring Peggy Roach and all women whose hidden lives remain the church's best and purest energy.

Richard Leach, dreamer of dreams

Dick Leach died in the Dallas airport, about to start a trip, at May's end. The obituaries described him as having amassed a fortune by making Barney a friend to children and a fixture in American television. But those who knew him understood that this wasn't half the story...

Dick Leach truly was a great American entrepreneur. With one of his daughters-in-law, he developed a genial animal figure into what commentators term a cultural icon. It made him rich, the remembrances say, a man who realized what the financial press still praises as the American dream, making it big enough to snub the world, if he had wanted to, and play golf forever.

But Dick Leach was rich in spirit before becoming wealthy in fact. Possessing the rewards of his genius, he was never possessed by them. And if he knew how to spin dreams, he was even more gifted at developing visions. Dick Leach's life was not the fulfillment of the American dream so much as it was the realization of the Christian ideal.

A Chicago native, he developed the Argus Press into a publisher of Catholic books and an array of media for school, family, and parish education programs. I was blessed to know him, and to spend time with him, for you *spent* time, rather than *killed* or *passed* it in his company.

He was filled with life, as was his home where he and his equally remarkable wife, Rosemary, raised five sons and four daughters, and it was wonderful to watch their Christmas card picture expand as their children married to fill the frame with children of their own. Of all that he left behind, his family was for Dick Leach the greatest of his accomplishments.

You could feel the creative energy humming within him, seeking the right project on which to spend itself. The Force was indeed with him, moving him to seek fresh ways to pursue his goal of giving a voice to Christian ideals in high quality products so that, no small vision, he might change the world for the better.

His lavish expenditure of energy did not deplete him as much as increase his enthusiasm. Being with him helped me understand the biblical jar of oil that, although used daily, was never used up. He brought to mind the Spirit's being *poured forth* on the earth, for he, too, poured himself fully into every undertaking.

No real entrepreneur, as the career of Dick Leach proves, needs to master any dark management arts. He was drawn instead to the light and, for him, being a businessman and a believer constituted one seamless calling. The faith he had in himself was fully integrated with the faith he had in God and he never broke a commandment in order to break a bank.

His deep inner life generated an optimism that was more of the Trinity than of the Rotary. Belief governed his choice of projects and his objectives. As he spoke, you felt that he was somehow easily connected with an unseen but very real world of the Spirit. Perhaps that is why he could say, with a smile, "Those who tell me I can't do something entertain me."

He did not mind those who assailed "Barney." He said that he was trying to reach kids rather than such critics. He understood his audience as when, a few years ago, he and his wife financed an extraordinary European production of a musical on Francis of Assisi.

The last time I heard from him, a few weeks before he died, he was rescheduling a dinner engagement he and his wife had with me and my wife because his travel plans had changed. He was heading for the Mediterranean for a reunion with his family. How right it seems that he died as he was about to embark on a journey, his plans well made, his bags packed, another adventure stretching before him with those he loved most.

How right that he would be thinking of the other side of the world, the one where night had already fallen, and where he would arrive with the dawn. He had spent his life thinking beyond the horizon, beyond the darkness, about the world in need of light.

McVeigh, revelation, and artificial tears

The Catholic Church teaches that revelation ended with the death of the last apostle. Timothy McVeigh died this week with his eyes open. How much did we see of bone-deep truths borne on television that allows us to see events and, the core of revelation, to see into them, too?

The squat federal prison suddenly morphed into the ancient Coliseum, and if there was little bread, there was a great media circus, the rows of satellite dishes turned to heaven like choir monks, covering Death's arrival. He would arrive any minute, but what did he look like, and would he take questions?

Terre Haute, French for "lofty land," is a flat and drear stretch, and in its French name it bears the terror domesticated in the huddle of brick buildings where Death waited patiently for its entrance. For *haut* is used of high treason, *haut trahison*, and of the executioner himself, *exécuteur des hautes oeuvres*.

The warden looked right as he told us so much by saying so little, standing, clipped and trim, in his best dark suit and as American as an astronaut back from the moon, tight lipped and terse, revealing how deep the journey had been by sticking to its technical surface, laying a cover on its uncomfortable mystery as one would on a dead child.

The journalists appeared subdued by the experience, telling us what they had seen, saying as much by their manner as by their overlapping descriptions of the redness of the warden's telephone and the whiteness of everything else, as if a fresh snow had smoothed every surface, making everything the same—the whiteness of the room and of the sheet pulled up to McVeigh's chest, the whiteness of his T-shirt and the paleness of his face and lips.

Almost all of the journalists reported that McVeigh had lifted himself to make eye-contact, seeking them out individually. Yet another witness reported that the glass was shaded and that McVeigh was squinting rather than finding the eyes of anybody behind the windows.

Had the media representatives looked into McVeigh's hard, dark eyes and experienced a revelation about the Mystery that had taken up residence there? Had they noticed that Death rather than the prisoner had looked back at them?

Perhaps the truest revelation was found in the glimpses of the memorial to those who died in the explosion, the 168 and three waiting to be born, so like us, so like our families and the people down the street. These were silent pictures of people embracing, supporting each other as they wept inconsolably, laying open for us the human hearts as shattered as the Murrah building, hearts broken and never to be quite mended.

This revelation was deepened even more by the statements made by the victims' relatives who had watched the execution from a different angle on closed circuit television. They seemed cried-out and, as one mother of a four-year-old who had been killed said—the incident had put a period to a sentence but there would never be anything like closure. It had been hard to accept the death of her daughter and for years she had looked into the faces of little girls, blond haired and of an age with hers, aching to find her alive.

Accepting her death didn't bring closure, she said, revealing it as a vain and empty effort to process Mystery so that it will not live on in us or disturb anyone else.

These revelations were interrupted by another, an advertisement that, unintended by its creators, offered a footnote to what was, after all, a visual event, a flood of images overflowing with revelation.

The product, the voice-over told us, was artificial tears, just like our own, that would do the work of real tears. But what is the work of real tears if not to vent the broken heart rather than soothe the tired eye? Still, what a revelation—artificial tears for a nation filled with weeping, technology promising relief by providing what, in their true and saving state, constitute a profound human language nobody has to teach us about the mysteries of love and loss in our lives.

Artificial tears may taste of saline solution. Real tears, like real blood, taste of salt, a fundamental element of life, and they both come from the heart. This salt makes our tears sting, making of our sight a sacrament of the great and sacred Mystery of Life and Death revealed to us in this event.

Stem cell debate: everything but wonder

During the Great Depression, General Motors inscribed on its Chicago Century of Progress Exhibition pavilion words from the British Catholic writer G. K. Chesterton. Their meaning echoes as truly in our time of abundance as in that time of want: The world will never starve for wonders; but only for want of wonder.

The ongoing debate about stem cell research reflects the wonders that science has achieved and hopes to provide for humankind. Glowing like a radioactive core hidden in the mound of discussions is the wonder of creation itself, ignored here, written off there, shouted down almost everywhere, and yet unyielding, abiding, eternal in its mystery.

This research means handling the stuff of life, a wonder profound enough to rehabilitate the idea of wonder, that aura, like the moon's ring gently buckled about it on a summer's night, that identifies the everyday magic and the eternal grandeur of creation. Moved to wonder, we are shaken briefly free of time and glimpse, as on a sudden turn on a mountain trail, the vistas that lie ahead.

The word *wonder* contains a lesson as it refers to some aspect of creation "that...arouses awe, astonishment, surprise or to a wonder created in time by human hands, such as the Seven Wonders of the World." Wonders blossom both from Mother Nature and from human nature.

This multi-dimensioned sense of wonder fits the stem cell discussion. It reveals what is natural in us—this reflection of the profound mystery of creation and of our natures whose pattern is sewn so deeply into these elements—as well as the wonders that humans can accomplish as we reach toward a destiny almost beyond imagining through the arts of science.

This intersection of the wondrous, this linking—like spacecraft from parallel universes of mystery—urges us to pause to allow their aura to settle into us and to hush voices that would conclude this debate before we understand its terms. As Leon Kass, a prophetic bioethicist, wrote, "...we face a mysterious and awesome power, a power governed by an immanent plan that may produce an indisputably and fully human being. It deserves our respect not because it has rights or claims to sentience, but because of what it is now and prospectively" (as quoted in *America* by Paul Lauritzen, March 26, 2001).

Pope John Paul II, our time's staunchest defender of humanity in its earliest stages, was very precise in his language to President Bush ruling out the *creation* of embryos for this purpose and, despite commentators claiming otherwise, did not condemn all such research. He left room for wonder and wonders as he did in his *The Gift of Life*, acknowledging that we lack exact scientific knowledge of when we become persons and that the church has not taken a definitive philosophical position on the matter. This suggests that our approach should follow his in reverence, perspective, and caution about making policies based on the nonexistent moral gravity of political or public relations slogans and techniques.

Some forces brutally politicize stem cell research solely to gain a victory or a defeat in popularity for the president. Some claim that no risk inheres in appropriating, cloning, or harvesting stem cells because their tissues may cure terrible illnesses.

Some endorse choice, valuing it in itself with no regard to what is chosen, as the supreme good in the matter. Still others close the case before it is opened, stamping as immoral in fact or in the future to conduct any stem cell research, including the use of embryos that will be discarded anyway.

We are starved for wonder by these approaches, conditioned by the immediate response of the trivialities that are our toys—televisions coming on, Internet searches, pick-up on the Mercedes—to regard time as the enemy and patience as a vice. Yet science and theology, two participants in this dialogue, have never been in a hurry to resolve weighty questions about humanity.

The recent National Institutes of Health document, reported by the *Wall Street Journal* (July 19, 2001), noted inconclusive tests and "the challenges...including difficulties in growing desired cell types in sufficient quantities and ensuring that transplant treatments don't cause side-effects. Where scientists have placed the undifferentiated embryo cells into laboratory mice, they have formed tumors...Scientists are still struggling to show that cell therapies can show any benefit at all."

The disastrous, irreversible side-effects on Parkinson's patients of cell transplantation prompt science to pursue this wonder cautiously. Science stands with the pope rather than with the headlines in proclaiming cures around the corner.

On no other issue, in our wonder-filled world, do we find ourselves so starved for wonder itself.

Good news for humans: genome still a mystery

As in the great full moon tides of summer, when the deep yields up treasures midst the flotsam and jetsam, the flood tide of news has deposited a gift of mystery on the beach of our consciousness. Deep inside its front section, the New York Times *(August 24, 2001) reported in a tone almost apologetic and just this side of being defensive, on an article entitled, "Human Genome Now Appears More Complicated After All."*

The lead tells us that "After a humiliating deflation this February, human dignity is on the recovery path, at least as measured by the number of genes in the human genome." In short, we have a corrective to the weeks of confident headlines about imminent breakthroughs, through stem cell and other research, on a vast catalog of human suffering. We humans were getting simpler, perhaps as easy to map and repair as integrated circuits.

Last winter's calculation of 30,000 human genes eclipsed the old textbook "guess" of 100,000 and made humans a lot less than the angels and not much grander than the round worm (19,000 genes) and the fruit fly (13,000 genes).

The February estimate "suggested that evolution had not found the design, operation, and maintenance of a person much more complicated than the job of running the microscopic . . . mustard cress (25,000 genes)."

But this judgment has turned out in August, much like pennant hopes for the Chicago Cubs every year in the same month, to have been off by at least a third.

The article explains: "It is now not so clear that the real number of human genes will be known any time soon. With all the estimates out

there, 'it has to be becoming clear to people it must not be simple,' said
Dr. J. Craig Venter..."

The news story, really an account of the way true scientists correct
themselves systematically and publicly, was also a secular documenta-
tion of our human mystery. While describing one exploration of the
human person in particular, it revealed something of the infinite complexity of the human personality in general.

Perhaps this information was not widely publicized because there
is nothing really new in it. We are as wisely suspect of full explanations
as we are of final solutions for anything. And while it is refreshing,
there really is nothing new in discovering that as we learn about ourselves we become more, rather than less, a mystery.

Both the great scientist Albert Einstein and the great theologian
Karl Rahner came from the Black Forest region of Germany. As Rahner
once expressed it to me in an interview, the mystery of the world that
frustrated the physicist was exactly what attracted the theologian.

A parallel universe of mystery opens on the other side of every
door opened by scientific research. That is the meaning of the revision
of the estimate of the number of human genes in the genome. Those
with a sense of the mystery of the universe will not be frustrated, as
Einstein was, but will be attracted, as Rahner was, by this constant
tracking of our unknowability.

This fresh opening on the future in every advance also offers a
corrective to those believers who are less interested in these ever new
beginnings than they are in spectacular endings. Lovers of apocalypse,
that is, of the universe being reduced to ashes, should learn the mystery in the word *apocalypse*.

The familiar religious word *revelation* comes from the Latin trans-
lation, *revelatio*, of the Greek word *apokalypsis*. They both mean
"unveiling," which is perhaps the best word we have to describe the
work of both the scientist and the theologian. They take away the veils
that block us from seeing into the endless mystery of the world.

The last day before the world changed

My wife and I had driven past the meadow in Pennsylvania where
United Flight 93 would crash and by the Pentagon on our way to New
York where we would be on September 11.

New York, New York. "The date," the ordinary looking lady said like a
seer, "is 911." An emergency for all of us, this September day in 2001
that, like a September day in 1939, ended a dream of peace.

The headlines in that Tuesday's morning papers are the last picture we have of a world unaware that it would never be the same again.
What people were excited about—who would be the next mayor of
New York, political deals to revive the economy, whether Barry Bonds
would break the home run record or Michael Jordan would play basketball again—were made suddenly trivial by Death's striking down
thousands and searing all of us with twin lightning bolts of terrorism.

That morning promised a day of ravishing beauty, better even
than the day before, that final ordinary day when the leaves whispered
of fall but the thermometer sang still of summer and a brief electrical
storm washed down Manhattan's dusty streets the way loosed hydrants
do for playing children on the hottest days.

The sky was clear and the buildings stood fine-edged against the
glistening Atlantic waters, promises, each of these, of the coming glory
of autumn in New York. One could look, as my wife and I did the
evening before, at the Trade Towers in the last sunset that would ever
gild their walls, and sense that the fall had made its move against summer and change was in the air.

The clarity of the atmosphere only sharpened the razor strikes of
the planes that slit the towers open like a man's wrists to lay blood

sacrifice on the altar of lower Manhattan. And there rose a pillar of cloud by day that would not, as it did in the Old Testament, lead us safely out of the desert but more deeply into one that we had never known before.

The ashes fell on all of us as we and our world were changed. For what we could feel was the edge of evil itself, evil not spread out in disguise by the devil, but evil brewed in the dark apothecary of the human heart, evil unleashed in its raw and indifferent power on the innocent, evil that did not come from another world but from our own.

This mystery seems as dark and impenetrable as the clouds of debris that brimmed above the lower buildings, rolled along the city streets, and finally totally engulfed the life we had shared until that moment.

What was altered on Tuesday morning was the ordinary, the everyday, life in its own seasons, complicated enough but sweetly simple compared to life under the shadow of dread, the feeling that, for reasons unconnected with them and perhaps by now beyond being understood by anyone, good men and women could no longer be sure that ordinary life, that ordinary time, as it is called in the Catholic liturgy, would ever exist again.

For most of us, ordinary time is all that we have. It is our chance for simple glory, for waking to the wonders of the world and of each other, for making friends and falling in love, for giving and encouraging life in a generation beyond us.

Ordinary times are the ones that we can never forget even though we are blessed with different ways of remembering them. Ordinary life is the scene and setting for the extraordinary miracles of everyday living, of forgiving each other for our failings and learning to love each other more, of facing hurt and doubt and setbacks together, of discovering that these are the way we celebrate the Eucharist of all the living and dying of each ordinary day.

We will learn, as the days turn into weeks, of thousands of ordinary lives and of the freeze frame in which they are now fixed—the good-byes of husbands and wives, and children, too, heading off on another day, the hundred moments that will forever break our hearts —our chance for goodness and our real glory in being human.

That world was lost with the thousands of dead, those legions of the ordinary who were so much like us. We will weep for them, as uncomforted as Rachel, and for the ordinary times that were killed with them on Tuesday.

Maybe *this* is the greatest generation

America's Baby Boomers recently discovered that their parents—survivors of the Great Depression, winners of World War II—were heroes. Ever since, these Boomers have paid them honor, in Tom Brokaw's phrase, as "the greatest generation." The Boomers have also fingered their guilt like rosary beads at never having faced greater tests than the SATS and whether they would get into the local country club. Until 9/11, that is . . .

Now they have been tested by terror as many-headed as a hydra, revealing that, beneath the surface of abs, SUVS, and stock options to which destiny had seemed to consign them, they possess at least as much, and maybe more, goodness, heart, and courage as any previous generation.

The thousands of stories set like diamonds in the black heart of this darkness tell us what the Boomers may be reluctant to admit: *theirs* may be the greatest generation ever to grace American life.

The Boomers, some younger and some older, were on the front lines of an attack so savage that nobody could have prepared them for it. The test was raw and fierce, a fulfillment of the scriptural vision of some being taken and others being left, and just so quick as that twinkling of an eye in which all will be changed.

They had nothing to draw on but themselves. And, in that split second of dread, they discovered for themselves the depths of their character, the beauty of their hearts, and the generosity of their souls.

Boomers, critical of their own self-absorption, were tried in the flames that burned away this superficial dross to show how they put away self-concern for the sake of others.

Perhaps they learned, as we have learned from them, why their parents never talked about their experiences. When the test came, they stepped out of themselves to find the true north of life as their minds and hearts turned to others. You cannot remember, and so you never talk about, those times when you completely forget yourself.

These Boomers, who seemed so wise about wines and, at times, closer to their black Labradors than to anybody else, found for themselves and showed us where their hearts lay, in those intervals, in airplanes and office buildings, in which they knew that they were going to die.

They also replied to a question asked for centuries but never really answered: What would you do if you knew that the world, or your world, would end in five minutes? A saint was celebrated for looking up from the billiard table and answering that he would go on with his game. But that is, literally, to play, rather than deal, with this proposition.

And who has not heard that, when we know we are about to die, our whole life will flash, MTV style, before our eyes? And how many times have we heard accounts of near-death experiences replete with tunnels, light, and a sense of peace?

But, until September 11, 2001, we had no sample of any size to tell us what people were like when they faced certain death. Now, however, thanks to dozens of cell phone calls, we know—and know beyond any doubt—what men and women do in these last seconds of their lives.

They forget themselves as they think of those they love, their spouses and children, their parents and friends. They do not complain or bemoan their fate. Neither do they pray for miraculous deliverance or even for the forgiveness of their sins. They do not think about themselves as they speak their last words.

They just want to tell others how much they love them, that they want them to be safe, that they want them to be happy, that their last will and their true testament is one of utter concern for those they cherish, that they break free of the grasp of death and judgment on their lives by giving themselves away so completely that, before time runs out, they are already immersed in the eternal.

The flaming towers and the skies were not filled with business travelers or tourists that last morning but with lovers, some laying down their lives for their friends, but all of them at their best, drawn fully out of themselves so that we see them as they really were all the time. Blessed are these Boomers, unpossessed by their possessions, saving us rather than themselves, loving their own until the end, as great as or greater than any generation we will ever know.

The voices in the ruins

Something profound, and not yet well named, has happened to all of us in the last few weeks. Many journalists are stranded on the near shore, stunned by the soaring tide that ravages and reshapes the land they thought they knew. Others, including the comfortless and those who try to comfort them, and maybe most of us, are in the sea itself, bubbles streaming around us as we swim upward from the depths that so suddenly clasped and pulled us down…

We surface on the far reaches of Mystery, at this place as holy as any shrine in the world. If the black boxes of the planes are silent, the hearts of those lost still transmit true signals about what happened to them and to us.

Some claim that myths swirl from the ashes—the water supply is poisoned, the C.I.A. knew about the bombing all along. The *New York Times* (September 25, 2001) tells us this under the headline, "As Thick as the Ash, Myths are Swirling." *Myth* is the right word used in the wrong way.

Myth, meaning "falsehood" or "rumor," beggars the human dignity of this event. *Myth*, from the Greek for "story," is that way of recounting the truth about us in human tales that are immune to the distortions worked on memory by time and chance.

Myth is also the language of faith. Jesus preached in the mythical form of stories because they are the native tongue of religious mystery. We humans find ourselves, our souls and our destinies, in *myths*, in the great stories told over and over about the links between love and courage and life and death. The primary significance of the great myths is always spiritual.

That is why people drawn to Ground Zero tell us that no pictures capture its truth. Ground Zero in Manhattan, along with the crater in Pennsylvania and the gashed side of the Pentagon, constitute Ground Sacred. They are now the center of the world of spiritual truth, places where so much seems to be lost but where everything important about us is also found.

Standing silent at the smoking ruins is a greater tribute than placing another wreath of clichés there. We must let this place of Mystery speak to us through its hundreds of stories, each one revealing something different and no two of them the same.

What do we hear if not the *myth*, that is, the *story* of the Hero, that hero, as Joseph Campbell wrote, "with a thousand faces," who stands for all of us who must, some in one way and some in another, pass through the same trial. First, such heroes must leave their own country and journey to one they do not know. There they must face and slay the fiery dragon of ignorance. Only then can they return home with boons for those they left behind.

Everybody who came to work at the World Trade Center on September 11 made this Hero's Journey. Many were not New Yorkers by birth, and many had come from other parts of the world, leaving behind home, neighborhood, everything and everybody they loved. They came, as bond traders and brokers, secretaries or window washers, to take on the dragon that waits for each of us at every dawn, that beast of what we do not know and cannot fully see that we must daily conquer to be true to ourselves and God's gifts to us.

Hero is another word for "saint," for they share a calling to which the rest of us are apprenticed—to live by the truth of who they are and what they do, thereby slaying the dragon that would feast on them if they were false. Then they can return home, having made themselves whole, another word for holy, through their work that day.

The stories of these hero saints are imperishably invested in the invisible shafts of space that still tower above the ruins: of people journeying every morning on the subways, commuter trains, and airplanes, ready that day for the tests they did not know would be given. These are stories of brothers and sisters, and whole families, too, noble hearts seeking the Grail, women weeping as warriors bear dead heroes on their shields, lovers reaching out to that other side of themselves, the beloved who finally made them feel whole; of sons seeking their fathers and fathers seeking their sons and mothers doing the same, every story about people just like us.

They entered the Mystery and defeated the dragon that only seemed to consume them, bearing back to us the priceless spiritual boons of what does and does not count in life. Those asking what to do with this now sacred place will hear the answer if they listen to these voices of the ruins.

The Site

We have learned again that we have not yet found the words to express, even to ourselves, Fate's rape and murder of New York City. "Unreal city," T. S. Eliot wrote in The Waste Land, *"...I had not thought death had undone so many."*

The Police, Fire, and Emergency personnel are reluctant to describe the Trade Center wreckage as *Ground Zero*. They call it *The Site*. They did not select this by vote or poll but by discovering that the phrase expresses what they feel but cannot yet fully name about these seared and sacred acres.

Site is as rich in meanings as Manhattan's lapping waters are with salt and memory. *Site* may seem a general description of a place or location. Yet it carries meanings like a flag. We sense this in its Latin verb of origin: *sinere*, "to leave, to allow, to remain."

This Amish-plain designation unearths an edge of the true feelings buried deep inside the workers who, as we say, tend the site. The horror of September 11 may resonate in *Ground Zero*, but its spiritual reality buds like a wasteland flower out of *The Site*.

We speak respectfully of an *archeological site*, that space set aside because it contains the everyday things of people who lived before us but were not unlike us. We feel a kinship with them at the hearths where they gathered, as hungry for food and story as we, and in the sprays of now withered flowers they placed with their dead to express a tenderness and love that make them cousins to us all. We protect such places from careless passage or violation because we recognize our family resemblance to those who once breathed and worked and yearned for love there.

Site is medicine's word for the place in the body where the blow was struck, the *wound* suffered. *Site* also refers to the place at which the fertilized egg attaches itself to the *womb*. *The Site* speaks to us of *wound* and *womb*, of a place of suffering that may lead to death and of a place of joining that is the beginning of life.

The Site is our Atlantis, this great place, silent although filled with sound, alive although filled with death, pure as only human hearts can be even in air fouled by the dust devils that are watered into grayish mud by the roving sprinkler trucks that stir memories of the long lost peace of summer streets.

The mood of loss fills this great amphitheater of wreckage as Tchaikovsky's Pathétique symphony pervades a concert hall. For if much has been removed, much remains. Great sections of buildings hang open like battered car doors, their contents exposed in jagged tiers, a freeze frame of their occupants' last moments so poignant that it seems sacrilegious to gaze at it.

The Site is our Coventry, a war-destroyed cathedral with a charred spire of tower facing propped in its wreckage. Around it, as in an ancient town square, huddle the structures that received savage secondary damage. Here are the scarred and boarded shops and schools, hotels and lesser office buildings, many of which will come to life again, much as we will, the same and yet never the same.

At the center of *The Site*, energy wrestles with loss like Jacob with the angel of death. Here the confident muscularity of America is at work lifting out the debris beneath the swaying white booms of the birds of prey machines, as majestic as the ruins themselves. Nearby stand the trucks, silent pall bearers waiting to carry away the tower remains.

And American organization is everywhere, in the tents in which the workers eat, and others in which they bathe, and others, as lively as those in an oil patch boom town, filled with everything, from fresh socks to a few moments of friendliness, and from new boots to rubdowns for these valiant harvesters of overwhelming grief and loss.

One grieves for New York, its suffering placed almost beyond grief by the crash of yet another plane into a neighborhood that had already offered its sacrifice to this darkest of autumns. Perhaps the only fitting thing that the New York Yankees could bring back from the World Series was loss, rather than noisy victory, to lay as a wreath of honor at *The Site*.

Listen, then, to the scripture for a Sunday in this season: "Today salvation has come to this house, because he too is a son of Abraham. For the Son of Man came to seek out and to save the lost" (Luke 19:9).

Revelations at Thanksgiving

We stand on the ridge, lighted palely by the fleeing sun, just above the dark, chill valley of winter. We have usually made our accounting with the year by now, knowing, as the farmers do, of the land now sealed until spring, how to count our blessings and mark where we stand with life...

This year, we are certain only that we are still absorbing the blow, that it will ache like a healing bone within us through the snowy sleep of winter, and that its pain, but not its mystery, may be less when spring's first light rises.

Still, a blessing is not the same as good luck. Blessings are never a bargain and are paid for in the currency minted in the soul by our surrender of something we have been holding back of ourselves.

Good luck, conversely, may be as cheap as a lottery ticket or as morally expensive as insider trading. If it adds to our bank account, it also increases our fear of losing it, and we begin to screen people better than airport security guards to protect what we have and hide who we are. Such fear, the scriptures tell us, casts out love.

On this first Thanksgiving after September 11, we may count as a blessing big enough for the nation what we learned about so many people who died that day. They were good at love, we learn, and, in their last minutes, they used their love to cast out fear.

They have heaped these blessings onto our tables and, as the scripture says again, into our laps, full measure, pressed down, shaken together, and running over. Blessed are they, and we through them, who thought not of themselves but of others and laid down their lives for them.

We may offer thanks that the Age of Revelation, said to have closed with the death of the last of Jesus' apostles, has been reopened in our time. *Revelation* comes from the Latin word that means "unveiling." *Apocalypse* also means "unveiling."

Scourges are the opposite of blessings and we know more about them now as well. Mythically and spiritually, scourges always slay love and beauty. They reveal in their thousand tactics—as in the Nazis breaking up Jewish families the better to breed terror—that if love is killed, the beauty of life is slain as well.

September 11 was a day not to destroy towers dedicated to trade as much as to massacre lovers as individuals, marked as plainly as hospitals by their good hearts, along with their families, their children, the simple times they savored and, finally, life itself. For these lovers breathed their spirits into the buildings, as Jesus did into the sick and dying, to bring them alive and to reveal their beauty at every dawn.

It is true that *apocalypse* seemed victorious as the curtain walls of the Trade Center fell into fountains of debris and dust dark enough to rob the day of the sun. So, too, its scourging horsemen seemed triumphant at the flaming Pentagon and in the scorched Pennsylvania meadow.

The *apocalypse* betrayed its own monstrosity by *unveiling* the beauty of those it destroyed. Seeking to rob them of time, it revealed what was eternal about them. Those who seemed lost have instead been found, and the simple beauty of their ordinary lives has been made into an imperishable blessing for us.

Our eyes have been opened because their tongues have been loosed and they have spoken to us of everyday values we thought long decertified by the post-modern world. Their stories are blessings of reassurance, not because they are so different from but because they are so like our own and those of our own families.

These men and women bless us by confiding in us. Some tell us again their own version of *Beauty and the Beast*, while others help us to understand the true meaning of the apocalyptic phrase, "the end of the world."

They tell us stories of how, on meeting, often by surprise, something was unveiled for them as they suddenly saw in each other a beauty so rare as to be saved for their eyes alone and so great as to tame the raging beast of loneliness in that moment. Their *world came to an end*, not through apocalyptic destruction but because their love allowed them to see together what they could not see alone, the infinite beauty of the world they now shared with each other.

And so an old world has come to an end for us as well and we count at Thanksgiving the ordinary human blessings whose power terror revealed but could not destroy.

The mystery of the world as it is

We are worn out from looking on the suffering of this year that is now dying with no last words, this long school term of daily examinations less on what we have learned than on whether we have learned anything at all, this long prison sentence in which time passes while it also stands still. "Yes, we have gone on living," many feel with T. S. Eliot, "living and partly living."

Those words, from *Murder in the Cathedral*, match the sense that the year challenges some central American longings. We love mysteries but also want them solved immediately. The idea that some mysteries cannot be solved, that they are forever beyond us, is disquieting. We protect ourselves against mystery by donning earphones, passing through museums more like drone planes than art lovers, never allowing the paintings to speak directly to—and possibly disturb—our own depths.

Our mystery-intolerance makes us obsessed with *closure*, with capping our experiences the way Americans cap burning oil wells, terminating the flaming overflow of such mysteries as death and loss. Some say that we need closure on the thousands of deaths out of due time we have seen this year, or otherwise their meaning may forever elude us and our mourning never be done.

These frustrated and frustrating longings are aspects of a larger engulfing drama of human experience in which we all have speaking parts. We suffer together the suffering world, that "stained glass," as the poet put it, "on the white radiance of existence."

We continue to witness this ongoing mystery that will not be solved even when its planners and perpetrators have been apprehended, found guilty, and punished. That is the easy part of this mystery that is the *sacramentum mundi*, the sacrament of our world, the symbol reflecting the image of the world back to it and to us.

The attacks of September 11 constitute, before our eyes and in our hearts, a mythical event in a myth-starved era, a tragic yet mystical orchestration of human experience that we enter, without explanation, solution, or hope of closure, to discover and recognize the mystery of being.

No other current event so captures the unfathomable character of our existence together, *as we are* in *the world as it is*. The "religious function of a mythology, that is, the mystical function" Joseph Campbell reminds us, "...represents the discovery of the dimension of the mystery of being."

Christmas is a mythical event whose story will outlast time's variations and history's vandals. It will even survive the ACLU because it tells us our story, the great human story we recall at the peak of every year.

God once looked at His creation and found that it was good. But Christmas tells us that He entered *the world as it is*, our world, the same imperfect world of pain, injustice, and sin that lies about us, this vast, tragic wonder of love and goodness ever terrorized by loss and death.

The September 11 attacks reveal, as nothing has since the Holocaust, *the world as it is*, this Mystery we can never solve, abounding in sins and flaws that reformers never understand and can never extinguish. We are never free of this pain and sorrow or of the love, ever outweighed and overmatched, that thrives on this imperfection, is found only in this imperfection, the love that makes life possible and conquers death itself.

September 11 symbolizes the religious mystery of our being. How unlike an angelic choir we are. In this mythical event we find everything that has ever happened in human history, every language spoken, every emotion of the heart, every age group, every degree of education, every state of health—from the gym-minted fit to the handicapped, every longing and every hurt, every dream and every delusion, every hope and every kind of plan, the timid and the brave, yes, and, above all and in everyone, sparks enough of love and self-forgetfulness to redeem it all—in James Joyce's words, "Here Comes Everybody."

As the next of kin, we cannot ignore this mystery. How could we miss the family resemblance and fail to recognize the Christmas religious mystery we can never solve, of our lives *as we are* in *the world as it is*?

The Seasons of 2002

What causes sex abuse by priests? Vatican changes subject

The scandal of sexual child abuse by Catholic priests has broken open as all long-suppressed truths always do, leaving everybody wondering how it could have occurred and been covered up for such a long time...

What explains the tragic worldwide explosion of sexual abuse by priests and other religious personnel? How could these men and women, trained over many years in seminaries and religious houses to understand and practice chastity as a condition of their calling, suddenly have found the same unresolved sexual problem bringing intractable pain to those they abused and incomparable suffering to themselves?

One could suggest that they were all simultaneously possessed by Satan, and that the smoking hoof prints of the Prince of Darkness link rectories and religious houses in a circuit of temptation.

That, at least, would be an answer. It would not be correct, because common sense and traditional Catholic teaching tell us never to look for preternatural explanations for events before we exhaust the natural explanations.

This troubling question of *why* is not even asked, much less answered, in the Vatican decision to place all cases of priests accused of sexually abusing minors under the jurisdiction of the Congregation for the Doctrine of the Faith. There, in secret, a forum will deal with such cases, thereby protecting, it is asserted, the rights of victims, the church, and the accused priests.

This instrument was crafted to avoid the central question by a silky smooth change of the subject. It deals not with *why* sex abuse occurs among the clergy but with the *what* and *how* of regulations and procedures.

It is comparable, therefore, to a government bureaucracy that, asked how mad cow disease could have infected the nation's herds, distributes rules to farmers on how to lock their barn doors.

The Vatican officials responsible for this policy statement are not from the line of the apostles. They descend from characters so crafty and puzzling that you wonder how they got into the gospels at all. You remember the crowd that made friends with the mammon of iniquity or covered themselves by cutting in half what debtors owed their masters. Their successors could exchange skin grafts with them as they distract us with discussions about which Roman department should handle sex abuse cases in secret.

The problem is not that these processes will be *in secret* but that these rules have been published *in public*. We need a large sign: DANGER, DISTRACTION AHEAD: FINES DOUBLED IN CHURCH BUREAUCRACY WORK ZONE.

It is insulting and embarrassing to Catholics everywhere that, a generation after a sexual crisis emerged from its century's old chrysalis to blossom as a flower of evil, the official response changes the subject and ignores the question of how and why this happened in the first place.

We waste our righteous indignation by claiming that these rules mask a *current cover up*. The *cover up* has been going on for years. It was abetted in many cultures, including that of the United States, through the cooperation of police, judicial, and media institutions that, in an era of privilege for social hierarchy, suppressed scandalous news about public figures and professionals, including priests.

The *cover up*'s collapse exposed the sexual problems of religious personnel, freed victims from the silent and private shame to which they had been relegated, and subjected priests and religious to noisy public shame for behavior they did not understand themselves.

This *cover up*'s sour fiction provided procedures, of which these new ones are cousins once removed, that obscured the real causes of sexual abuse so that church personnel moved like free agents from one assignment to another, like Draculas freed to find fresh blood.

The new rules are the old rules that postpone mature resolution of a problem that has ravaged the lives of victims and perpetrators and has laid the church itself open to charges of hypocrisy in its public teaching on sexuality and the primacy of all that preserves and promotes life.

The tragic outcome of this obfuscation and delay is now being acted out in Boston. Not a rosary's worth of new regulations can spare Catholics the embarrassment of witnessing former priest John Geoghan face criminal and civil penalties for sexually abusing minors through four decades of being caught, supposedly treated, and transferred to other parishes without a warning label of his danger to the young.

Had the question been *why* instead of *what*, this terrible story would never have been told. Neither would Bernard Cardinal Law have been engulfed by a storm that had broken before he came to Boston. The church can expect more of this sadness until it asks *why* and *how* this problem came into being.

Don Hanifin

Make you to shine like the sun...

Once more we gather to say good-bye to a dear friend, a man big in every way, a man who delighted in mischief so that nobody was surprised when the fire alarm went off during his funeral Mass in Naples, Florida, and the fire department officials later reported that it must have been triggered by an invisible hand.

Don Hanifin appeared to me in church last Saturday. Right over there. As the people were singing a familiar hymn. *And He will raise you up on eagles' wings / Bear you on the breath of dawn/ Make you to shine like the sun*... And there he was, shining like the sun, as he did in life, defiant as a turret, beaming under his suntan and damn the dermatologists...

If you intone the name Don Hanifin, the choir here in Pelican Bay, in Naples at large, and in cities along the coast all the way to New England—in places too many for us to count but none too small for him to visit—that great choir responds, *EVERYBODY knows Don Hanifin.*

If Don was easy to know, he was also hard to miss. He stands in our imagination right now, in his bathing suit and baseball cap, a combination of a Christmas tree and a Sumo wrestler, waving a greeting, come over here, there's plenty of room, smiling, mostly in welcome but partly in mischief. Sit down, he bids us, I've saved a chair for you...

Everybody knows Don Hanifin. Yes, I said to myself as, like you, I thought of all these bright mint years in which we knew and were known by him. But, as I thought about him and that great hospitable presence we recognize, I found myself asking, *Did I* really *know Don Hanifin? Did you* really *know Don Hanifin?*

In Thornton Wilder's *Our Town*, one of the characters says, "If you want to know the truth about somebody, you have to *overhear* it." In this place that he did so much to make into *our town*, what truth did you hear and what deeper truth did you overhear?

Would anybody contest that Don was an Irishman, a contesting Irishman at that? Is he lessened in memory or in truth if someone applies to him an adjective applied to many other Irishmen as well? Was he ever, do you suppose, *stubborn*? Did anybody ever sense that, like a mountain accommodating opposite energies deep within itself, he could, at one and the same moment, be both the irresistible force and the immovable object?

Does the dictionary definition of *stubborn* ring true here: "determined to exert one's will, not easily persuaded, obstinate"? Is that how we *heard* him at times? Or does a further definition tell us the fuller truth that we must *overhear*? "Characterized by perseverance, persistent"?

How much richer that word becomes, how much better applied, when we read the dictionary example of *stubborn soil*. Because, of course, out of such soil crops grow to nourish us and flowers bloom to brighten our lives. We are grateful to one who perseveres in working the soil, who does not give up on it, who has faith, we might say, in the treasures that may come from it.

You knew, or perhaps you overheard, that Don began as a florist, that he persisted against his parents' plans for his college education, taking leave of Syracuse University the very day his father left him there, to follow the artist in himself as a pilgrim without a map would follow a single star, and that he persevered in a calling that harvested floral beauty out of the reluctant soil, then visions out of the stony New England earth in the interiors that he first imagined and later designed?

Research tells us that creative people can balance seemingly contrary forces within themselves at the same time. So, yes, that irresistible force was ever engaged with the immovable object within him in the dynamo of his creativity, the source of his confidence in himself, his faith in God, in his family, in his friends, in the possibilities every day held for good work and good times.

The shore was the right place to meet Don Hanifin, for at its edge the elements of all life intermingle—earth, air and water and, for fire, friendship and good conversation. In these elements, he was in his element. He bore watching when he entered the waters. When the Gulf inched just above 60 degrees, the men of St. Maarten, raised on Northeastern Atlantic shores, were about the only ones in the surf. It could have been a mildly corrupt Boston Law Firm—*Hassett, Healey, Kennedy, and Hanifin.*

Don operated in the water even more nimbly than he did on the land. You remember that interlude when he had purchased a new condominium at the Grovesnor but still had one to sell at St. Maarten? We entered the water together one day. Bobbing nearby, I listened as he struck up a conversation with a stranger. The swell rose to obscure them but each time they came into view, Don had elicited more information from this man: his name and occupation, his address and phone. Could his social security number and Mastercard be far behind? The men disappeared behind a shield of blue water, then popped up like corks again—now Don had his origins, his family, his career, have you ever thought of living in Naples? Had the fellow not been hailed out at that moment by his wife, I swear Don would have closed the deal on the next swell. Vintage Hanifin, you might say, this magician of the Gulf where, every day, he turned the water into wine.

Everybody knows Don Hanifin. And everybody has a favorite story about him. Perhaps your favorite is that of the consolation prize he bought for himself after a bad day on the stock market—a gorilla suit that he donned before he went calling on his neighbors. When Marie Pearl answered his knock, he swept her up in his arms and carried her around her apartment, King Kong and Fay Wray heading for the Empire State Building again. You all have stories—of Hanifin the movie fan getting you to go to the theater and Hanifin the movie critic stomping out before ten minutes of it had unreeled—of laying plans for a St. Patrick's Day extravaganza and presiding, his green tam perched on his head and a large Manhattan clutched in his hand, noting with a cheerful lack of modesty that the evening had been a *Hanifin Production.*

But did you really know Don Hanifin? Children see right through us to who we are and what we are really like. What did we overhear when Wally and Carol Gross's grandchildren awarded him, as they did to nobody else around the pool, the honorary title of *Uncle?* And what did we overhear when we learned that Don and Joan had quietly begun to support a poor seminarian from an even poorer country so that he could finish his Roman studies and be ordained a priest?

And could we really know Don Hanifin if we did not know him and Joan together? Like the greatest art, the deepest love seems so natural and so unforced that it looks easy. So Don and Joan seemed, so they *seem*, for we cannot speak of their love except in the present tense. Yet what prodigies of ingenuity, foresight, human understanding, and planning must dear Joan have worked in order to make safe the way for the Hanifin production of his own life—that great three-ring circus with calliope music, sawdust, noise, clowns, barkers and the MGM lion himself—as he turned into the driveway to their child-filled home every night? How much we learn about love from just such people, and how much we learn about God's love, as full and fitted to each of us as theirs was to each other.

We are not surprised that the sun should bring him to mind. The sun, of course, is the symbol of eternity, as the moon that pales and disappears is that of time. For the moon gets all its light from the sun as we, in time, get all ours from eternity. God teaches us something about the eternal in people who so splendidly reflect the sun. Eternity seems less strange, less distant, for all the dear people we have come to know and love in this blessed sunlight. Don Hanifin would want us to remember them as we remember him, for he is in their midst. There is Kitty Bitterman, yes, and Walter Rogers, too, and Phil Daniels, and two Pats, McGee and Grant. Come over here, there's plenty of room; I've saved a chair for you...

How much we have learned of eternity from all these people we loved and were loved by in time. They are here this morning, just as Don is. Can't you sense them, can't you feel them? For God has lifted them up on eagles' wings, borne them on the breath of morn, made them to shine like the sun, and holds them in the hollow of His hand.

The ashes of mystery

We wear the same ashes, each and all of us, this year, the ashes touched to our foreheads on September 11 like a time stamp, signifying the moment and the morning when Before ended and After began...

The clock of time has been reset, of course, but most of us have not. We feel different. We have not gotten over it, somebody says, and we nod, yes, that's right, as we read the latest explanation for why we feel the same and yet changed at the same time.

A famous clothes designer says that people have become more "sincere" and that "sincere is not good for high fashion." Decorators claim that where once we favored the casual, we now demand a "new formality" with chandeliers and antiques (*Wall Street Journal*, January 18, 2002). Travel agents say that we want to go away and stay at home, too, and cruise ships now hug the homeland shores. Some artists "were stopped in their tracks, paralyzed by the loss. Others turned out rapid-fire, quick-reaction work, as if to control psychological damage" (*New York Times*, February 1, 2002).

They are reading the after-shocks of mystery, the thousand ripples still radiating from that moment when summer held its breath and the seasons collapsed around us. What we, and they, are feeling is the pull of eternity in the things of time, turning the everyday and the commonplace into the surreal and distorted. Salvador Dali painted distended and melting watches that puzzled his contemporaries but speak to us of how time, that we think to trap in jeweled cases and atomic clocks, turns into mercury once it has been invaded by the eternal.

Ash Wednesday will also feel different to us this year. September 11 was so thick with ashes that they erased the day, so that one fire rescuer would say that only the first filtered light told him that the world had not ended, that he was not buried in midnight. And his comrades tell how they felt "unmoored from reality," taken out of time itself, in the choking veil where, at one moment two would be standing, and, in the next, one would be left (*New York Times*, January 30, 2002).

The ashes distributed next week will link us to the mystery of that event and, in the symbolic language of rituals, will bring us into communion with the lost and those who loved them. Ashes symbolize penance and reconciliation and their origin lies in the Jewish custom of sprinkling ashes on the head a sign of repentance (*Encyclopedia of Catholicism*, edited by Richard P. McBrien, HarperSanFrancisco, 1995, p. 100). Ashes are also used in the dedication of a church.

We are not surprised that the root of ash, *as*, means "to burn" or "to glow," and that its Latin form, *ara*, means "altar" or "hearth." Ashes carry our human and religious history, for they whisper of the hearths where our families gather and the altars where our prayers are offered, of why we build churches in sacred places, and of every glowing forge of the human in which time and eternity are melded together.

Thousands of people come to view the site in lower Manhattan. The magnet of the eternal draws them mystically, for ashes also mean ruins. Along with the gashes in the Pentagon and the Pennsylvania hills, this place of ashes is the hearth on which we build our love. And it is an altar where we can leave the wreath of loss that is the price of our being able to love at all. It is a church in which time and eternity can never be separated from one another.

Lent is a compound of these elements. Easter, like Passover, is determined by the first full moon after the spring solstice when day and night are equal and the sun, symbol of eternity, and the moon, symbol of time, stand across the sky from each other. Our timepiece moon reflects us, dying and rising each month, receiving all its light from the eternal sun.

Lent means spring, and its Easter climax recognizes that time is lit by the eternal as the moon is by the sun. Next Wednesday's ashes symbolize more than our mortality. They are as rich as the sea in what humans need, of glowing hearths for love, of sacred altars for our losses, and of time ever flooded with eternity.

Priest sex abuse a moral issue before it is anything else

The vacuum of leadership among the nation's Catholic bishops since the 1996 death of Joseph Cardinal Bernardin has in the midst of the clergy sex abuse scandal turned into a black hole much like the black holes described by astronomers. They give off no light as they draw everything nearby into their dark whirlpool of energy.

Catholics want to admire and support their bishops but, as the latter find new ways to bungle the clergy sex abuse crisis almost every day, believers wonder if they are being deliberately tested to see how strong their faith really is.

Bishops need not worry about that. Look down from any Catholic pulpit at the people gathered for worship and you will see men and women who have already faced every imaginable trial that life can offer, from the sudden loss of children to death to the slow loss of loved ones to Alzheimer's disease. Do not preach to them of suffering, for they know it intimately in its every form.

Catholics understand and can accept tragedies in the public life of their church. They have spent their lives doing that. They now indicate, in polls taken in Boston recently, that their faith in Catholic teaching is not shaken by the sex abuse crisis. If their faith is not shaken, their confidence in their leaders is.

These leaders have been operating more as bureaucrats than as bishops and, as a result, ordinary people react to them, as they do to IRS agents and Enron executives, with a skepticism earned through betrayal. The bishops have made their people doubt them by first treating pedophilia as an exaggeration, then as a financial matter, next as a legal matter, and now as a justice system issue.

They have not confronted it for what it is, a moral problem that involves their priests and implicates themselves.

They have begun to refer to it as a crime and to hand the names of accused priests over to prosecutors. This reminds me of two things. The first is the puzzling gospel story in which the debtor is handed over to the jailer until he pays every cent he owes, an improbable solution with an unlikely outcome.

The second is the Russian novel imagery in which children are tossed off the well-blanketed sleigh by adults anxious to satisfy the bloodthirsty wolves pursuing them across the snow, expediency sacrificing morality along with the children.

America's bishops have paid almost their last cent and it is has been reported that the church in Boston is examining its portfolio of properties with a view to selling some to try to find a permanent solution to the pedophilia crisis considered as a *financial* problem.

They threw the abused children off the sleigh for a whole generation, fighting their claims vigorously by countersuits in some dioceses, such as that of Bridgeport, Connecticut, when New York's Edward Cardinal Egan was its bishop. He also made priests into "independent contractors" for whose actions the diocese had no legal liability. That is how the crisis was made into a *legal* problem.

Now bishops are tossing drivers and footmen to the wolves, naming priests' names faster than the movie moguls did those of suspected communists in the "Hollywood Ten" days. That is to make this crisis into a *criminal* problem.

An appalling new version of the cliché that war is too important to be left to generals tells us that morality may be too significant to be left to bishops. They are appointed, after all, to be teachers of faith and morals. Morality is the elephant sitting in the sanctuary, hard to move and hard to ignore. The congregation can see it and is astounded that ecclesiastics have called in stockbrokers, lawyers, and district attorneys to utter magic formulas over it to make it disappear. Instead, it trumpets its distress louder than ever.

The generation-long crisis of priest pedophilia is, in its unexamined origins, its manipulated history, and its present tortured and torturing manifestations, a *moral* issue that must be defined as such before any true resolution can occur. A venerable theological saying tells us that if we want to know the morality of something we should ask what the majority of healthy people hold on the issue.

The bishops have these available in every parish, the pure-hearted and long-suffering people who could clarify and resolve this moral issue for them without effort and without charge. That resolution will come from the faith they have in the church and may restore the confidence they would like to have in their bishops.

Searching for our wholeness

America's cardinals went to pieces in public last week, in part because they had lost touch with the wholeness of human beings. Simultaneously, the great religious revelation of our time continues at the wound in lower Manhattan. There the mystery of our longing to be whole is celebrated daily on that rough altar as solemnly as a Eucharist by men searching for the remains of 9/11 victims, this is my body, yes, and this is my blood and we do this in remembrance of you.

So uneasy did our cardinals seem with the human suffering beneath the clergy sex abuse scandal after their two-day Roman meeting that one wondered if they had ever been parish priests, if they had ever bent over the beds of the dying, blessed a child, or stood fast with people in their deep and wordless grief after incomprehensible loss.

Perhaps that is why several did not appear, inventing, even as you and I have when we really didn't want to be somewhere, "previous engagements." This may have been the only moment in which these princes of the church achieved the "transparency" that some have lauded as the way prelates should relate to their people. Transparent, indeed, for we could see right through them.

The cardinals seemed, ordinary Catholics said, in their simple pure-of-heart reaction, "out of touch." Out of touch as much as those still longing to find the bodies of their loved ones lost on 9/11 are in touch with the sacredness of human intimacy at the core of both tragedies.

So urgent is our healthy human need for contact with those we love that the "largest forensic investigation in United States history is pressing limits of biomedical research to identify victims of September

11 terrorist attacks" (*New York Times*, April 22, 2002). Experts plan to use new scientific techniques, such as DNA analysis, to match individual names to remains so that they may be returned to their families for burial.

The darkness of this amphitheater of ruins is dispersed by the light in the eyes of the searchers who know that a true fragment of bone can restore whole individuals to those who still love and long for them. Here the story of Lazarus is re-enacted every day as the dead are bidden to come forth, to be taken in the hands that touch them as tenderly now as they once eagerly embraced them in life.

The great religious mystery of intimacy is held in this search as gently as the seeds of next spring's growth are in autumn's last flower. We stand at the edge of this site that may not be as broad but is just as sacred as St. Peter's Square. We feel the enormous pull of the elementary particles of our human existence in the energy of love that lifts off these remains: here I am, find and touch me, draw me close to your body, let me feel and be felt in the wonderful freedom and simple need of that intimacy where we are safe together, take me home, yes, find me, hold me close and take me home.

This daily sacrament of recovery affirms what many ecclesiastics doubt or do not understand: we are not souls serving life sentences in bodies that betray us, nor are we spirits locked in tense combat with the flesh. We are not divided against ourselves so that we rush to the attic of intellect to be safe from the earthy goings on in the cellar. We are unified as persons and there are no higher or lower parts to us, one that is all virtue and the other all vice.

Our sacredness lies in our wholeness. Touch someone's body and you touch all of them, violate someone's body and you make sacrilege of their wholeness. The revelation of 9/11 opens us to the eternal that we experience when we are unguarded in each other's presence and give without taking and so possess more of ourselves and of each other.

The experts searching for the flesh and bone that restore human wholeness stand in sharp and saddening contrast to the cardinals who seemed so unfamiliar with intimacy or the mystery that is violated when a clergyman touches someone else not to give but to steal some-thing for himself. They seemed outside this simplest of human experi-ences; kiss my ring, that's close enough.

Perhaps that is why they have decided that this is a mystery that only the police can solve. It is instead a religious Mystery of human wholeness, their business, and it baffles them. The sadness is that they are too out of touch to be touched by or to recognize it.

Build anything, Ground Zero's spirit will still be there

We stand with the living and the dead at Ground Zero that now resembles, in its vastness, emptiness, and mystery, the hidden desert that Jesus entered for forty days, the sweet desert that showered manna on the questing Jews, and the harsh desert that echoed with John the Baptist's proclamation that one greater than he was to come . . .

The 9/11 site sings of its mystery as softly as the spirit does as it shuffles the desert sands. Here, we have spent most of a year like novices in a new religious order born out of the pain of history itself. What have we seen and what have we heard?

That the secular city is filled with faith, that the greatest of its wonders is ordinary and human sized, just big enough to be borne in the heart. And that religion is not, as Bible-abusing preachers urge, a function of the will in training for title bouts with temptation.

The ordinary saints of 9/11 reveal that religion, like love, belongs to the whole personality, turning us toward rather than away from other people in searching for God. Religion enters us gently through our imaginations rather than tensely by way of the will. Faith, like first love, enters through the eyes, possessing us and leaving us hungry for sacraments, the loaves and fishes, the vigil lights in a lover's eyes, the body embraced and embracing, water to cleanse and wine to warm, oil to heal and salt to savor, each as right as love is for the earth. "I don't know any place," Robert Frost says, "it's likely to go better."

These elements are the open secrets of 9/11, the things the dead carried with them that morning, tethered with us on the lifeline of spiritual mystery that was no mystery to them. Moments of silence at the site are as filled as late night radio traffic with their plainsong litanies of wonders whose simplicity and purity blind us with their revelation.

Revelation has its origin in words for "unveiling." Life's mysteries are out in the open, unveiled in every true human exchange, as in the thousands shared with us on 9/11. Religion is found in the last words of the ordinary saints of 9/11, in the final impulses, deep enough to sum up whole lives, and the law and the prophets, too, biblical vessels poured out but never emptied, all these men and women longing to tell someone else one more time, "I love you..."

The city's great newspaper says of the cleanup, "It is nearly done," and tells of retired fire captain John Vigiano who "has kept vigil there ...ever since his only children —a police detective and a firefighter— disappeared in a summer morning's roar" (*New York Times*, May 3, 2002).

Captain Vigiano is our Everyperson whose sacramental presence at the site cannot be missed. We read that "construction workers, police officers, and firefighters have formed a protective cocoon around" him. After they shake his hand, "they are slow to let go, as though some of his grace might be transferred through touch." As it has now, to all of us.

The eternal lifts off the site as well. We feel it as construction worker Jack Mirto did when, after working his sixty-five-ton excavator there for weeks, he found that "time had lost its meaning, how Thursday could just as well be Tuesday," and how laid off workers were anxious to get back to that zone of mystery, pleading, "Get me a day, get me a night..."

Whatever is built to replace the towers, these spiritual realizations that link love, work, death, and eternal life will always be in this place. New buildings will be vessels of mystical truth, made sacred not just by memory but by the energy of human love, the central mystery of all religion, so lavishly expended here on 9/11, that will charge the air here forever.

Why can't it be then?

Two events, charged with mystery and memory, gently intersect in this coming week, Memorial Day and the end of the rescue effort at the 9/11 site. We cannot fight off, or, in the sacrilegious postmodern phrase, "bring closure" to the experience of loss that is both so profoundly human and religious at the same time.

We deal with the deepest of life's mysteries not by unraveling them but by surrendering to them. We give ourselves to them less as Hercule Poirot than as poets, artists, or lovers and saints do in their daily work and ordinary lives.

If lawyers style themselves as *advocates* in representing our interests, artists, poets, and saints are our *forerunners,* our *scouts* who sense and find their way into the enormous mystery found in every moment to tell us about it and open a way for us to enter it safely ourselves. They are not, however, museum guides, telling us what we must see for ourselves, the *Mysterium tremendum et fascinans,* the *mystery,* as we may freely translate, so *overwhelming* and *engulfing,* of the world exactly as it is.

Ordinary people understand that we gain love not by conquering it according to the tactics suggested by glossy magazines and patent medicine psychologists but by surrendering to it, entering the mystery on its terms rather than ours.

That, of course, is the part that gets us, that surrender that requires us to raise our hands and make our way, undefended and vulnerable, into the transforming mystery that exalts us but makes us suffer, too.

The mystery quickly teaches us that, if we may be hurt, we may hurt others, too. Real intimacy—living and loving at the closest possible range with another—is a religious mystery rather than a psychological trick, because lovers find their true lives only as they lay them down for each other.

Love, despite the promise of a bad old movie, does not mean "never having to say you're sorry." If we really love someone, we must be ready to say we are sorry all the time. If real love needs tenderness, it needs tending, too. As Ann Landers once put it, "Marriages may be made in heaven but the maintenance is done down here on earth."

All lovers are vulnerable to time, a great mystery in itself, because as mythologist Joseph Campbell explains, "Where there is time, there is sorrow." Time works away at us relentlessly, mocking the footnote efforts of Botox to transform faces that look as if they had lived into faces that look impossible to live in. The main text mainlines the mystery inlaid in this week of memory.

The Trade Tower site, filled in or built upon, remains an altar as sacred as St. Peter's, on which the mystery of loss, inseparable from the greater mystery of love, will be offered until time is no more. The rescue phase ends on May 30 at the mid-morning moment when the second tower fell. Bells will toll, measuring out in time our eternal longings, investing the air with mystery, like that at Gettysburg and Normandy, to which we can only surrender.

We drink here the cup of the greatest religious mystery of our time, of the gains and losses known to everybody fully alive, to everybody who ever loved anybody. All 9/11 sites claim pre-eminent mystery not because saints from heaven appeared there but because ordinary people living in ordinary time loved each other there.

We feel, as with the harsher mystery of the sex abuse by priests, how we bleed with eternal longings when we are caught on the sharp edge of time. We yearn fiercely to manipulate time, to turn the master clock of the universe back to before either of these terrible events began so that we could prevent them from happening. We confront ourselves, unable to ride our appetite for the eternal through the veil of time, drinking that cup already taken by the poet, the artist, and the saint, *"Why can't it be then?"*

What is affirmed, as the rescue effort ends at the Trade Tower site, is the mystery that abides—the simple wonder of things in the world exactly as it—the extraordinary mystery of the goodness of ordinary men and women, swimming upstream to the eternal, overcoming the current of time—that will sing forever in the air here.

We pass to each other on this weekend the cup of the sacramental mystery of ordinary life, of loving and trusting and hoping in each other. These are eternal because they conquer time, and they are unmistakably divine because they are so unmistakably human.

After Dallas/going home

The Catholic bishops conclude their meeting after adapting measures to deal with the sex abuse crisis among the clergy. Dallas might as well be Dodge as they hurry to get out of it. It is always in the going home after a decisive event, of course, that we discover what happened and what we really feel about it.

The father gives his daughter away in marriage and uncovers all the misgivings he has failed to express as he drives away from the reception. "I just hope," he sighs to his wife, "that she'll be happy." And it is during the ride home from the cemetery that our ambivalence about the dead rises from the place inside ourselves where we buried it, "I wish I had one last chance," we muse, "to talk to him again..."

On the ride home, each of us with our own deep thoughts speaks softly and elliptically, if we speak at all, and the background music is the Being Human Blues. Peace can be our companion, too, but, now that the grave deed is done, we may ask whether we did enough or could have done something differently.

What will the bishops hear in the lonely quiet of their long journeys home? If they have passed tough sanctions against priest sex abusers, will they wonder what they have really done? Some voice, innocent as that of an abused child, may ask them, "Do you think you have healed me, and all the others, by dealing only with a symptom of a larger disorder in the church?"

As they gaze out at the clouds, they may wonder whether, in finally erecting this dam of penalties, they have diverted the thundering waters, or will they learn, as engineers recently have in the Southwest, that a dam once thought a triumph for a river may so alter the ecological balance that it is a disaster instead?

This is the hour when everything we don't want to think about rises anyway to ask prelates what they have really accomplished. Have they had a massive, unintended impact on the inner life of the church by handing over their pastoral responsibilities to the criminal justice system? Will Catholics who sacrifice to teach at lower pay in Catholic schools learn that they are suspect from the start and that their names may be entered casually into the eternal life of a criminal database?

Will the angel of regret visit the bishops as they doze to inquire about their reliance on lawyers to draft their principles? Lawyers are advocates and their style is adversarial. They bring not peace but a sword to problems. Their style disrupts trust and clouds truth. What is their effect when the problem is trust and the victim is truth?

The homebound traveler stirs at the pilot's voice: We will land in twenty minutes. What then, the inner voice asks, what do you do if, by the law of unintended consequences, you have turned the church from a family into a virtual police state?

Familiar sights appear below the airplane's wings as the bishop tries to shake another voice out of his head. But the voice persists, as eerily as the ghosts to Scrooge: What of the past? What of the future?

Bishops may react as many politicians do, in the present, solving today's problems, and, if they cause a problem for tomorrow, solve that tomorrow. But the haunting raises a vision of the Bishops' Meetings Past: What about all those times when you denied, delayed, or postponed dealing with the sexual abuse problem that has now dealt so decisively with you?

The homebound bishops' vision reveals the centuries in which, to untold suffering for ordinary people, the official church taught a distorted image of human personality in which sexuality was Satan's instrument and good people were made to feel guilty for being human and many marriages and many homes were racked by the resulting pain. The inner voice continues: Look carefully and see if some of these victimizers, whom you now cast off, were not first victims themselves of households in which sex was so repressed that, wounded sexually, they bore their open wounds like a cruel stigmata into the priesthood, to transfer to the innocents in their care.

"Going Home" is a folk song that catches our pain and yearning. Its bittersweet mood of reverie makes us think about where we have been and why we went there and to face whether we have been the mythological hero who has slain the dragon of ignorance and can bring home truth, or whether we avoided the great battle and bring nothing but our own child-like need for comfort with us.

It is in the quiet going home after the noisy event that the truth sits on our shoulders, whispering into our ears. Bishops hear what we all hear: What have we really done with our chances and how will we live with our choices from now on?

Dear Ann Landers

That familiar salutation also serves as a valedictory description of a great and good woman. She was dear, as genuine treasures are, to the millions to whom for nearly fifty years she gave common-sense advice on everything from broken hearts to broken plumbing…

And she was dear, as true friends are, to those who had her for one. My wife and I were blessed to have places in that circle that expanded and turned double and triple deep around her without anybody's losing their place or their eye contact with her.

She often said, in that voice enriched by its high Iowa plains origin, "All the good people in the world eventually get to know each other." She worked hard to implement that idea just as she encouraged individuals to bring out the best in themselves without postponing it for a later day when the conditions would be perfect—sunny, dry, the track fast—and the risk would be low.

Eppie, as she was as instantly known in Chicago and elsewhere as only the one regarded famous can be, *Eppie* understood that, for us humans, the conditions would never be ideal, and the risk of our talents must be taken even on muddy tracks and under sullen skies, or we would miss the race altogether.

She understood that we might have only one chance to do the right thing, or say the right word, or respond to true love, and that our fulfillment and happiness depend on our readiness to seize the human moment, in which we might lose, rather than fool ourselves with daydreams we never win, such as cashing in on the lottery.

That is the risk she took when she won the 1955 contest to become Ann Landers in the Chicago newspapers. She brought the same spirit to a speech at Harvard Medical School. An audience member asked in the plainchant of snobbery, "What qualifications do you have to speak to us?"

Eppie did not skip a beat. "None at all," she replied calmly. No, she had no graduate degree, no advanced training, just the God-given common sense with which she entered the world. Then she proceeded to wow the audience with her lecture.

Eppie's open secret was that she knew who she was and that she never tried to be anybody else. She was the Jewish girl from Sioux City who went on to become the world's most widely read columnist and one of its most famous women. She learned how to wear diamonds and furs and how, in arriving at any gathering, to make an entrance that drew all eyes to her, but she would laugh hilariously in describing herself afterward.

That ability to skirt the bonfires of the Vanity and avoid being singed by the flames was one of her great strengths. With a good-natured wink, she could have spoken the line delivered by Katharine Hepburn in *A Matter of Gravity* (Enid Bagnold, 1976): "Nature has left some marks but I have removed them."

About to go out, she would glance in a mirror at her hair, as secure as an ironclad against any potential breeze. "Pretty red tonight," she would say with a laugh, making the world an amused co-conspirator in her evenly matched battle with time.

She understood time as only somebody with a deeply religious sense of life could. Time is the currency of life, she understood, and there is no saving it for a rainy day. Spend it generously, especially on others, fill it with the good work you can do now, not tomorrow, invest it in the next generation, why are you putting off love when it is the only antidote to time?

Of the thousand memories, here is one from behind the scenes. In 1975, she announced in her own column that her husband was divorcing her. Speaking warmly of Jules Lederer and their thirty-six-year marriage, she asked her readers to understand its goodness even though it "did not cross the finish line."

The night that he left, an Eppie the world would never see spent the evening assembling socks and shirts and shorts to send to Jules. He always forgot these things, she said, he'll need them now.

That is how I remember this tiny woman, larger than life but down to earth, following her own advice, don't cry over it, you still love him, do it now, time is all we really have to spend on each other.

Why do babies cry in church?

How is it, you may have wondered, that babies seem to know where we are going to sit in church and, like divining rods seeking subterranean water, move those holding them to settle in the pew right behind us?...

This phenomenon, noted in temples since the first light spread beneath time's door—why do you think they sacrificed doves if not to drown out the nursery chorus?—may also be connected with Mystery, that Capital Letter energy of the Divine that pecks restlessly at the inner shell of all creation.

Babies who cry in church are, by the harshest of judgments, a mixed blessing. They sometimes seem to possess that intuitive timing that allows a great baseball player to choose the exact split second in the pitcher's motion to break away from first base and successfully steal second. Infants, who only seem unknowing, sometimes howl at that split second when preachers open their mouths to wing it through another sermon.

The ensuing contest—like that between choir monks who have been in the monastery too long, exchanging antiphons like hand grenades—is usually indecisive, as preacher and babe raise their pitch in attempts to prevail over one another. Some in the congregation wonder why the crying rooms in the back of churches are no longer used; did they go out with the Latin Mass? Others root for the child in swaddling clothes, as if he or she had the effect of old-time indulgences that could decrease the time they have to spend in that special purgatory of not-quite-prepared sermons.

Which is harder to take, the questioner asks in the style of the parable, the sermon in which the priest describes in lesser words the story he has just read aloud in the gospel, or the child crying, on behalf of the whole congregation, for mercy?

But infants do not cry in church to vex priests, the finest of whom are vexed enough these days. They do it because their cries and gurgles are sacramental in themselves as they plead the human case in God's house. They pierce our distractions, arouse us from daydreams, rescue us from our all too idle musing, bring us back to real life, alerting us to its Mystery and wonder, allowing us to hear the mystical sound of a child taking on life, grasping and engaging with it, singing of creation's depths, and opening us, if we let it, to the experience of the sacred that the interior of the church and the celebration of the liturgy are meant to provide.

We must peel away the bitter rind of the child's cry to taste the fruit from the tree of life within. Think, if you will, of all the pro-life sermons you have heard, and of some bishops relishing their self-righteousness in bearing down on Catholic politicians who adopt a pro-choice position, canceling invitations, forbidding such politicians to speak on church property. *There*, they say, *that* is what pro-life means.

Have you ever heard a sermon, as I once did, preached in that same self-justifying tone by a priest who could not hide his dislike of Americans as he thundered out phrases like, "You are a nation of murderers!"?

Do either of these approaches deepen your sense of life and your commitment to defend it? Do they open you to the simple wonder of life and growth that is at the very center of all religious Mystery?

Think for a moment of the great vault door to religious Mystery that opens gently, voice-activated by the cry of a child making an eager claim on existence, the miracle of life refreshed and renewed in our hearing. Think of the parents who brought the child into the world at no small cost and no small risk. Think, as you survey, of the couples who take on the task (often underestimated and under-credited) of collecting, bathing, and dressing their children so that they can attend Mass as a family. There is religious wonder in these vignettes of parents working small miracles in the midst of their share of illness, setbacks, and discouragements, putting their families first, allowing us to see in life the kind of wholehearted sacrifice remembered at the altar.

Why do babies cry in church? Because we need them to sound that human note of transcendence that is more true in its tone than the tower bells or the filigree notes of the great organ. Babies cry in church because it is the right place for them to say yes to the Mystery of life and to remind us to do the same.

Who goes to church anyway?

Surveys regularly tell us how many people attend weekly religious services. Along with crime rate and stock market surveys, indicators easily confused with each other these days, they fluctuate and disclose little about who worships and why.

We already know who worships and why. This information is contained in the gospels, written so long ago, and are on display in most houses of worship—and certainly in Catholic churches—right now.

Many experts on prayer suggest that, to establish contact with God, we should wipe away all distractions, bow our heads, and close our eyes. Divine conversation, they imply, begins only after you shut the world out.

Would you, however, tell artists that to contact their Muse they should deny themselves the sight of the world? Real artists consume the world with their eyes and their souls. They understand intuitively that, if they do not observe everything, they will not see anything, that to starve them of sight of the world deprives them of their unique vision of it as well.

We need to keep our eyes open if we want to find out who really goes to church. A sacramental faith like Catholicism is made to satisfy, if not satiate, our senses and, even then, as Paul tells us, the eye will not be filled with seeing. The sacramental symbols are culled from the primary colors and everyday staples of God's creation: water and light, bread and wine, salt and oil. They have been found around every hearth at which humans have taken warmth and nourishment throughout history.

These elements stand next to each other on your kitchen shelves, some in sacks half filled, some with their labels half torn away, some in packages that bear the smudged fingerprints—how human, we say—of those who have used them and put them away casually.

In fact, these sacramental elements resemble the rows of people sitting around you—in front and behind you, too—in church. If we want to contact the Divine, the thing to see is the Human spread sacramentally about us, some of us half filled, some in packages with bursting seams, or labels hanging loose, and all of us with the smudges and scars we have acquired in being used, now this way and now that by life, the source of all true asceticism. When we live with our eyes open, we never have to invent a sacrifice for Lent.

Indeed, the great sacrament is the congregation itself, these good people, each a bearer of religious mystery, all of them gathered not to find faith in church but to bring their own there to be reflected in the Eucharist, this symbol of the everyday sacred, the dying and rising of falling in love, raising a family, working and loving in endless cycles. How much we miss if we do not look at the faces of those around us, in which we can read their lives and understand why they are in church.

We notice, in this shambling concourse of sacred humanity, the very people found in the gospel. Do you think that these children, clutching at their parent's pants legs and summer dresses, are any different from those on whom Jesus smiled and said, to his followers then and us now, that of these his kingdom is composed?

Coming down the aisle for Communion is the man born blind, a white cane like a shepherd's staff gripped in his right hand and his wife's hand in his left for guidance, how like one person they have become, communicating by the slightest touch, how filled with light they seem.

Look around at the widows—they are everywhere in churches because they are everywhere in the gospels—some with only sons, some with illnesses, all of them having taken their final vows in the mystery of loss.

Perhaps we can see the man well pleased with himself and his donations. He has stood complacently in every temple and chapel throughout history, thanking God that he is not like the rest of men. We are glad that he is not like them, too. But his complacency is redeemed by the man next to him who, asking for mercy on himself as a sinner, does not recognize his own goodness. How common that is among the truly good. They forget themselves in life and so they cannot observe or remember the good they do for others.

But we can, finding a revelation that no survey can deliver, in the people all around us, lost to the thousand tasks of living, vulnerable to hurt, thinking of what they must do next, but here, just as they are, bearers of the sacramental Mystery of being human and of all of life. Blessed are those who keep their eyes open, for such visions will be theirs.

The architectural equivalent of "closure"

The recently displayed plans for rebuilding the World Trade Tower site disturbed many and disappointed everybody else. Now there has been a call for new designs. What can the latter learn from the failures of the former?

The spurned designs convey no awareness of what occurred humanly on September 11. Their renderings bear no traces of anguish or of any effort of the spirit to enter and speak in their own language of the mystery of love and loss that still aches to be remembered at the now cleaned out but still painful wound in lower Manhattan.

Instead, they delivered Late American Cliché, buildings designed to lull rather than to stimulate, surroundings without discernible character, the concrete counterpart of the national pseudo-psychological imperative never to offend anyone, to live on the surface of events, and to deal with tragedy by saying *I feel your pain* without feeling anything at all.

Enter the cathedral of the mall, these bland buildings urge, where every line and hue is carefully chosen to stimulate the conditioned response of shopping, the operational Prozac of the masses. This rejection of mortality threatens to transform the World Trade Center site into Forest Lawn East, death denied in the sunshine by protoplasmic promenades and spaces non-specifically called *memorials*.

Denying death is not the same as affirming life, so these schemes cannot symbolize the human tragedy of last September. That site will never become a place for the living until we can, for those whose family members and friends were killed, and for ourselves, by way of word and symbol, express the revelation of death and life that took place, and continues to take place, at the site and in ourselves.

How intuitively the rescue workers sensed 9/11's mystery of love and loss as they sought out the dead, covering them with flags and flanking them with honor guards, to bring them, as the living have borne the dead throughout history on shields or in shrouds, to those who loved them. How right the keening of the pipes at their burials with their uncomforted laments for those who died out of due season. With what dignity these rescuers in rough clothes used simple rites to recognize that 9/11 is the sacrament of the love and loss that are at the heart and core of being human.

The dead have spoken to us so that, for the first time in history, we know what large groups of men and women do when they know they are going to die. Facing eternity, they plunge into time. Facing death, they invest themselves in life. They forget themselves, in the buildings and the airplanes, and want only to call up their spouses, parents, or children to tell them that they love them. They are still calling, *I love you, Keep the family together, If you tell me that you love me, I'll come home, I love you* forever...

September 11 is the *Titanic* of the twenty-first century, the great vessel with all classes, from busboys to millionaires, revealing to us what ordinary people are really like when, at midnight or mid-morning, Death rises out of the sea or the sky. These men and women were and are our surrogates—filled that morning, as are we all, with idle thoughts and passing interests, with piled up plans and work to do, along with tides of feeling, some sexual, some sad, and some of great unnamed longing, washing through them—the everyday human flotsam riding the deeper current of their goodness, their generosity and bravery, their capacity to love, which were the truest things about them as they were called forth by the immense tragedy to be themselves.

Memorials are not to make us forget but to help us to remember, not to bring spurious closure to loss but to open it fully so that we may know what has happened to us and to those thousands of persons who died that day with last words not of regret, or of pleading for themselves, but of love for others.

The initial plans, with their fatal giveaway preoccupations—*mixed use, commercial space, rental income*—fail because they do not look at, comprehend, or symbolize the profound mystery of love and loss that lies at the center of the tragedy of September 11. What would these architects envision for the now unadorned Normandy beaches, a resort with a reflecting pool? And what would they build on the bone-strewn fields of Verdun, a *faux* French village with time-shares?

You cannot speak to the place if you cannot hear the place speaking to you. The planners have not listened to the silence and have not heard those last minute phone calls still resonating in the great space where the towers once stood. September 11 was the great human spiritual experience of our time, and without that insight as its cornerstone, no structure can ever symbolize successfully the love, loss, and glory of that day and that place.

I was at the Last Judgment this week. I'll bet you were, too

The Last Judgment has always been dependable theological theater. It has all the elements of an Alfred Hitchcock film—attractive characters, a love story, drama and danger, some humor with, of course, suspense, and, if possible, a surprising finale. Please, the movie ad urged, do not divulge the ending and spoil it for others.

Nowadays, the Last Judgment is the picture with the "buzz," that is, the one that everybody talks about even though it hasn't opened yet. It is the great coming attraction. Don't, we are warned by a series of apocalyptic novels, be "left behind."

But all of us have already attended the real Last Judgment. It is showing at churches and temples throughout the country. I witnessed it at Mass this past weekend. It will be showing again this weekend, in case you missed it.

It does have attractive characters and more than one love story. It also has a measure of danger and drama, plenty of humor, and an ending that surprises everybody. You can talk about it as much as you want and you won't spoil it for others.

The cast of non-professionals excels at the one requirement for their roles. They have to be human. Their clothes come from their own closets rather than the costume department. There are no special effects, for the small miracles are not contrived by computer but generated from real hearts.

Just by coming to church, ordinary men and women make themselves vulnerable. They come with a feeling of confidence. They are not intimidated by coming, as it is said, into the presence of God but do so freely and without putting up any defenses. They seem comfortable and hopeful as they take their places in God's sight. This may be Judgment Day, but they do not look afraid.

Nobel laureate Saul Bellow speaks of a writer's need to leave his isolated desk, to go where people congregate, in the park or on a subway, to be refreshed by what he calls a "humanity bath."

That is the first and essential feature of Judgment Day. We are bathed in humanity, in its vast and broken history, in its gains and losses, its tragedies and its triumphs, in what we look like assembled, never quite in even rows, falling down, getting up, pulling somebody else up, too, thinking we are finished and finding that we must start over.

To enter our humanity by immersion, all we need do is to look at the people around us. Everybody is here, young and old, just like Judgment Day. Some are dressed for it and some are not or, as I heard a priest say with a forgiving smile at an early Mass, "Some of you dressed in the dark because you'd never look like this if you had the lights on."

God sounds much more like that than like the hanging judge some claim He will be. He recognizes how much we stumble around in the dark in our lives, may note it publicly not to condemn but to embrace—and allow us to accept—how endearing and forgivable we are when, even floundering, we give our best to life.

Search the faces as DaVinci did to find those to sketch as the apostles and other followers of Jesus. They are here, too, completely unaware of how they reveal themselves—and thereby judge themselves —as they say their prayers.

Drama abounds in these faces, and character, too, and the lines and scars are judgments on them and the pain they have faced without complaint and the love they have given without charge. Every one of these love stories is a judgment proclaiming how, despite trials that only they know, they have loved so deeply that they seem, in an anticipation of each other that great dancers would envy, to have become one while remaining separate individuals at the same time. Judge us, their bowed heads silently say to God and the world, too, for here we are, just as we are, there is nothing hidden.

The church is filled with such people like this, some married a long while, some anticipating it, some remembering the dead who live in the sparkle of their eyes, yes, and young people setting out, bravely making themselves vulnerable to plot twists and endings that neither they, nor we, can see now.

The surprise ending is that this *is* Judgment Day, and that, since these people offer themselves in evidence every day, they don't fear God now, even if they come late or look as if they dressed in the dark. As with the crowd in church, Judgment Day turns out to reveal how good, not how bad, ordinary people are.

The Seasons of 2003

Whose contemplative life is this anyway?

Where, people ask in a noisy world, do we find the contemplative life these days?...

Catholicism has long honored contemplation as a calling thought as tough as digging tunnels beneath the seas. Contemplatives, which is what the men and women who accept this vocation are termed, quarry a seam of the eternal out of the riverbed of time and fill it with meditation, a prayer that finally transcends the images and incidents that obsess us and leads them to their goal of a wordless union with God.

The men and women who seek this objective have traditionally closed the door on the world softly and turned the key as silently as the corridors and cells of the monasteries in which they spend lives cut off from the concerns that absorb the rest of us in time.

So it is not easy to meet these mystics because they often dwell in distant places, some of them behind grillwork more discouraging to intimacy than the glassed-in penitentiary niches through which the next of kin visit prisoners.

Except that it is easy and we need not journey to cloisters to identify them. They are, as Jesus spoke of his union with even two or three gathered in his name, "in the midst" of us and we already know a lot of them by name.

If we cannot casually enter the *enclosure*, as the sealed-off areas of monasteries are termed, we can easily look around at the other people in church. Catholics do that all the time anyway. They just do not realize that, while they are checking out hairstyles, clothing, and whether and what others drop in the collection basket, they are often gazing at contemplatives, too.

Indeed, church is the best place to find people living intense lives of union with God, as the elected existence in isolated abbeys is described.

These ordinary men and women are often unaware that, in the tumultuous world, they are on the easy terms with God that monks strive mightily for in self-imposed exile from the same noisy mainland of humanity.

That lack of self-consciousness has always been the invisible sign and seal on any life that can be called holy. This explains why, in the famous gospel story of the Last Judgment, the men and women who are saved are also completely surprised and are full of questions: *When was it that we saw you hungry and gave you food, or thirsty and gave you something to drink...?* (Matthew 25:37).

There is a simple reason why they cannot recall these moments of intense union with God, these instances when they broke out of time to touch the eternal. They cannot remember because they were not thinking about themselves when they responded with food, drink, and comfort for others.

These people—caught up in contemplation they cannot name and do not even think about—stream by us in church aisles every Sunday. They lead mystical lives without knowing that they were ever called to them.

Our best prayer after receiving the Eucharist is not made by closing our eyes and struggling to look into ourselves as we do down darkened cellar stairs. If we open our eyes and look at the people all around us, the stress and the fear of falling disappear and we become contemplatives by contemplating them.

The first thing that strikes us is how embedded they are in time, that is, how willingly they have assented without complaint to its conditions of aging, chance, separation, illness, and death. These people we call ordinary live their whole lives without ever having the home team advantage. They give their all—as they do before our very eyes—to each other, to the next generation and often to the previous generation, and they are so absorbed in this daily handing over themselves to and for others that, emptied of themselves, they are filled with the Divine.

And the wonderful part—and the revelation for us—is that, like artists lost in their creations, these men and women are also lost in loving each other, working hard, and raising children, so that in the world itself they achieve, as a side-effect, the union with God that earnest contemplatives seek, with the world put aside, as the main goal of their lives.

Almost home

America is again made hostage to mystery on a day, heartbreakingly like that of September 11, whose promise of loveliness is broken before dawn has come full on the land. And once more we can barely absorb the images of this spacecraft cutting one wake, then two, and then a cluster of them against the sky and into our souls.

We are hostage to the mystery of what went wrong and how could it happen, a mystery for which we will get answers as painful in their subjunctive, *if we had known*, as the facts are in their flat declarative, *this is what happened*. We can solve such mysteries and make sure that they never happen again.

Then there is the Mystery for which we do not even know how to ask the questions, that Mystery, *tremendum et fascinans*, freely translated as "overpowering and inescapable," that is the religious mystery in which all our lives are set.

True religion reveals itself in these moments. Unlike the New Age, ancient faith is made for real life and does not provide Hollywood endings. It asks questions more than it gives answers as it mocks pollsters who cannot imagine any "role" for it beyond being an "influence" in American life or politics.

The pollsters satirize themselves after 9/11 with their surveys that center on whether religion gets a lift out of that event and whether it is just a "bubble" or a "blip" that will soon disappear.

Pundits betray condescension when, after the Twin Towers fall or the shuttle explodes, they invite religion to give *meaning* to these events. Religion, however, is not a consumer good that sells better in sad times, or a source of meaning, or simple pious explanations, such as those uttered by people hurrying past our grief. *Maybe it's better that it happened this way...*

Real religion summons us into and symbolizes for us the over-powering and inescapable mystery of being alive here, in this time and no other, with these gifts and these chances, with the possibility of love that is but a membrane apart from loss. Yes, that is the Mystery for which there is no one-paragraph S.A.T. essay of meaning and no full disclosure, for it bears no label we can check for its contents, nor any bar code we can scan for its cost.

We can only drink this chalice of suffering, because religion does not give us the *meaning* of life but it does give us a chance to *experience* life. The tremendous mystery of these terrible events shatters the crust of distractions that people sometimes mistake for life or indulge in to avoid the experience of life.

On such days, television holds up real life, the stuff of real religion, in this Mystery, the same on February 1, 2003, as on September 11, 2001, the same yesterday, today, and tomorrow. Americans have been conditioned to reject this Mystery in a culture that devours winners and has no taste for loss. But loss is an essential part of this Mystery, *our* mystery, this sacrament celebrated in our sight again as the host is broken above the flatland altar of Texas.

The mission is almost over, and the men and women of the crew sit in for us, revealing our common pilgrimage and condition, this state we enter so often that we hardly notice its depth—almost finished, almost paid up, almost grown up, almost where we want to be, almost home...

These men and women author a great sign in this vehicle that flames like so many across biblical skies, this vessel, bearing all of us, as it dives away from the sun that symbolizes eternity and we see through the eye of the earthbound video camera the spiritual imagery of what is happening.

For the screen is suddenly scored by high electrical lines that symbolize the net of time to which the *Columbia* is returning, time that grasps us all and mothers all our sorrow. And, just as suddenly, a tree's branches spread across the screen, a tree in winter whose buds, filled with new life, offer a sacramental frame for this vessel and for the great Mystery of life-as-it-is in the world as-it-is for us humans as-we-are—almost home.

Possessed by mystery

What is it that we feel together, living in a sanctuary that offers none,
our ears filled with the plaint, Peace, Peace, and there is no peace,
hostages to a moment in history in which we can barely breathe,
haunted by the cowled pundits in the choir stalls—and no really
wise, much less holy, man among them—chanting endlessly the
same antiphons of risk and death and doom?

We pray as best we can, tormented and distracted prayers for a terrible swift sword of war if war there must be, for all those servicemen and women who are our human shields, in harm's way in a cause that, if as well defined as many others that have summoned ignorant armies to clash by night, remains a source of conflict for some, of great deeds for others, cheap and sacrilegious politics for still more, and a weight as heavy as the world for the rest of us.

What is this that has taken charge of us as roughly as a man grabbing and forcing us to go someplace against our will? Have we ever experienced a more brutal irony than this reality whose blood-red dragon's eyes do not blink as we steal a glance at what we think are our lives flashing before us in the pseudo-adventures and second-hand sinning of reality TV?

At times like these, we feel the pulse of life as it is, that rhythmic beat that is lost in the white noise of our distractions and the discharge of our daily routines. We inhabit and are inhabited by Mystery, not the Hercule Poirot kind, but the spiritual mystery of being alive that sums up religion pure and simple.

We are experiencing what the great saints wore themselves out with vigils to achieve, a direct encounter with the Divine. St. John of the Cross wrote of the human puzzlement at what he learned by scaling heroically to the summit of mystical prayer, *There is no way here.*

No way, he learned and we already know, by storming it through fasts and penances and other punishments for our human condition. We never lay siege to the Divine by laying waste to our humanity.

Perhaps John of the Cross learned that it was simpler than he thought and, if he wrote that *there is no way here*, he may have concluded that *there is only your way here*, in the pilgrimage you make through your own life; that, accepting the religious mystery of life and death and loss found in it you discover that you are at the center of God already. You make this pilgrimage by way of the simple ascetic of everyday life and have no need, and, indeed, would feel self-conscious at falsifying yourself so much, to try out for the Sanctity Olympics of self-destruction through self-denial.

These intense moments return our attention to the sacred places that are so simple and often homely that we do not have names for them. They include lovers catching sight of each other after being apart, the feel of the wind or the sun on a walker or a runner on a spring day, and the innocence lifting like grace off the crib of a newborn. At such everyday points that do not seem intrinsically spiritual and that demand our total immersion in time, we embrace the Spirit and drink from the cup of the eternal.

We live the great Mystery out in these human ways, though we are so absorbed by them that we seldom think of them as our real lives in God. But, in these events, we recognize that the transcendent lies in the simple, that the eternal signals from the core of time, and that everything and everybody we love are at risk every day.

We are best defined as believers as those who are possessed by Mystery. We are on such easy terms, nodding to it like a neighbor in everyday life, that we do not feel how it overflows our depths until war casts its terrible light on them. We are winded because we have already made the climb to John of the Cross's summit and have found there what we brought with us, God face to face, the Mystery we feel so keenly this week.

Reality TV/Revelation TV

A month ago, a headline informed us that "TV Networks Plan Flood of Reality for Summer" (New York Times, *February 24, 2003). Co-opting the computer's function of "garbage in/garbage out," programming executives planned—and note the word carefully—"to unleash at least two dozen reality shows from June to September."*

Unleash gets it just right, for the more honorable executives understand that they are masters of the hounds who are setting dogs loose on the public. You'll need a rabies shot after being bitten by Roseanne Barr who pitches "a cooking show to cable networks and searches for men on a Jewish Internet dating service." Flea powder goes with *The Simple Life . . .* in which a pair of privileged young women . . . move in with a hardscrabble farm family."

That was before Reality took over TV from Iraq, taking us over as well and bidding us, better than any retreat master could, to look into ourselves by the light of this pale pagan god's eye that stares at us everywhere, America's longings on display in the living room, the restaurant lounge, the airport gate, the airplane itself, and now—as an option to keep children from asking "Are we there yet, Daddy?"—the back seat of SUVs.

But we are there now and television, so easily criticized for its flirtation with bogus reality, redeems itself by unveiling un-retouched reality. Television pans the world for human folly and shallow sensation. Then, like an amateur with a video camera who catches the airplane crash, it gazes suddenly on the grandeur of life in views of our common humanity that touch our deepest sensibility.

Reality comes from the Latin, *res*, the "thing," the "being," the "possession." And what does television's unediting eye, so like our own, see if not, as it takes in everything, the *somethings*, like a pair of discarded goggles or a flyer's abandoned helmet, that throb like an electrical line because they were *someone's* things, a fellow human being's *possessions* still holding the charge of the hands of a man or woman as filled with simple dreams as we are.

Television has become an unwitting agent of the Age of Revelation that has never ended despite claims that it closed with the death of the last apostle. Yes, we can believe that and believe something else, too, that revelation has not ended any more than the moon, the symbol of time, has ended its *pas de deux* with the sun, the symbol of eternity and source of all light.

It is by that light of eternity that television allows us to see into the spiritual radiance of the men and women we too often look at without noticing our family resemblance to them. If we masked their faces, would our supposed six degrees of separation dissolve in what we could see of their eyes? We seem to be immersed in war news but we are really witnessing the Good News, that of the kingdom of God spread on this earth, made plain in the lives of all these people who stand out in the desert background as if they had just heard Jesus speak of how blessed they are.

Television redeems itself when it calls off the dogs of reality shows and allows us to see the dogs of war set loose so vividly and the mystery of suffering and loss that, along with the poor, we always have with us.

It has been a season of revelation, for we seem to have been in all these places before, at the Tigris and the Euphrates, yes, and, not far off, at the places searched for the fragments of the *Columbia* shuttle as diligently as the household was searched for the lost coin.

That search and this war are taking place in the fields that men were always buying in the parables of Jesus, and in fields that can be called, with the one in which Judas was buried, fields of blood.

And there are hillsides, such as the one on which Jesus spoke to the hungry crowds, and the one in Texas where the data recorder of the *Columbia* was recently found and we, like that long ago crowd, long to hear what this box says now to us.

Television has happened into these places where, as we learn in the gospel, our treasure and our hearts are to be found, and we realize that this remarkable medium may never be able to return to reality TV from covering this reality of life and death and destiny. Television is not covering the war as much as it is covering the spiritual mystery of human existence.

The eyes of our Lenten war

We have followed Dante, on these explosion-striped nights, into an Inferno and we cannot look away. Shown more than ever, our eyes, as the scripture tells us, are not filled with seeing. It is as if a much heralded movie has finally opened but are we watching the beginning or the end? Or is it, like so many post-modern films or a round-trip bus ride in a strange country, all middle with a stop but no real ending?

There is, of course, a difference between what we look at and what we see. And, if this is an age in which many feel that being televised rather than baptized is the sacramental initiation of their lives, is there some sense, at the edge of our consciousness, that this Lenten war is a transaction in which we see and are seen at the same time?

Or is that sensation as old as we are, so that we should not be surprised that, as we watch life and death in the valley of the Euphrates, we recover that intuition of being observed ourselves that moved the psalmist to pray, "Let the words of my mouth, and the meditation of my heart, be acceptable in thy sight, O Lord..." (Psalm 19:14).

What was written in the *Canterbury Tales*, "the feeld hath eyen and the wode hath eyes" ("The Knight's Tale," 1.1510) is fulfilled in this televised war, reminding us of the mysterious reciprocity of seeing and being seen that is basic to our unbounded spiritual longing and to our cheapest self-deception.

An eye looks out at us from the scriptures. If our "eye is single," we learn, our whole person "will be filled with light." And we count it a blessing, or at least good fortune, to "fall in love at first sight."

As strong a stand of virtue as we know grows out of the Chaucer's field that we recognize as everyday life, for we find a trustworthy sig-

174

nal of truth when we look directly into someone's eyes or do not blink when someone looks into our own.

Sight is squandered by those who look no deeper than surfaces and who feel that perfection at that level delivers true love and lasting happiness. If working on abdominal muscles is a minor vanity, it nonetheless foreshortens our ability to see that our attractiveness and our strength come from our depths and by their light we see what is lovable in each other.

It has been a long human journey to see ourselves whole and free ourselves from the images pressed upon us throughout history, images that have been as damaging for us as the graven images of false gods were for the Israelites. These views divide personality into good and bad elements, making us experience guilt for being human and having all the feelings that go along with that.

Our religious pilgrimage is not to a place where someone claims a "vision" as much as to one where we can recover the vision of our *wholeness* that is fundamental to our *healthiness* and our *holiness*.

How strange is the alert to our mystery that flashes on the television screen when a laser-guided weapon searches out its target. An unsteady white-lined template is pressed on the grainy black and white of the earth below. Its coordinates contract and expand and a white dot jiggles now this way and now that at its center, fixing finally on a target that explodes beneath our gaze.

We do not tarry as these ghostly lines of the gun sight—this roving eye that finds—fix on and bring terrible swift judgment to an oblong blob we can barely see. No wonder we cannot tell if this is the beginning, the end, or the measureless middle. And what of this sense we cannot shake that in this Mystery Play we are being seen even as we see, that the pale eye of this gunsight is roving across us, bearing a judgment for us as well as for the land below?

Changing the subject, or why victims still suffer

A recent conference at Boston College's School of Law chronicles the natural transformation of once human events when they are translated into the nation's new native language, legalese...

The agenda centered on such issues as whether the sex abuse scandals in the Catholic Church have become a "threat to religious liberty," the meaning of "criminal liability for a diocese," whether dropping the statute of limitations in these cases was "utterly absurd," and whether churches should share in the same protection granted to the media under the "speech and press clauses of the First Amendment" ("Scandal Called Threat to Free Worship," by Adam Liptak, *New York Times*, April 6, 2003).

These topics generate so much conversation and comment that many people may not notice their smoke-screen effect or how exchanging opinions on these issues takes you, at rocket lift-off speed, through cloud-land levels of abstraction that leave the real world of sex abuse behind like an abandoned and forsaken planet.

These lawyers are not talking about the debasing experience of those who have suffered sexual violation by a person they trusted. They are talking about *their* experience in de-hydrating and diluting the raw and wrenching reality of being abused by forcing it into the limited and limiting vocabulary of the law, the process and precedent and "may it please the court" protocol that makes something else out of a trespass on intimacy that is like nothing else. No wonder so many victims feel that so few of those who represent the institution in which they were hurt have any understanding of that hurt or any capacity for or interest in responding to their unhealed wounds.

Lawyers did not pursue the sex abuse crisis like the ambulance chasers of old or the class action collectors of the present. The bishops invited the law, first civil, then criminal, into the everyday life of Catholicism last year in hopes that the law would save them and solve their problems at the same time.

The result, of course, has been a fulfillment of the old Mexican curse, "May your life be filled with lawyers." The bishops' calendar of events, once printed in diocesan newspapers, was an advertisement for the busy shepherd confirming here, banqueting there, and laying a cornerstone over there. Now it is a court docket of appearances for depositions and testimony in criminal cases and it does not carry the same intoxicating champagne-like deference that once bore the bishops along weightlessly through their rounds.

If it is not pleasant for them to be forced to take an oath that they will tell the truth, it is a grim realization of the occupied country they have made out of church life through their handing of its management over to lawyers.

Their discomfort is nothing, however, compared to that of victims who still feel their wounds but also feel that they have been left behind by the law that so often talks to itself about itself instead of to and about them. Even their ablest advocates sometimes quantify them in their dealings with them, because even they do not understand the concept of damages unless it is embossed with a dollar sign.

The deconstruction of sexual abuse into a legal text occurs when people do not understand what really happens when a trusted person takes sexual gratification from a vulnerable and unsuspecting child. Predators rationalize the erotic manipulation of the innocent, of course, often shifting the responsibility for the action to the victim, and moving away so fast they can barely remember or give names to those they harm.

The psychological or human truth about such transactions can never be abstracted successfully by lawyers. That is because the wound in such sexual violation occurs not in the fleeting moment of consciousness that it represents for the victimizer. These blows are bunker busters of personality and they penetrate and lacerate the unconscious of those who suffer them. In the unconscious, however, time does not pass and a wound inflicted in this everlasting now is as fresh twenty years later according to the time we measure in consciousness as it is at the moment when it is inflicted. People don't "get over" unconscious wounds. Such injuries are not soothed by a bishop's cliché or a lawyer's abstractions. The terrible burden of victims is that they feel *now* the full demeaning force of what a priest called "Father" did to them, according to the calendar, twenty or thirty years ago. There is no statute of limitations in the inner lives of victims. Their suffering is only intensified by those who press time's crown of thorns into it, especially by the progressive abstractions of the law. When the law ends up discussing whether bishops and dioceses should be regarded under the First Amendment on the same media plane with CNN and the *National Enquirer*, we finally understand the scriptural phrase, *the last state of that man shall be worse than the first.*

Grieving for David Bloom

I did not know David Bloom and you probably didn't either, except in the way we know so many hundreds of people on our television screens, their images carried away in the great media tides that flow through our homes each day. We forget most of them immediately and, if we recognize the wan public images of politicians, pundits, and game show hosts, we don't feel that we know them or even want to know them.

Yet that is not how many of us feel about NBC-TV correspondent David Bloom, as we discovered when we learned of his death of a blood clot in the Iraqi desert. "Only thirty-nine," we heard against the sudden squall of shock, "leaving a wife and three young daughters." Yes, and leaving us, too...

What was it about David Bloom, that strapping, smiling man we last saw standing in a sandstorm, wearing goggles, his hair streaming like a chariot rider's or a young god's swimming in the deep, a figure from myth in a land of myth where the Garden of Eden was said to have been found near where the great rivers, the Tigris and Euphrates, flow?

Why, in the welter of death and waste of war, were many surprised to find, as they put it, that they felt "so bad" for this correspondent, that they were touched by this man as if he were a lost friend or family member who tuned their souls to the sad music of wonder that this should be so, *David, we hardly knew ye.*

Besides watching him on television, I had a contact with him, quite indirect and yet memorably human. I heard someone else talking about him and perhaps I should have recognized then the small mystery of this second-hand connection that met the measure of playwright Thornton Wilder's observation that we have to "overhear" the most important truths in life.

It was against the low buzz mingled with the soft clashing of knives and forks at a brunch in Naples, Florida, that I heard a couple describe their own son's friendship with David Bloom who was in the city at that time. The correspondent had left a message trying to arrange a tennis game and the good natured post-script said that he would be out, he was going to Mass.

It was a curling whitecap in the swift moving flow of conversation and, like so many things we make note of even when they are none of our business, this background vignette about the man who gave the news and hosted the weekend *Today Show* was that truest revelation of a man, the one he does not know that he is making. What kind of man would leave such a message unless he was pure in the richest sense of that word—as unaffected, direct, and truthful as a good boy answering his father's question about what he was doing?

We are not surprised to learn that the name *David* means "beloved," for so he clearly was to many whose lives he entered to a depth they did not understand until they heard that he had died. Nor are we surprised to be reminded that *bloom* means "the condition of being in flower" and "a condition . . . of vigor, freshness, and beauty" or "prime." The word's root is related to the concept of "powerful masculinity."

David Bloom was all of these, this man who, undefended himself, allowed us to lower our own defenses, not as a surrender but as a welcome to someone who seemed to be what so many strive vainly to become, a true man.

Yes, there is something about this man whose goodness resonated in the voices I could hear of people I could not see, sitting behind me in a crowd never gathered before, or again, in such fashion. In short, a seemingly passing moment that was really a vessel bearing something of the mystery of this man, the *mystery* in which we feel his vigor, *his* mystery, *our* Mystery, *the* Mystery of Death and Resurrection in which we live together every day.

Times editors and the bishops separated at birth

Are we really surprised that great establishments, as seemingly different as a newspaper that roots itself in the news of the passing moment and a church that rests itself on eternal verities, should occasionally harmonize on the same off-key Institutional Blues?...

Was it just a year ago that the *New York Times* was reporting the Catholic Church's crisis of sex abuse among some of its priests? Some bishops had reassigned priests, attaching no warning labels about their having forfeited their trustworthiness by sexually violating children. The gods of irony winced as the bishops stamped these priests approved, *This is a fine priest in good standing with the institution...*

The church scandal surfaced first in Boston, the *New York Times* of archdioceses because of its long tradition and the clout of its archbishop, Bernard Law, who gained power through his relationship with the pope, whose program of restoring authoritarian hierarchy he implemented.

Bernard Law is a finely mannered, white haired man who justly gained a reputation as a progressive leader by challenging the forces of segregation when, as a young monsignor, he served as editor of the Catholic paper in Mississippi.

At the height of the furor about his seeming to have ignored warnings about errant clergy, Cardinal Law apologized, said it was his responsibility, and that, no, he did not see his own resignation as part of the solution. Boston priests reported widespread demoralization and dissatisfaction with his leadership and a large group signed a letter asking for his resignation. What Law said he would not do in May, he did in December, ending his great career, giving up the power and the glory for the good of the institution he served in hope that it would restore confidence in the church.

Was he separated at birth from another mannered, somewhat more theatrically white-haired man, Howell Raines, the executive editor of the *Times* who, it is said, achieved his clout-filled position through his long relationship with the publisher and exercised it, according to *Times* staffers, in an authoritarian, hierarchical style? An Alabaman, Raines gained notice for his journalistic challenge to the same culture of segregation that Law confronted a state away.

Now the *Times* is publicly suffering the same institutional convulsions that the Catholic Church experienced a year ago, and for the same reasons. Despite many warnings from various editors, a young reporter forfeited the trust of his calling by serially abusing the readers, seducing them with made up or copied work, earning new assignments despite fifty published corrections, *This is a fine reporter in good standing with the institution...*

During the height of the furor, the demoralization of other *Times* writers has been reported and, to a question from one of them at a staff meeting, Mr. Raines said that, no, he did not see his resignation as part of the solution. He apologized, he took responsibility, he hopes to restore confidence at the *Times* and in the *Times*.

Perhaps, as a result of these tragedies, we can develop a greater measure of sympathy for, and patience with, all institutions and those who must manage them. The achievement of great power is one thing. The ability to exercise healthy authority is another, requiring a deeper set of values and a capacity for self-observation not often found in men who think that they must control their world hierarchically or it will fall apart. Was it that vain effort to control everything that made the worlds fall apart at the *Times* and in Boston?

Times editors and American bishops are amazed to find themselves companions in woe, fallen titans sitting on a park bench wondering how they lost track of the trust that their institutions run on and how they could have kept reassigning the untrustworthy.

Perhaps, after years of looking suspiciously at each other, they will now look each other in the eye and re-learn the lessons of trust together. Then they may be able to look their people in the eye again, too.

Midsummer madness/midsummer mystery

July is ever the midwife to madness, offering its stage to anyone who wants his or her ten minutes of fame right now when, because of the season, the days seem to last longer than in the bitter broken-off light of late December...

How preoccupied we are at mid-summer with time—from the reports of scientists who dream a Frankenstein's vision of conquering it or reversing the swift flow of its current that we know as aging to the jester's efforts to fool it with what is now called hair coloring and whose pitch is that you look older than you are and that a touch-up is no more vain than resetting your watch to the correct time.

And, as we feel the season slipping by and wonder if it's too late to have a good time, we behold senators blowing platitudes as Moby Dick did gouts of sea water, *Come*, they urge, *back to* the lost and gone time of Watergate, *What did the president know and when did he know it?*

And then, on a day savored by the greater and lesser gods of frivolity, we learned that the *New York Times* had a new editor, Bill Keller, who had to wait, in an example of the large and cruel mystery of time that envelops good men, to receive the job that went to another person two years ago.

Time's lesser summer markers flowed in quickly: the date was announced, August 28th, on which the miniscule mystery of the Publishers' Clearinghouse annual million-dollar giveaway would take place. It was also *half time* for the baseball season and the All-Star Game was played.

In the ecclesiastical counterpart of moving a manager out of the minor leagues and to the Yankees, Archbishop Justin Rigali was transferred from St. Louis to Philadelphia. The *time* he had anticipated as eagerly as ancient prophets did the coming of the Messiah had finally arrived and he could at last wire the Roman tailor who had taken his measurements long before to make the cardinal's robes that would soon be his.

Then, like an electrical storm at dawn, a simple revelation illuminates these varied madnesses, and our own, and breaks us out of time altogether, forcing us to gaze into the true face of Mystery at midsummer.

"Crew of *Columbia*," the headline shouts, "Survived a Minute after Last Signal" (John Schwartz and Matthew L. Wald, *New York Times*, July 15, 2003). We learn that the "*Columbia* astronauts lived for almost a minute after their final communication with mission control, well after signs that the craft was in serious trouble... the onboard sensor recording system... continued to function far into the breakup of the *Columbia*..."

After months of analysis, the investigators of the explosion of the *Columbia* last February 1 concluded that the random piece of foam that had struck the vessel's wing had caused the wound that later took the vessel's life and the lives of its crew. These weeks of testing had, to some extent, depersonalized the disaster, for the discussion and the simulations of the event were all of material and described in the language of engineering.

But now human beings, men and women, are suddenly seated again at the controls, our surrogates in this myth of gigantic risk, noble effort, and numbing failure. It is a tale repeated endlessly in the long story of the human family, told also, in lesser ways, in the lives of all of us, in the losses and gains of our best efforts, in the destiny that uncoils around us, as it did around the astronauts, biding its time as it counts out what we have spent, or what we have left to spend, of our own in any great love or work.

The crew's men and women are at the center of this mystery, the mechanical parts the least of it, for this is a Mystery with a capital letter, a religious Mystery in which, months later, we can sit with them and feel the pressure of the last minute bearing down on them with all the weight of time, time reasserting its claim until that itself is snapped by the grip of Mother Earth pulling them back to her breast, Mother Earth beneath Sister Sun and Brother Moon breaking time open, scattering its sorrows, and opening the eternal to them.

To us, too, of course, if, at this midsummer, we can push aside the madness and see that human persons are still at the center of the Mystery, that sacrament of our lives in which we feel the pressure of time and the pull of eternity every day.

Remembering Peg

Our next door neighbor died, a woman who, pert and lively as a spring bird, wore a black bow in her hair into her last years. She was filled with good sense, good humor, and great understanding of the human condition...

Hearing the news that Peg Reynolds had broken free of time's grip loosed a flood of memories in everyone who loved, and was loved, by her. Indeed, so many are the bright images of this pert and perky lady that, as in sifting through forgotten family pictures found in a desk drawer, we are hard pressed to choose the one by which to remember her.

But, if we spread these favorite photos of ours on the table, what would we see? We would quickly discover that, as in all things and persons faithful, even though we looked on her from different angles and at different times—some of us seeing her as family, some as friend, some as neighbor—we all saw the very same thing, this remarkable woman, small in physical presence but very large in her encompassing heart, who grew old in one way but remained so young in all the important ways that it seemed unfair that she, still vivacious, witty, and alert, should be called away out of what seems to us due time.

Let me open the album my wife and I were blessed to have as long-time neighbors and friends. Peg is standing at the door—a double door to match the hospitality within—in her caftan and with a bow in her hair, waving us into the house whose warm wood interior matched the genuineness of her greeting and the fire of hospitality kindled there long ago by her and Dick that, as you know, glows there still today.

It is, of course, impossible to see her without Dick at her side, or coming through the door, a marching band in himself, the never quite old man in from the sea with the catch of the day.

You who nod at the adjective *pert*—yes, you say, *pert* to the end—will be interested, but hardly surprised, to learn of its origin, for its appropriateness may make you smile as it surely would her. Its root is *wer*, that survives in the English *weir*, and means, rightly enough for the woman who loved and married Dick, "a dam" or "a trap for fish."

How many tales tell themselves to us again as we recall her role, not only as wife, office manager, and homemaker, but as a kind of keeper for this jolly polar bear of a man who might be anywhere with rod, rifle, chain saw, or—love of his energetic life—a front-end loader. Can you remember the wry good humor with which she allowed him to implement his war against ground hogs, chipmunks, or, perhaps most typically, the robin that soiled his picture window once too often? Peg smiled indulgently as he devised his plan: He spread a sheet of foil on the ground below the window, attached electric wiring to it, and waited patiently for the robin to touch down. When the bird did, Dick threw the switch and, as Peg would recount dryly, *the robin flew away and Dick blew out all the fuses in the house.*

Her real name tells the story of her life and tells us, too, why we look on her as a treasure and value her so highly. The name *Margaret* comes from the Greek *margarites* and means "pearl." And we know of both Margaret and pearls that if their beauty is unsurpassable it is also hard won.

For a pearl is a gift from the deep that achieves its shape and its opalescent beauty from the grinding of sand within a shell where we cannot see it, for Nature does not give us such glory cheaply. And Peg did not achieve her never faded beauty, her presence and grace, by any cheap or easy route either. The depths are the right setting for talking about her, because you could not know her without sensing the depths within her. And you could not behold her comeliness and self-possession without sensing that she had achieved it, as the pearl does, out of accepting and living through suffering that we could not see either.

But that pearl that was Peg gleams still for all of us because it is eternal and is not touched by time or Death. Margaret, pert, yes, and perky, too, for this was the eternal shining through as well, the Peg who is the Peg of all our hearts, and a pearl beyond price for all of us. We have gathered to remember you and have discovered, instead, that we can never forget you.

John Geoghan, his own executioner

If ever a man carried the seeds of his death within him it was John Geoghan. In his long hidden life as a priest sex-abuser, his soft, once anointed hands filled children's eyes with terror as he stole a few flickering seconds of gratification for himself and wounded them forever.

Moved from town to town, he came at last, a convict, to the prison at Shirley, Massachusetts, where his own Dickensian fate was fulfilled in that terrible last moment as his own eyes filled with terror at the swift rough hands of a murderer on his own neck.

The facts are simple but the speculation, in a sadly fitting manner, will make more of him in wretched death than he ever was in the small rounds, like those of a milkman from another time, in which he delivered grief and sorrow at the back doors of ordinary families all across the archdiocese of Boston.

How faceless are the leading players in the great damaging episodes of our time. Stand John Geoghan next to Lee Harvey Oswald in the glaring lights of a line-up and they would merge into each other like the pale tones on the palette of a watercolorist. And yet how deep the blows that such seeming nobodies strike into the people and institutions around them.

Listen to the whispers from the Paranoid Ferris Wheel as it raises fresh plots against the sky: The murderer could not have acted alone, it was an inside job, somebody opened the cell door for the killer, the neo-Nazi was a dupe, set up by the real killers, prison workers who had sworn an oath to "get" Geoghan. No, no, the chorus directed by Oliver Stone responds, Geoghan knew too much, the orders for his killing came from that famous source, as mysterious as that of the Nile, "Downtown."

As long as there are checkout counters in supermarkets, it will be hard to avoid this first-class craziness generated by the infantile life of this poorly developed man. In fact, sixty-eight-year-old John Geoghan may never have escaped from his boyhood, for he is remembered by those who knew him in the seminary as "boyish," a word whose origins help us to understand this bedeviled man and the destiny to which he was drawn.

For *boy* is related to old French, Latin, and Greek words that mean "to fetter" or "to shackle" and, indeed, John Geoghan paraded his destiny of being fettered, or yoked, by his stalled inner growth so that the seeming charm of his external "boyishness" was not a beguiling virtue but a side-effect of the stunted development that he sought to complete through feeding on the innocent children in his care.

Poor Geoghan backed into the protecting priesthood, blessed by the institution that rewarded his passivity, was pleased by his inability to question or rebel, and reinterpreted his immaturity as docility and obedience, just the man we want, someone who will go along and make no trouble with celibacy. Even after he had repeatedly violated children, he transmitted passivity like a death ray as it stimulated the paternalism that moved him now here and now there on the ecclesiastical chessboard. His *I'm no trouble* passivity moved even Cardinal Law to a pity for him that ignored the terror he struck everywhere he served as a parish priest.

While commentators often say that "violence begets violence," it is actually *passivity* that begets violence and, from early on, passivity, shielded by official passivity, was the buzzing magnet for the fate that finally found him in a prison cell on Saturday. But not before it took down many others, from Cardinal Law who tried to protect him, to a cohort of officials who covered up for him, to an institution that shrugged and refused to examine the causes for clerical sex abuse and now wonders why it has lost the confidence of its people.

The passivity of this man/boy sent out signals summoning his death in a cell in which he was supposed to be safe just as he violated children in a church that was supposed to be safe for them.

John Geoghan was the agent of his own death, a man who in a mean place met the terrible destiny that he sought all his life, this man whose fate lay like a prophecy curled in the *boyishness* that was his identity card. The term *boy* comes from a family of words, as we have noted, that mean "to fetter" and, cruelly enough, can mean "a collar." If his passivity earned him a Roman collar, it also delivered him to that last murderous collar to which he yielded the last breath of his sad and shadowed life.

With the Mass, it's not the manners but the meal

You can tell when an organization is dying by the way it looks away from what is essential to obsess about details.

Fast talking telephone or wireless companies apply the hard sell for call waiting and caller ID, incidentals about as useful as stock market tips from your barber. Is this what a phone company should be doing? Did they really break up AT&T so you could send pictures or play video games on your phone?

The main business of the phone company is to connect you with others, not to interrupt you or, God help us, to entertain you. The main task for churches is to connect you through the symbols that reveal, on the Sabbath, the religious character of your experiences during the rest of the week.

It is not, as some suburban churches think, to extend mall life in a structure that owes more to the builders of multiplexes than the builders of cathedrals. The food courts, day-care centers, shops, and cup-holders in the plush theater seats do not help people to see beneath the surface of suburbia but push their faces into it. If you ever wondered what it would be like, *this* is purgatory.

The Catholic Church still suffers an agonizing crisis of sexual abuse by some of its priests and one can understand that its officials may want to distract the people, who are theologically the real church, from the fact that this problem has not been solved, nor has an even more important one, the disappearance of the Eucharist, the central sacrament of Catholicism.

Father Willard Jabusch describes it as the "Vanishing Eucharist" in the magazine *America* (May 12, 2003), noting that "in place of the Mass . . . there are now some Bible readings, a few hymns and possibly a homily and distribution of previously consecrated Communion hosts." Many Catholics, he continues, "find it...scandalous that this sacrament should be allowed to disappear..."

You would think that these administrator-bishops whose karma is canon law would know that canon 213 declares that Catholics have "a right" to the sacraments. Unable to link that to their obligation to provide them, they are presiding over the disintegration of the sacramental system. But they speak gravely about the manners connected with receiving the Eucharist, the ecclesiastical equivalent of call waiting.

At their recent St. Louis meeting, they described the big sacramental problem as the diminished attendance at Mass, rather than the disappearance of the Mass itself. Their new directives are the equivalent of their missing the bomb that blew out the stained glass windows but issuing new rules on how to sweep up broken glass.

I swear to God I am not making this up. New rules will soon require Catholics to bow or genuflect before receiving the Eucharist. Suppose they refuse, as some surely will, to do so? Will they be refused the sacrament? After communicants start tripping over each other, how soon will the lawsuits for the bruises and broken hips begin?

The bishops have also announced that, while we thought they were trying to check clergy sex abuse, they were carrying on an official exchange of letters concerning new Roman directives requiring Catholics to *stand* after receiving the sacrament. You will be relieved to know that, as a result of this lengthy bureaucratic inquiry, Catholics can also *sit* or *kneel*, as, with common sense, they would do anyway.

The latest is the holy day lottery that, according to the bishops' Committee on Liturgy, works this way: "This year because All Saints Day, Nov. 1, falls on Saturday, the usual obligation to attend Mass that day is abrogated...The Mass obligation remains for the Feast of the Immaculate Conception, Dec. 8, even though it is on a Monday..." Your Catholic blood will race to learn that "the committee reflected at length on the widespread confusion resulting from the present practice..." and they will do "further research."

You do not need the Hubble telescope to see the black hole into which the Eucharist is disappearing. That church officials are focused on making rules for non-existent problems tells us sadly that if their eyesight is bad their vision is non-existent.

James Shannon: A man for all seasons

Jim Shannon broke free of the framework of time on August 29, entering eternity as easily as a man who had been there many times before. Any guards on duty smiled and waved him through, for how could a barrier be raised against this extraordinary man who spent his life breaking them down?

He stands in memory as a mediator, a priest, and a bishop forever, even though he resigned from the official side of these titles before half the Catholics in the country were even born. He was always in the midst of people, often in their joy and always in their woe, that confessor who always had the long lines as he listened first to his left, then to his right, reconciling people to themselves, to each other, to lives that may have seemed ordinary to them but never to him.

He left the official church but he never left the Catholic Church that he identified always as his home even during the generation and a half through which he waited for Rome to grant permission for him and his beloved Ruth to be married in a Catholic ceremony. Even then he scrupulously followed the Vatican's conditions.

They drove a hundred miles to a place, as Rome specified, where he was supposedly unknown and could give no scandal. He complied with this demeaning condition because he loved the church and, although he could see through these parole officers' dictates, he could also look beyond them to the human structures whose flaws did not surprise him and whose unifying function he would never dishonor.

Jim Shannon left the administrative church because he was not only an educator and a bishop in Minneapolis but also a downtown pastor who listened to and learned from his people, gaining a first-hand sense of their efforts to love each other and live good lives. He felt their anguish to ease their hearts long before politicians began feeling their pain to get their votes.

Shortly after Vatican Council II, he accepted a request by a fellow bishop to appear on a national television program about the church and his comments revealed his pastoral understanding of why so many Catholics rejected, in good conscience, the official ban on birth control.

The late Francis Cardinal McIntyre attacked him, demanding that he be censured. His own archbishop, thinking of the promising ecclesiastical career that lay before him, warned Jim that, if he persisted, he would never become a cardinal.

This was an excruciating time for Shannon, who loved the church but loved its good people even more. He once told me of a pastoral incident that symbolized the great fissure that had opened up between ordinary hardworking people and their bishops.

A young laboring man told him of coming home on his birthday to find that, even though he and his wife had been scraping along, she had made him his favorite dinner and baked him a special cake. When they were cleaning up later, he reached over and clasped her shoulder gently. She froze in place, lowered her head, and looked away. Beyond all the theological arguments and abstract instructions, Jim saw into the hearts of a young couple and felt the coldness of the official shadow that fell across their lives to kill the simplest and most profound of their moments together.

He followed human experience back to its headwaters where he found the truth missing from the humanity maps drawn by many church leaders to control people and, of course, further their own ecclesiastical careers. Not many of them would have kept faith with their conscience, as Jim did, after being warned that he would never become a cardinal that way.

Jim Shannon was as squared off and Irish looking as Spencer Tracy, who said actors should know the lines, be on time, avoid bumping into the furniture, skip the fancy stuff, just concentrate and speak the lines simply and truthfully.

Jim Shannon, never even tempted to fancy stuff, entered everybody's troubles at the right time. He didn't bump into the furniture, but many bishops, once critical of him, have since tipped over everything in the sanctuary.

Jim knew his lines, because they were right out of the gospel, and because he spoke them simply and truthfully, they had the power to comfort, encourage, and heal everybody who heard them. In the gospel question, which of these men was justified in God's sight, the men-for-one-season bishops who once condemned him, or Jim Shannon, the man for all seasons who never became a cardinal but never stopped being a priest?

Pope John Paul II

On September 11 let the pope listen to America

The pope is unhappy with Americans... again.

The world, as in the "world, the flesh, and the devil," is the problem in general, according to the pope, who locates the problem in particular in America and in Americans. The pope reminds me of the elderly lady I once accompanied to select a casket for her husband. To the undertaker's question, "Which one do you like?" she responded, like an Irish mother of sorrows, "I don't like *any* of them!"

So the pope seems to feel about Americans and their culture, as Cardinal Avery Dulles reminds us in a recent reprint of a lecture given last April at Fordham. He doesn't like *any* of us.

Did Dante know about this papal vision of America when he wrote the *Inferno*? Our country sounds like a hell of a place, in which "dissent" is described as "rampant," "religious illiteracy" is widespread, and "liturgical laws are flouted." Oh, yes, and "Catholics have little appreciation of their mission to spread the faith" in this country where "religious practice is falling off."

Americans don't do anything right, as in "sex outside marriage, abortion, divorce, the use and marketing of drugs, domestic violence, defamation and financial scandals, such as falsification of records and embezzlement." And, on a wonderful ecumenical note, Cardinal Dulles passes on the word that "the morality of Catholics all too often sinks below the standards observed by Protestants and nonbelievers."

If I were a Roman official making these accusations, I would watch out for lightning bolts. This inventory of our woes gives people who want to believe them a dizzying paranoid high.

There is no shortage of sinners in America, of course, but perhaps, in this autumnal season of reflection and remembrance, we could examine what apparently the pope has missed about this land and its people.

September 11, 2001, was, in fact, the great sacramental event of this new century, for what it revealed, and continues to reveal, in its unfolding and inexhaustible Mystery, is the extraordinary goodness of people we mistakenly term "ordinary."

Real Americans, a great many of them Catholic, did not realize that as they left home on September 11, as beautiful a morning as any a lingering summer can bestow, they were entering Judgment Day as we all will some day, not dressed for the occasion, thinking of something else or of someone else, boarding the planes and riding the elevators in the midst of strangers, all of whom had made long journeys to arrive at just that place at just that moment, not just to face death but to reveal to us how filled they were with life.

What did we learn, and what might the pope himself learn, if he listened to the simple stories of these people, so like us and those we love, husbands and wives, sons and daughters, who spoke and speak now of their lives to us?

He would learn what people actually do when they know that they are going to die. They do not cry for mercy but do something profoundly human and therefore profoundly spiritual: They call up somebody else to tell them that they love them. Yes, and something profoundly religious, something so simple it escaped the attention of those who, concentrating on the flaws of Americans, miss their goodness completely.

For these people were found, on that morning, as most Americans are found on this morning, as men and women living less for themselves than to care for others, absorbed hardly at all with their own needs because of their commitment to the needs of their spouses, their children, their parents, and their friends.

So, too the Police and Fire Department personnel who did not look for a way out of that inferno but for a way into it, brave and true and clear eyed as they lay down their lives that day for others. They, along with all the others we now remember, can be classified under only one title, for if they would all admit that they were sinners, they were, first and foremost, lovers who revealed to us, better than stone-carved commandments in a courthouse or the easily given judgments of popes and prelates, what faith looks like in real life.

Does making the sign of the cross get you a hit?

The greatest wonder of this year's World Series is that the ACLU has not sued major league baseball to stop managers and players from making the sign of the cross, kissing religious medals, and pointing heavenward after home runs to invoke or to acknowledge divine assistance.

After all, baseball is the national pastime and, if the late William O. Douglas could find "emanations" from the Constitution to generate a "right to privacy," it should be a cinch for civil liberties lawyers to claim that praying during the nation's game violates the separation of church and state.

What are average non-litigious fans to make, however, of the imprecations of athletes in general and of baseball players in particular? We can easily read their lips when they use God's name to damn the fates or the umpires, and even ACLU purists understand that such utterances are not prayers.

When the Florida Marlins' "Pudge" Rodriguez makes signs of the cross as rapidly as an old monsignor at a Latin Mass, is this superstition, an obsessive ritual to ward off demons, or as clean and clear a prayer as the double he then hits off the left field fence?

And when the Marlins' manager, Jack McKeon, says, of St. Theresa, to the *New York Times*, that, "she in our church is the prodigy of miracles, and I've been praying to her to work on a miracle that she, so far, has been delivering," are we watching baseball or a religious revival without a tent but with at least as much faith as the outdoor Vatican ceremony of the same day in which the pope has invested thirty-one new cardinals?

What we are viewing, of course, is something profoundly human. Perhaps the ACLU understands that it cannot sue persons for what they think or believe, or perhaps its lawyers, busy with Christmas cribs and the Ten Commandments on stands as big as kitchen islands in courthouses, haven't figured out a way to do it yet.

Nothing, however, is more human than prayer, an effort as old as humankind to make a relationship with a Higher Power. Prayer becomes difficult only when experts try to teach ordinary people how to do it. Instruction in obsessive ways and methods as finely drawn as battle plans to storm the divine fortress leave most people exhausted and feeling that they are falling short of an unattainable ideal.

Good men and women pray all the time, often wordlessly, often when worried about their families, or spontaneously, when they are struck by the vast and inexpressible beauty of creation or by an episode of great loss, such as that of 9/11, when they sense that we all belong to the same family.

It is also very human to employ obsessive rituals to guarantee success or to keep bad luck at bay. These reveal how we place ourselves at the center of the universe so that the outcome of everything, including the World Series, depends on our wearing our lucky hat or touching the slats in the front fence in prescribed order. We think we have the power to disturb the balance of the galaxy by doing something, such as turning on a light, and instantly changing the outcome. "If only I hadn't done that," we murmur, confessing that *we*, not our home team, lost the game.

Yes, all these, along with superstition, conspiracy theories, and feeling destined to win the lottery, are small features of our large human nature. That they get scrambled up with prayer does not make prayer less or diminish our imperfect but inborn hunger to find the Divine in all of creation. That is sacramental, but so, too, is our ability to smile at our own self-importance and to forgive ourselves and each other for being so endearingly human. And that is very religious, indeed.

For Thanksgiving, take a humanity bath

America's great novelist and Nobel laureate, Saul Bellow, once told me that, because of the solitary nature of the work of writers—"We labor like silkworms," he says of our elected exile—he often leaves the copy books he fills first in graceful longhand and the ancient electric machine at which he types the next draft, to take a "humanity bath."

"I am drawn," he says, "to where ordinary men and women gather, riding the subway, walking the busy streets, anyplace where humans reveal themselves..." In such places, we may witness what he describes in *The Adventures of Augie March* as our "universal eligibility to be noble."

Writers are not the only ones who can be washed clean in the pool of our common humanity, of course, and, in a week in which it is hard to avoid advice about what to serve or how to cook Thanksgiving dinner and how to act or what to watch in and around the feast, the only way to escape is to take a bath in human wonder ourselves.

No training and no preparation are needed to exercise this birthright that allows us, in this last of the year's clearings before winter, to discover the spirit of the feast in the faces of those who sit near us at the candlelit table on this day or who stream by us in the commuting crowds on almost every other day.

Taking a humanity bath is nothing less than immersing ourselves in the great religious mystery of our lives. It is here, on our everyday rounds, rather than at the end of pilgrimages to shrines or in the cool quiet of cathedrals, that the essential Mystery flows over us like a gentle tide or a warming southern wind.

This Mystery fits us as human beings, so beware of those who say that we must overcome our humanity in order to make room for God.

We can understand the Mystery of God's love and presence because we experience it with those we love, and who love us, all the time. We do not love each other because we are perfect but because we are imperfect, the essential condition for being lovable.

And what is the great revelation about the way God loves us that can be found in the way ordinary people love each other? They resist each other's efforts to improve their looks or their manner by saying, "I love you just the way you are."

That sentence sums up the way God looks on all of us and bids us to recognize this mystery of His Love in the only place it is ever found, in our relationships with each other. A humanity bath immerses us in our depths, as vast as those of the sea, in which we send and receive the true soundings of being alive together.

The great religious Mystery is not one of a solitary sack-clothed figure who flees the world to make room for God in a soul scrubbed free of the least residue of a human touch, those "attachments" to persons and places that spiritual writers of a certain period labeled as harmful to our spiritual health and obstacles to our union with the Divine.

Thanksgiving is celebrated at a table just as the Eucharist is, and for the same reason. We group around the table, giving thanks for finding God—like the gospel treasure in the field—in and with each other. That field also contains weeds that are not without their stunted wonder.

Stunted wonders, that's us, and Thanksgiving is a humanity bath that, like a Turkish bath, reveals rather than hides our humanness. Indeed, in the humanity bath we find how we actually look in the sight of the Lord, and the very image we angle away from confronting in the mirror, or that seems so lacking to us, turns out to be just what He has been looking for all along. Eucharist means Thanksgiving, and in our imperfect tableau we break bread with the Lord who loves us just as we are.

A Christmas meditation on cathedral pews

Social scientists speak of "unobtrusive measures," that is, spontaneous behavior that reveals the truth as well as or better than carefully devised tests and interviews or, God help us, exit polls.

We stand now at the North Pole of the year from which we look down the path we have traveled and choose the way we will enter for the next phase of our journey.

Our pockets and desks overflow with unobtrusive measures of ourselves. Check book stubs and credit card bills, for example, are virtual autobiographies at our fingertips. They provide an irrefutable account of what we bought and where we went.

Each entry asks the same questions: *What were you thinking? Why did you buy this? Why did you go there?* Judgment Day will not reveal our motives and intentions any better than these unobtrusive measures.

Similar measures exist that allow us in the Christmas season to forgive ourselves and each other for being so chronically human and to renew ourselves for our passage through the coming year.

These are the "markings" that the men and women we mistakenly term "ordinary" make in time that manifest what is eternal in them.

They include the hearts carved in trees, signs that speak of love that remains fresh through generations of every kind of weather. These symbols may be stretched and altered by the strains of growth and the smiting of sun and storms, but they endure, as true love does the battering it may at times receive in even the closest relationships.

Ancient trees survive the storms because of their deep roots and may be the best symbols of our abiding love for each other. They bear the entwined hearts of many generations, surviving the defacement of vandals and the chainsaws of foresters, as unobtrusive measures of our deepest longings and truest selves. Do not miss these trees for the forest of distractions around us.

We can't search for these unobtrusive measures. They present themselves to us as they did to me in Chicago's Holy Name Cathedral. This great old limestone church is filled with great symbols, from the stained glass windows to the dead cardinals' ceremonial headgear hanging high above the main altar.

The best measures are far less spectacular. These include the markings on the pews left by generations of parishioners. Even varnished over, they stand out, unintentional engravings made by the shifting and kneeling of a million ordinary men and women over the decades.

While some small initials may have been scratched by restless children, most of these irregular lines and spheroids have been embossed accidentally. Some of them were made by umbrellas, others by dropped objects or the unintentional swipe of a ring as someone reached for a wallet. Tiny phone numbers or names tell us where the longing hearts of lovers lay as they engraved the markings with a fingernail, a key, or a pencil stub during a long sermon.

The gold in King Tut's tomb cannot rival for richness this maze of human signals that speaks so poignantly of people who have assembled in joy and in sorrow or just with their ordinary problems that fit the liturgical season of Ordinary Time. Most of these measures, like those on our own hearts, come from everyday wear. They are sacraments of the ordinary, signs of life, just the right present for each of us to open on Christmas Day.

The Seasons of 2004

John Gregory Dunne: Good-bye, dear friend

Nobody better fulfilled Henry James's definition of a writer's calling than John Gregory Dunne, who died as the old year ended. James's ideal was to be as someone on whom nothing is lost.

Nothing was lost on John Dunne, nothing of our human longing for the transcendent despite our sin-hobbled pilgrimages through the human condition. "A writer," he once said, "is an eternal outsider, his nose pressed against whatever window on the other side of which he sees his material" ("John Gregory Dunne, Novelist, Screenwriter, and Observer of Hollywood, Is Dead at 71," by Richard Severo, *New York Times*, January 1, 2004).

John Dunne was, in Saul Bellow's classic self-description, "a first class noticer," and this gift enabled him to recreate the world and its inhabitants in swift, deft phrases, not telling us what people were like but allowing us to feel their deepest and truest resonations just by letting us overhear them in conversation.

Speech as human revelation is found as high art in his masterpiece, *True Confessions*, a novel also made into a movie, in which post–World War II American Catholicism, the Church Triumphant after generations of immigrant struggle, comes to life in Los Angeles in the story of the Spellacy brothers, one a monsignor on the move to higher things and chief aide to the cardinal, and the other a detective immersed in lower things on the vice squad.

In this tale of Irish brothers, a subject whose joys, sorrows, and readiness for combat and reconciliation he knew well from being raised in a big family in West Hartford, Connecticut, we read the story of hard-won Catholic cultural ascendancy by the cultural paths then open to its sons, through the church or through the Police Department.

John Gregory Dunne

The novel contains the whole of that now lost world at that moment and can be read not only as a touching and stirring entertainment but as a three-dimensional display of Catholic energy and achievement as it challenged and shattered the restraints of a wary W.A.S.P. national culture in which even President Franklin D. Roosevelt, who depended on Catholics' political support, thought that appointing one to his cabinet or to the Supreme Court was about as far as he could go in rewarding them.

Those who want to understand Catholicism on its vigorous way toward electing John F. Kennedy may well consult this book rather than dried out statistical reports or tranquillized historical accounts. This novel, like no other, captures the muscular church on its march from sea to sea, building churches and Catholic schools, and expressing itself and its understanding of human compromise and sin in the uneasy relationships that developed between Catholic hierarchs, contractors, politicians, and police departments.

John Dunne was not only a great writer but also an extraordinary friend whose last message to me came in a phone call to my wife while I was in the hospital for serious surgery at Thanksgiving time. He wanted to know how I was and wanted us to know that, when he had been in Paris with his wife, Joan Didion, he had visited his favorite church, Sacre Coeur, and they said a prayer and lit a candle for me. In the classic tradition he knew so well, John had remained for Mass and Communion on my behalf.

I was not then able to speak to him, but I hear his voice often now. He spoke, as he knew, with a slight hesitation at times, retrieving half a word or half a sentence as a juggler might to rebalance them and fashion them artfully into a dazzling sentence. That is what he did all the time, snaring shards and pieces of our glory and meanness and transforming them into words that became like mirrors in which we could see and judge ourselves less harshly as humans.

He and his wife Joan, against the grain of modern marriage tactics, were together all the time, joined, as it seemed to me, as flavors are in a salad so that, without losing themselves, they also constituted a third and wonderful thing, a man and woman in love and devoted in every moment to each other and to their daughter, Quintana.

John Dunne broke free of the restraints of time to enter the eternity with which he was as familiar as he was with Boyle Heights in Los Angeles from which the Spellacy brothers of *True Confessions* arose, or the Frog Hollow of West Hartford from which he and his own remarkable siblings arose. He had drawn down on his intimate knowledge of everything human, and, since nothing was lost on him, caught the sparks of the eternal in all of us so that he entered easily into its full and brilliant light.

Super Bowl half-time show: nobody grown up enough to sin

CBS should know that commissioning MTV to stage your Super Bowl half-time show is the same as hiring the ACLU to do your Christmas decorations...

Witnessing the show may be likened to overhearing a group of teen-agers in their first exchanges of what they think are "dirty" jokes. You are embarrassed at their fumbling efforts to shed their innocence when they are not yet mature enough to commit a real sin.

Real sin is well beyond the range of our synthetic celebrity class and way beyond the football and network officials now professing to be "shocked, shocked" at what occurred.

This lack of sin means a lack of any grand passion for any true cause or real love for any true person. These are the defining emotions of those who shear through the folds of their own narcissism to make contact with a world separate from their own petty fantasies and to enter relationships whose flourishing depends on putting away the things of children to become adults.

The Super Bowl incident would be a passionless crime except that, by the measure of its sponsors and performers, it was, at best, a passionless misdemeanor.

Adult men and women are capable of real love, courage, great art, heartbreak, and sin. These go together in the risks that adults must take every day as they face the moral complexities of the theme, the "freedom to choose," a tip-off, as America's most used and least examined slogan, about the gaudy emptiness of the half-grown half-time display.

Don't blame the performers. They frolic in a low-class garden of Eden for a living and, because they spend so much time looking at themselves, have not yet even noticed the tree of the knowledge of good and evil, much less been tempted to eat of its fruit.

The so-called adults—CBS, MTV, and the NFL—those behind the half-time show who also okayed commercials that made men's room graffiti look like Shakespeare—are now trying to restore their virginity by promising investigations to rival those into the pre–Iraq War intelligence estimates.

Incapable of sin or genuine relationship with the public, they play the role of the teacher who, having missed adolescence, identifies with the students, taking sadly shallow pleasure in their plans to dismay adults because they are still allowed to embarrass themselves.

So what did MTV do when the NFL complained of the rehearsals, "about suggestive dancing by… Nelly, who grabbed his crotch repeatedly…"? MTV, according to spokeswoman Carole Robinson as reported in the *New York Times* (February 3, 2004), "gave notes" to performer Kid Rock, "one of which he honored, two of which he didn't." And as for Nelly, well, "he made moves on the air that he did not display during rehearsals." Sounds more like high school than high dudgeon.

Officials, including NFL Commissioner Paul Tagliabue, who vows "We'll change our policies," take on the role of the hapless but enabling high school teacher on whose back the students, in final triumph, pin a "Kick Me" sign.

What did they expect when the MTV web site promised something "shocking" during Janet Jackson's performance with Justin Timberlake to a song, "I gotta have you naked" that hid its *faux* shock in a fig leaf of unintelligibility?

Their high school excuses should have blamed the dog for eating Jackson's costume instead of the "garment malfunction" her spokesman, Stephen Huvane, blamed for the brief exposure of her right breast. Timberlake, he said, "was supposed to 'peel away' Jackson's rubber bustier, 'to reveal a red lace bra…but the garment collapsed.'"

And so should we, in laughter at the spectacle of these network heads and football league leaders revealing what we already know, that they have no taste and that they go on high moral alert only when the cash register doesn't ring.

Their worst hypocrisy is their pretending that something *bad* happened at half time. The mid-winter madness lacked *gravitas*, any true sense of what sin can be like in its bitter flavors of betrayed love, flouted truth, or deliberately shattered trust. To sin at all, you must first be an adult who knows what it takes to love. That kind of robust sin can be forgiven. But there is no forgiveness possible for the feigned outrage of the Super Bowl overseers at the adolescent follies they created in their own images and likenesses.

Picasso and the passion of Madrid

The only seemingly long dead Spanish artist Pablo Picasso gazes with us at Madrid's wound of terrorist shattered railway carriages, mass funerals for the ordinary people overtaken by Death on an ordinary morning, a political revolution, and a gate slammed shut on an older way of life...

In his 1937 painting, *Guernica*, he paints—for there is no past tense for someone speaking so vividly to us in the present—a view of carnage and loss inspired in time by the Spanish Civil War that, in its timeless symbols, evokes not only the closing of an age but the Mystery of what happened before our eyes last week in Madrid.

The smoke rises from the 3/11 ruins of Madrid's commuter trains to mix with that above the 9/11 ruins in lower Manhattan, Washington, DC, and a Pennsylvania meadow, the biblical pillar of cloud by day that matches the tower of fire that is the night sacrament of all our losses. We must look for ourselves before we look with Picasso at the essential Mystery of these interrelated events that reveal our relationships with each other.

Picasso depicts carnage in the imagery of the Spanish bullring, in which "a horse and its rider," as Joseph Campbell describes it, "lie shattered and a bull stands mighty and whole" (*The Masks of God: Creative Mythology*, 1968). This represents, as 9/11 and 3/11 do, an end and a beginning of historical periods. The central figure of the bull surviving in the midst of death helps us understand this newest panel in the Mystery into which we have all been drawn.

Madrid and the Trade Towers are separated, in time, by exactly 911 days. In the eternal field, they are twinned in a Mystery, *the* Mystery, *our* Mystery, that is, of us-as-we-are in this world-as-it-is, with love our fragile armor in our daily skirmishes with loss and death. We turn to Picasso because our journalists, busy with fragmentary details and hurried interpretation, do not even dream of such possibilities. Nor do we hear of them from most of our religious leaders.

They are out of touch with the Eternal because, by living according to the 24/7 news cycle, journalists and prelates reveal their enslavement to the cycles of the ever-changing moon, that symbol of Time that, lacking light of its own, must catch it from the never-changing sun, the symbol of Eternity. Reporters and church leaders often seem to lack light of their own to shed on the great events of our times. Lacking a sense of theological Mystery with a capital *M*, they specialize in conventional interpretations of mysteries with a small *m*. Platitudes, in short, instead of Beatitudes.

So the tragedy in Madrid has been reported more as a story about politics, as bad timing for President Bush's policies, rather than as Eternity breaking through the binding of Time. The same weekend brings us an indirect definition of the same Mystery. Designers replacing New York's Trade Towers, face "three colossal forces...gravity, wind and...fear" ("High Anxiety," by James Glanz, *New York Times*, March 14, 2004). Those who enter will not only be haunted by what occurred on the site in the past, they will also be apprehensive about what could happen again."

The Mystery of Life and Death and Destiny cannot be vacuumed out of that sacred space. The devices of time may tame gravity and wind, but fear is the breath of the Eternal rippling across our souls, our natural reaction to finding ourselves immured in the great Mystery of living and loving and dying, the Mystery we share in common that reveals that, even with different looks, we belong to the same family.

This is the Mystery of what American poet Robinson Jeffers prophetically called the "Tower Beyond Tragedy." And the master artist Picasso, weeping then as now for his country, sees what reporters and bishops cannot, the Eternal in the heart of the Mystery of loss. The bull, Joseph Campbell explains, is "symbolic of the ever dying, self-resurrecting lord of the tides of life" (*The Masks of God*).

Madrid's wrecked rail cars now take their place with the fallen Trade Towers, the rebuilt Pentagon wing, and the healed over Pennsylvania field as symbols of the unreported and un-preached about Mys-

tery with a capital M that stands at the center of our lives, overshadow-
ing all the over-reported but petty mysteries with a small *m*. Picasso
paints a bull for us so that, in the ruins of Madrid and in our own, we
may recognize "the vehicle of the appearance of an eternal present in
the field of passing time..." (*The Masks of God*).

Reports: American priests are American men

As if we were riding the buffeted African Queen rather than the ever-steady barque of Peter, we are heading toward a cataract of reports and responses about American priests and the sexual abuse problem that exploded in their ranks two years ago.

Established by America's Catholic bishops, the National Review Board will release on February 27 the results of the John Jay College of Criminal Justice census of the incidence since 1950 of sexual abuse by American priests along with its own analysis of the factors affecting the scandal's uncertain origins, delayed identification, and clouded management.

The Catholic League for Religious and Civil Rights has already issued its own assemblage of information, "Sexual Abuse in Social Context," in order "to put the recent scandal in the Catholic Church in perspective," and "to guide the discussion that will follow" the distribution of these reports.

The Vatican is about to issue a 220-page report, "Sexual Abuse in the Catholic Church: Scientific and Legal Perspectives," urging church authorities "to work more closely with scientific experts to identify potential perpetrators and make sure they cannot harm the young" (John Thavis , Catholic News Service, February 19, 2004).

CNN claims that the National Review Board's report will reveal that, over the last half century, 11,000 abuse claims have been made against Catholic church personnel and that 4,450 clergy have been accused of molesting minors.

The Catholic League maintains that by most estimates the percentage of priests involved in sexual abuse is relatively small (roughly 1 to 2 percent), and, asserting that "children are much more likely to be sexually abused by family members and friends than by anybody else," it suggests that "the incidence of the sexual abuse of a minor is slightly higher among the Protestant clergy than among Catholic clergy, and that it is significantly higher among public school teachers than among ministers and priests" ("Sexual Abuse in Social Context: Catholic Clergy and Other Professionals," Catholic League for Religious and Civil Rights, February 2004).

The League maintains that the problem is not pedophilia, as the media have described it, but homosexuality, implying that the latter is the true but overlooked cause of the church's woes.

When the last words about the nation's priests are uttered this weekend, they may not go beyond the first words of the report of the extensive psychological research commissioned, along with sociological, historical, and theological investigations, by America's Catholic bishops over thirty years ago: "American priests are ordinary men."

We will learn this weekend what all good priests know: They are ordinary men in the sense that their experience of being human and being sexual is more like than unlike that of American men in general. Take an inventory of male American sexual conflicts, uncertainties, fantasies, and anxieties and they will be, as they must in the human condition, a tissue match for those of priests and other men of the cloth.

Nobody can deny that expectations on the behavior of clergy are legitimately higher than on those of other men, but it would also be hard to deny that the realities of the inner lives and longings of these groupings do not radically differ.

Television's *Sex in the City* ended with a whimper rather than a bang after six years of chronicling the loneliness not only of the long distance runners but also of the short sprinters pursuing sex poorly nourished by human relationships. The Superbowl half-time is infamous, not because it revealed America's "pushing the envelope" of mature sexual expression but because it documented our immaturity with a display of barely adolescent sexiness instead.

What tells us more poignantly of America's struggles with growing up, Justin Timberlake's high school sophomore's pawing of Janet Jackson, or "Iron Mike" Ditka's commercial hawking of a sexual stimulant for men "to stay in the game?" Or is it the news that women think they are now "empowering" themselves by producing pornography from their own viewpoint rather than that of its traditional consumer, the leering, curious male?

The forthcoming reports, and their subsequent analysis, will tell us no more about priests than they do about ourselves, that, despite our vaunted sophistication, we remain far from understanding human sexuality fully, indeed, far from appreciating the even deeper mystery of human personality, that we need more sympathy than censure for all of us who think that everybody else understands sexuality better than we do.

The weekend's reports will tell us not just how human priests are but also how human we all are. We need to ponder these reports, priests and us included, in the spirit of psychoanalyst Harry Stack Sullivan's famous observation that "We are all much more simply human than anything else."

An Easter voice from a modern tomb

*The rock was long ago rolled away from our modern tomb, that place
cut in the rock where the Trade Towers once stood and where the great
sacramental revelation of the goodness of ordinary people took place…*

Now a voice filled with life speaks to us from the tomb that, like the
tomb of Jesus, only seemed to be seized by Death. We hear a valiant
woman speaking to our depths, "a calm voice," as the *New York Times*
put it, "as disaster unfolded in the sky" (January 28, 2004).

"Betty Ann Ong," reporter Philip Shenon writes, "a veteran flight
attendant for American Airlines, could not have sounded much calmer
on the morning of September 11, 2001, as she tried to describe the may-
hem aboard Flight 11."

We will hear this voice as long as we remember this day, for Ms.
Ong addresses us, as do prophets and God in the scriptures, out of the
whirlwind and the burning bush, revealing more about the nature of
the event than a Congressional Commission ever will and explaining
why architects have had such difficulty in designing a memorial to this
greatest event of our time.

Earlier in the year, the Congressional Committee investigating
9/11 played a portion of a tape of Miss Ong speaking, from the back of
the doomed plane to airline ground personnel, demonstrating, according to chairman Thomas Kean, her "heroism" and the "duty, courage,
selflessness and love" evident in the midst of that day's chaos.

A voice, we now understand, of life unafraid of death, a voice of
Resurrection.

"My name is Betty Ong," she begins, "I am on Flight 11." Recapitu-
lating what happened after the jet's highjacking out of Boston, she says:

"Our first class galley attendant and our purser are stabbed. We can't get into the cockpit. The door won't open."

Two and a half years later, her voice intones the horror that has been lying wide awake within us ever since, untouched and unrelieved by the passage of time. Miss Ong tells us what we already know, that we still feel the pulse of this event within us, that it has broken free of the clasp of time, that it belongs to a category of Mystery that transcends the mystery that the Congressional Committee is trying to solve or the one with which architects grapple as they try to fuse profound loss with the renewal of art and the resumption of commerce.

The memorial problem, according to critic Michael Kimmelman, arose from the democratization of the design contest. This "populist palaver" gave a bad name to the "elitism" that he sees as a "blunt term for expertise" ("Ground Zero Finally Grows Up," by Michael Kimmelman, *New York Times*, February 1, 2004).

Kimmelman brushes Mystery with his sleeve in describing Santiago Calatrava's Trade Center PATH terminal design as "ecstatic," referring to "its soaring wings and cathedral-like space, opening to the sky" and saying that it "may be the best memorial we have. It certainly brings people together."

But it is Ms. Ong's even voice that opens us "to the sky" as she speaks from a plane with "soaring wings," a place that is a "cathedral-like space" because it bears a cargo of Mystery—the mystery of these ordinary men and women, so like us, "caught up in the air, in the twinkling of an eye," revealing their simple goodness to us in the face of locked doors and stabbed crew members and an ending that they cannot know but that we now do. This Mystery brings us together because it confronts our fragility with everything that threatens to tear us apart.

Betty Ong's is a clear voice speaking directly to us from the heart of the Mystery that is the great sacramental revelation of our time, Mystery defined by theologian Richard McBrien as "reality imbued with the hidden presence of God" (*Catholicism*, HarperSanFrancisco, 1984, p. 1245).

She speaks for us and our condition, always one of knowing "in part, in a glass darkly," telling us, "We can't seem to get to the cockpit. Nobody can call the cockpit. We can't even get inside."

"Is anybody there?" she asks at one point. A reservations agent answers for us all, "Yes, we're here." And Miss Ong replies, as she does now to us, out of the whirlwind, the burning bush of Mystery, in a voice as clear as Easter morning: "I'm staying on the line as well."

True confessions

This piece tells the story better than I can summarize it. It is the talk I gave at Andrew Greeley's fiftieth anniversary of being a priest...

I have known Andrew Greeley almost as long as anyone here. That emboldens me to ask this question: How well do you know Andrew Greeley?

It is hard not to know him, of course, because of his achievements as a priest, a writer, a teacher, and, as he confessed to me his ambition just before we both turned forty, as a *savant*, a word that means a "learned scholar," a "wise man." And he has long since earned that description.

But how well do you know Andrew Greeley? As a successful novelist who has instructed and entertained millions of readers? As a sociologist of religion who has found the glass of data half filled while so many others see it half empty? As a public speaker with enough Irish charm to turn the Chicago River green without any help from the men who pour dye into it every March 17th? As a columnist with ideas to inspire or infuriate you on men and events? As a frequent guest on radio and television when a sensible opinion on things Catholic is needed? Yes, you will say, thinking of the many faces of our celebrant, nobody will ever be able to say, "Andy, we hardly knew ye."

It seems only yesterday that he and I were young priests together, and only a little after that, that he was celebrating his twenty-fifth anniversary of ordination at a South Side gathering. Many great people came for that event, including the late Daniel Patrick Moynihan, who fixed his blue eyes on my own blue eyes and spoke the only sentence he ever addressed to me, "Where did you get that drink?"

But how well do you know Andrew Greeley? Andrew and I were born in the same year, along with theologians Hans Küng and Johannes Metz, historian Martin Marty, and, yes, Shirley Temple. As Franklin D. Roosevelt wrote to Winston Churchill, "It's fun being in the same decade with you."

If you think of us as Irish brothers—and some of you here might just understand that concept—you will not go far wrong. Irish brothers, as we know, love each other deeply. They stick together in the long run. The problem, of course, is the short run, for if in another of Andrew's favorite quotations it can be said of the Irish that "all their wars are merry and all their songs are sad," then it can also be said that the closest of Irish brothers can fall into the deepest of estrangements, the worst of battles, and the stoniest of silences.

How well do you know Andrew Greeley? Well, I know him from a thousand adventures, including our grand battles for renewal of the church after Vatican II, and our memorable speaking tour of the Orient during which, among other things, we shared accommodations in a Japanese inn with boiling lava in the backyard and South Korean digs with a garbage dump in the backyard. I can still see him standing, in his Japanese garb and slippers, studying the fifty-foot buffet of various kinds of seaweed, perplexed for one of the first times in his life. And I recall him lecturing at a university along the way. It was June, it was warm, and the windows were open. I had lectured first and the sun was just setting as Andrew began to speak. Within a few moments, creatures, everything but Godzilla, began to fly in the window and attack him. He stared them down, batted them away, and waved them off, somewhat like King Kong under attack on the Empire State Building. And he did it with good humor and an Irish twinkle in his eye.

How well do you know Andrew Greeley? Well, let's get back to the falling out, for this is the tale I would tell you today. That, along with the fact that, of all his accomplishments and all his titles, it is being a priest that is most important to him. For, yes, in the tradition of all real Irish brothers, we entered a place where the trade winds of friendship died down and we drifted almost out of each other's sight if not out of the sound of each other's voices. Regrettable, one felt, remembering all the good, yes, but what could or would be done about it?

It was Andrew who did something about it and that is what I want to tell you about on this day of celebration. I do not know how he learned that I had prostate cancer and was in Northwestern Hospital, but I do know that the day after my surgery, as my wife and I sat quietly in my hospital room still stunned and sorting out the sudden turn of events, Andrew appeared at the door and entered with the greatest gift a man could give—and one that took a great man to give it—for it was the healing gift of reconciliation expressed, as the Irish, usually so in love with words, express it best, by the deed, by the gift outright of himself, by slaying the dragon of misunderstanding and wordlessly making us brothers again.

How well do you know Andrew Greeley? I thought that I knew him very well until that November morning when I got to know him as I would like to celebrate him today. For Andrew, fifty years a priest, and a dozen other callings fulfilled along the way, revealed himself that day as that we would all long to be—a Christian to his depths and a light to the world.

How well do you know Andrew Greeley, my Irish brother and friend, who remained that all through the years as long and uninviting as that Japanese buffet? He has driven away those demons as he did the invaders who flew in the window of that university on the other side of the world. And it is Andrew my brother I celebrate this day, fifty years a priest, a great Christian, a light, indeed, to the world.

Pope not infallible when he calls America "soulless"

Pope John Paul II might as well be French for the studied distaste he expresses about America. He recently warned a group of Midwestern bishops that their people "are hypnotized by materialism, teetering before a 'soulless vision of the world'" (Chicago Tribune, *May 29, 2004*)...

Perhaps the pope, like many a priest climbing the pulpit without a prepared sermon, merely made a hasty withdrawal from his memory account and, as in improvised homilies we have all heard, one association ignited another until the resulting blaze roared with heat while giving little light.

Giving America bad reviews is a standby of popes. Pope Leo XIII (1810–1903) criticized the vaguely defined ills of "Americanism," including "idealizing the separation of church and state."

Leo XIII, called "the Great," is a good starting point for re-examining whether the church should condemn or listen more carefully to America. Leo XIII claimed, in an 1890 encyclical, *Catholicae Ecclesiae*, that "almost nothing was more venerated in the Catholic Church...[than] that she looked to see slavery eased and abolished."

In fact, and unfortunately, the Catholic Church in a number of conciliar decrees and papal statements supported the status quo of slavery. Popes Urban VIII, Innocent X, and Alexander VIII "were personally involved in buying Muslim galley slaves" and, in 1866, after the thirteenth amendment to the Constitution abolished slavery in America, the Holy Office stated that "Slavery itself...is not at all contrary to the natural and divine law...For the...ownership which a slave owner has over a slave is nothing more than the perpetual right of disposing of the work of a slave for one's own benefit..."

While America was debating the evil of slavery and plunging toward a Civil War to end it, numerous anti-slavery tracts were placed on the Index of Forbidden Books. Perhaps Abraham Lincoln's Emancipation Proclamation would have ended up there as well. It is clear, however, that while Rome was burning with indignation at "Americanism" it was also still fiddling with medieval concepts of slavery.

Where was the moral high ground? In America, bloodying itself and fighting on for another century and more to undo the evil of slavery, or in Rome where, as historian Diana Hayes tells us, "the Roman Catholic Church did support and maintain with all its power, secular and spiritual, the enslavement not only on non-Catholics but of its own Catholic faithful"?

Pope John XXIII bade the church in Vatican II to listen again to the world that approached learning and morality on the basis of its experience, thereby discovering truths about ourselves and our cosmos that ecclesiastical leaders had rejected to the grief of the pioneers it condemned and to its own grief as well.

The Vatican left Galileo condemned as a heretic for four centuries because he challenged the notion that the earth was the center of the universe. Repeatedly, the struggles to understand the world and ourselves, whether carried out by Darwin on evolution, by Freud on the unconscious, or by America itself on overturning slavery, have been ignored or condemned less by the pure Catholicism of the gospels than by the alloyed Catholicism of benighted church officials.

These same officials tell the pope that America is a terrible place as they close the windows to the world that John XXIII opened in Vatican II. Perhaps nothing better illustrates the difference between America, condemned by the Vatican as sexually relativistic, and the Vatican itself than the long covered up sex abuse scandal among the clergy.

The Vatican had to learn from America that pedophilia is not only a spiritual and emotional failure but also a crime. America gets to the truth and calls it by its right name. Until Rome overcomes its reluctance to do either, Pope John Paul II might well learn from rather than lecture to America about moral superiority.

Even cardinals have bad days

Father John Jay Hughes, a distinguished Catholic scholar, recently
reminded me that if we could read the mail that crosses a bishop's
desk every day, we would be more sympathetic to bishops and more
understanding of the statements they make and the orders they give...

What, then, passed across Francis Cardinal George's desk or path that
convinced him that the very best thing he could do on Pentecost, the
founding feast of the church year, was to order the good priests at Holy
Name Cathedral to deny the Eucharist to homosexuals wearing rainbow sashes?

What theological revelation exploded like old-fashioned flash
powder to wash the cardinal's mind with its light that he decided that
taking a stand against sash-wearing gays was the perfect public way to
celebrate the church's enlightenment by the Spirit?

He claimed that "...the order...wasn't a condemnation of homosexuality, but a declaration of the Eucharist's sanctity" (*Chicago Tri-*
bune, May 31, 2004). Even Catholics sympathetic to the cardinal's
daily pressures are hard pressed, not to say puzzled, at how sash wear-
ers could threaten the Eucharist's sanctity by presenting themselves to
receive it.

And they may think that the cardinal needs more time away from
the office after his explanation that "Communion is about Jesus Christ.
It's not supposed to be any other kind of statement... They can receive
Communion, but not by protesting."

Protesting seems to be the operative word in the cardinal's insight.
He expressed great distress a few years ago that gays were demonstrating outside Holy Name Cathedral and ordered that Communion
should not be distributed to any of them. The then cathedral pastor,

Father Robert McLaughlin, intervened, expressing a fairly Catholic thought, "We don't deny Communion to anyone at Holy Name." That's the kind of Christian behavior, according to some observers, that led to McLaughlin's departure, by way of a one-sentence letter from the cardinal, some months later.

Homosexual Catholics, along with all other Catholics, have a right to the sacraments, according to canon 213 of church law, and the cardinal, along with all other bishops, has an obligation to provide them.

Gay Catholics wear rainbow sashes to identify themselves publicly as believers who want to practice their faith and to be nourished by the sacraments. These men and women did not roll raucously down the aisle on the floats of a Gay Pride parade. Nor did they carry placards, shout, wave, or set fire to anything. They did not disrupt the liturgical celebration but only presented themselves, as all Catholics do, as sinners seeking forgiveness, as humans hungry for the bread of the Eucharist.

Gays have grounds for protest, of course, especially after a Vatican document claimed that they bear within them "an intrinsic disorder," and the pope's spokesperson speculated that homosexuals may not be capable of valid ordination to the priesthood. Many commentators have attempted to make them the scapegoats for the entire clergy sex abuse scandal that has brought so much grief in recent years.

But they were not protesting, or inscribing heretical theses on the cathedral doors. They were being Catholics, like every other Catholic in the cathedral, aware of their sinfulness and also aware that one of the effects of the Eucharist is the forgiveness of our sins. Jesus said that his mission was not to those who do not need a physician but to those who do, that is, all of us on any given Sunday.

The cardinal may have acted after a bad day to give gays a worse morning and it is hard to see how his conspiracy theory of protest holds up. Is there, we might ask, a less Catholic thing to do than to give these men and women a handshake in place of the sacrament?

How many Knights of Columbus or of some papal order have entered Holy Name Cathedral wearing sashes over hearts as hardened and corrupted as any in the history of Christendom? How many murderous gangsters have been borne down this aisle to have priests bury them with a Mass and a last blessing if the most basic thing about Catholicism is not its willingness to face and forgive sinners?

How many clerics, wearing sashes of their own on their cassocks, have been more hypocritical than these sash-wearing gays about themselves and their lives? Perhaps we can understand that even cardinals have bad days, but these should not lead them to demean people who have been demeaned enough already and to make Catholicism seem the abode of the perfect when it is best understood as a home for sinners.

Disputes about Eucharist contradict its nature

Denying the Eucharist to Catholics of various minds and in various circumstances is a hot topic that generates even hotter opinions. Not since his community at Corinth provoked St. Paul have we had believers misbehaving so publicly in relationship to the central mystery of Catholicism...

Some bishops are angry that legislators who vote pro-choice thereby align themselves with abortion rights, directly flouting a long term teaching of the Catholic Church. They thereby break the unity of the Christian community, moving themselves away from its table, so that denying them the eucharistic food from that table is as much of their making as it is of bishops who want to deny them the Eucharist.

As a PS, some bishops suggest that Catholics who vote for pro-choice candidates should not receive Communion either.

Others just as angrily contend that the situation is more complex, that Catholic legislators must uphold the Constitution that allows women choice in these matters, and that they should not be branded as public sinners by being denied the Eucharist when they seek to receive it at Mass.

Some question whether bishops and pastors are really spiritually gifted enough to read the minds and consciences of anybody on a Communion line and why Catholic legislators are the only ones targeted for this harsh, singular, and, some say, medieval treatment. And, since everybody on that Communion line is a sinner, who draws the line and where does one make the cut?

Does the church deny Communion or Christian burial to other categories of sinners, such as those who lie, disregard, or disguise the truth in questionable marketing, advertising, political campaigning, or the generalized skullduggery of putting the fix in here and there? Is the Eucharist to be denied to those who operate gambling casinos that take away families' rent and food money? Has any bishop denied Communion to a legislator who is pro-life but votes pro-gambling?

This issue has been turned into street theater during this election year as, on the one hand, hecklers assail Catholic John Kerry after he leaves Mass, and, on the other, they attack Washington's Cardinal Theodore McCarrick for saying that the Eucharist should never be used punitively. Still others shrug the bishops off as dangerously involving themselves in politics in a period when, after they defended the questionable choices they made about the clerical sex abuse scandal, their own credibility, especially on sexual issues, remains at a low point.

That isn't a cloud of incense rising above this but a smoking mixture of bitterness, self-righteousness, generalized irritation, and specific score settling. It reminds one of Nietzsche's old complaint, "If only these Christians looked as if they were saved."

The American church needs a cooling-off period in which Catholics in general and cardinals and candidates in particular may meditate on the meaning of the Eucharist itself.

Listen to Franciscan Father Kenan Osborne, perhaps America's foremost sacramental theologian, as he gently tells us (*The Christian Sacrament of Initiation*, Paulist Press, 1987) that "the Eucharist is seen as a great moment of reconciliation... 'This is my body, which is for you ...This cup is the new covenant in my blood...' are all indications of forgiveness, of salvation, of reconciliation, of justification—a multiplicity of terms, but all with the same meaning: in Jesus...in his own life, death, and resurrection, and in...the Eucharist, there is reconciliation."

Before any of us says one more word to criticize either bishops or candidates, we might well meditate on Father Osborne's conclusion: "...the Eucharist, next to Jesus and the Church, is *the* sacrament of reconciliation, not the sacrament of penance, not even the sacrament of baptism. The Eucharist, because of the centrality of Jesus, must be seen as the sacrament of reconciliation."

Maybe the next time we are tempted to yell at each other about the Eucharist, we Christians should remember Nietzsche and at least try to look saved.

Catholicism not adrift or foundering

Catholics everywhere worry about whether there will still be a Catholic Church to serve their children and grandchildren. They would take great comfort from the analytic work of Joseph Claude Harris.

While others search its surface only for dead bodies, indictments, and bankruptcy papers, Joseph Claude Harris pans gold out of the Mississippi of information streaming from the headwaters of American Catholicism. The almost daily reports of the church's death, he concludes, are greatly exaggerated and, in fact, the church is functioning quite well.

The Seattle based research analyst notes that "For the last two or three years it has been very hard to find anything good about the church in the headlines. The sex abuse has been a gruesome scandal but, if you look at the data found in the Catholic Directory and the research at CARA [Center for Applied Research on the Apostolate], you find good things and no evidence that we are going out of business.

"People speak of a vocation crisis," he continues, "but from 1995 to 2002 parish leaders hired an additional 6,674 professional parish ministers. A staffing transition is happening with permanent deacons replacing priests and religious. Parish life continues, the sacraments are celebrated, and lay people have management responsibilities. If there were a crisis, you would have negative numbers. For example, my daughter is a youth minister in Seattle's Holy Rosary Parish. Her mentor is a liturgy director who is a layman and the parish business manager is a woman. That vocations come in a different way now than they did then is not a negative sign. Had we lost almost 6,674 parish ministers in that period, you could speak of a crisis. You can't with these positive numbers."

What about the donations that many claim are on the decline? Harris issued a report last fall analyzing Sunday collections for the last three years. "Donations to parishes increased by $259 million between 2000 and 2001 and $374 million between 2001 and 2002." That's a healthy sign.

The Catholic population increased by about seven million between 1995 and 2002. The proportion of Catholics to the total population increased from 209 per thousand Americans to 218. America is gradually becoming more Catholic.

"The Church has the financial structure to support this growth and function and is doing the same things, if in a different way, that it has always done. Take the sacramental life that defines the Church. Catholic baptisms represent 25 percent of all American births; 85 percent of these receive their First Eucharist eight years later. And 59 percent of this baptismal core present themselves for Confirmation.

"The funeral rate for Americans is 8.6 per thousand. The Catholic funeral rate is 7.8, about what you would expect given the reported number of 62 million Catholics. The funeral rate for Episcopalians is 13.8 percent per thousand registered members.

"The sacramental life of the Church has remained constant or actually improved over the last few years. There are no numbers to support the notion that Catholicism is adrift or that it is foundering.

"What we might call the Catholic Educational Market Share has remained constant for the last ten years. For primary years, 61 percent of the baptized Catholic population is in schools or religious education programs, and for secondary, it is 36 percent.

"These American numbers seem to amaze Europeans. How can Americans be so successful at, as they put it, 'doing Church'? One of the basic reasons is due to our American traditions. We are usually free of politics and they have a history of being tangled up in them."

Isn't the priest shortage undeniable? "We have many ways to respond to this that have not been tried. With a little imagination, the number of priests could easily be increased. Andrew Greeley proposes the institution of a Priests Corps on the model of the Peace Corps. And there is no canonical impediment to ordaining some of the 14,002 permanent deacons to the priesthood."

Harris's work is refreshing and reassuring about American Catholicism. "The information is all there," he observes, "it's just that nobody has looked at it as a measure of the historical success and fundamental soundness of American Catholicism."

If you want to feel encouraged about your children and grandchildren, consult his web site: www.josephclaudeharris.com. His analysis of Catholic contributions is a book of revelation, but it certainly isn't the Apocalypse.

Autumn's song of the human deep

Perhaps the world adorns itself with the superficial things of time—
the Emmy Awards, box office receipts, Brittany marries again—
to distract it from the Deep within it, vast and rich as the sea,
whose currents are Eternal.

Our lives are an interplay between our consciousness of, and constraint by, time and our awareness of, and longing for, the eternal. We experience both every day, but they are often so intermingled that we cannot, or do not, identify those moments when we get a glimpse of, or ride on, the surge of the Eternal in the quotidian.

The liturgy of worship is designed to open us to the eternal rather than to punch our time cards of religious duty. That is why it has always used the native tongue of the eternal—music, art, and metaphor—to tap into the Mystery beyond reason.

Those without a sense of art's capacity to escape time imagine religion as driven by clocks as much as commerce is. That is why the medieval church got into trouble selling indulgences as so many years or months off from punishments that have nothing to do with Time.

The time-bound also picture God as an old man and visualize St. Peter as a gray-bearded bureaucrat checking a ledger at the very gates of eternity. Goodness cannot be measured in units of Time. Goodness is where we meet the eternal in others, it is what allows us to be friends, fall in love, or transcend ourselves. It cannot be time-stamped or bar-coded.

Time and eternity are in a constant *pas de deux* in our experience. It was not, therefore, an accident, or just the calculation of a programmer who long ago made friends with the mammon of iniquity, that NBC-TV showed *Titanic* on the last Sunday before the beginning of autumn. Time-harried executives, unaware of why they were doing it, responded to movements in the Deep within themselves when they picked a film about the mystery of loss, love, and memory that are of the essence of autumn itself.

We are not surprised to learn that, on the deck of the dying *Titanic*, the brave musicians did not play "Nearer My God to Thee" but an English piece called "Autumn" ("A Night to Remember") by Walter Lord. They felt the tug of mystery that we all experience in the Deep within us when the earth tips halfway back from the sun to spread shadows across our busy lives as surely as it does across the infield of World Series games.

We keep time but eternity keeps us, and, although the fall (as it is also mysteriously but rightly called) is when the year seems to begin in school openings, new seasons in the arts, and getting back to work again, its mood is that of things coming to term, of leaves turning and harvests taken, of the passage of time, *all* time and *our* time, too.

Fall comes from the Germanic *Fallen*, evoking, with an unsentimental and Teutonic finality, the leaves not just coming to rest but completing their destiny, and some cycle we all feel in our Deep, by falling to the earth.

It is fitting that the liturgy encompassing this season is called Ordinary Time, that plain and homely prairie relieved here and there by holy days even as our ordinary lives are by baptisms, weddings, and birthdays, so that we breathe in and out with the universe whose groans of longing were written of by St. Paul. What he really heard was us—our sighing and longing on behalf of the galaxies for the eternal. That is what St. Paul knew "in part, in a glass darkly," and we do, too.

So the very small mystery of NBC's selecting *Titanic* for the eve of autumn is really a sliver of *our* Mystery, *the* Mystery that we experience in the cycle of every day, of every journey, and of every year. Listen to and draw up freely from the Deep, the well of eternity within all of us.

The forgotten commandment for the elections

Supposedly secular America has had no lack of moral advice and no small appetite for it during the election campaign that, like a villain who keeps rising from the dead in a horror movie, will breathe its last gasps of hot breath and hot air next week...

No group of voters has received more moral counsel, this way and that, than Catholics. They have been told by bishops and theologians that it is immoral to vote for candidates who support the pro-choice position on abortion, and that, for "proportionate" reasons, such as a candidate's support for overall Catholic social teaching, they can vote with a clear conscience for such candidates.

Catholic bishops backed uneasily and in a sideways motion away from their denial of the Eucharist to pro-choice candidates and those who vote for them. They have continued to insist, however, that, so central is the teaching that "abortion trumps everything" that Catholics should apply this in their moral estimation and electoral endorsement of the candidates.

Perhaps, as we stare at this soon-to-be-interred monster of a campaign, the bishops and other moralists would have helped the country in general, and believers in particular, more with a notion rooted in the Commandments themselves: "truth trumps everything."

"*Thou shalt not bear false witness against thy neighbor*" is about as basic a moral prescription as we are likely to find and, despite all the attention given to commandments concerning sex, it is the one most in need of rediscovery and restoration in both church and state. Indeed, American political campaigns, and other venues of American life, are now based at least as much on bearing false witness as on telling the truth.

Bearing false witness has been so domesticated by the advertising/ public relations complex that runs political campaigns as well as other large aspects of American culture that we hardly take notice, much less object, to the practice. Lying in public about products, services, and politicians has been given the less electrically charged name of *spin* and Americans have been conditioned to accept it as a high art rather than a low practice. Thus, after the presidential debates, correspondents identified their location without apology or blush as in *Spin Alley*, a baptized venue for transforming, hiding, or glossing the truth of what candidates either said or intended to say.

The highly paid reverse alchemists of our time—those who turn the gold of truth into the base metal of distortion—are true figures in the great chorus of sellers, entertainers, and con men who understand that, as philosopher William James once observed, Americans are ready to believe *anything* and would believe *everything*, if only they could.

"Hello, Sucker," the Prohibition era greeting of New York night club hostess Texas Guinan, is the slogan of the packagers and publicists who intend to shade if not obscure the real state of things. As a public relations expert once told me, "The art is to take the apartment building that collapsed because of negligence and call it 'urban renewal.'"

Maybe your father taught you what mine taught me, "Tell the truth because it is the right thing to do and it is also easier to remember." It is very hard to remember a lie because it is cut free of any connections to reality. That is why politicians so often contradict themselves or try to make a virtue out of taking several stands on the same subject.

As we know from knocking on a solid wall, nothing sounds like the truth. The chief architects of popular morality—scratch a public relations man and you discover the quintessential moralist for the American culture—have so conditioned us to the shadings and spin that were once known as lies and distortions that as we head for the polling place we need to remember that in this campaign, as in life itself, Truth should trump everything else.

The secret cause of the Ebersol tragedy

Sorrow hides itself within holidays, the better to break our hearts. So this Thanksgiving it stowed away on the Ebersol family flight that symbolized the deepest meaning of life and love. For love enters us into a two-sided mystery, that of discovering how to come together to give and share life and the other of accepting the inevitability of letting go of each other, the mystery, in short, of tasting eternity while living in time...

This mystery carries with it always the same question: How could this have happened to these good people, what is its cause?

Thanksgiving is our feast of the American family, of people coming, as they are described in the Bible, from a far country, prodigal sons among them, with room enough always found for them at the inn called home so that they break through time and touch what is eternal in their relationships with each other.

That is why, as the sun sets on a holiday, people ask, *Where did the time go?* Or, *Do you have to leave so soon?* We enter big religious mysteries in the small rituals of such reunions. When people love each other anywhere, eternity holds off time for a few hours, giving us a quick glimpse at what counts and what is worth holding onto in our lives together.

Robert Frost calls home that place where, "when you have to go there, they have to take you in." Home is not the superficial and socially undemanding "place" described in the old TV comedy *Cheers*, "where everybody knows your name." Home is the place where everybody knows us *just-as-we-are* and forgives us, or, at the very least, overlooks a lot and loves us enough to celebrate the mystery of being a family together.

Family gatherings are therefore previews of the Last Judgment, for the knowledge of each other's flaws does not blind us to the evidence of each other's goodness. As the pilgrims came upon Plymouth Rock, so we come upon our humanity on Thanksgiving weekend.

That is why, just as we are glad to see each other arrive, we have mixed feelings when everyone departs, for the shadow of the central religious Mystery falls across us every time we say good-bye to those we love. We do not say it out loud, but we feel the risk that anything may happen, and in that knowledge we sense the possibilities for loss and pain that are the real measure of how much we love each other.

"Pity," James Joyce writes, "is the feeling that arrests the mind in the presence of whatsoever is grave and constant in human sufferings and unites it with the human sufferer." But terror "is the feeling that arrests the mind in the presence of whatsoever is grave and constant in human sufferings and unites it with the secret cause" (*Portrait of the Artist as a Young Man*, 1916).

We may identify the public cause of the death of Martin Luther King, Jr., as a rifle shot, but its secret cause lay in his taking the risk, years before he was killed, of leading the movement for racial justice in America.

The very Thanksgiving setting of the tragedy of the Ebersols allows us to see past the public causes that will be argued for weeks. Was it icing on the wings or some other mechanical failure? We can see, and perhaps see the best of our own possibilities, in the secret cause of this heartbreaking event.

The secret cause at the heart of this essentially religious mystery is very simple: the Ebersols loved each other and made the journey, complicated for each member, to be together at Thanksgiving time. They took the risks that ride in every day for lovers, that all may be lost if we take this chance. We recognize the love that was in their hearts as they began to split up and head back into pursuit of their seemingly different destinies that turned out to be our common destiny as members of the same family living in the same Religious Mystery.

America's Christmas distraction: the body

Many wonder at the stubborn resistance to the idea of Christmas this year. "Winter Music Festivals" replace "Christmas Music" and a great Manhattan department store forbids its employees to wish customers a "Merry Christmas."

Theories abound at this superficial embrace of secularism, for, at its root, the celebration, as an overwhelming percentage of Americans profess, is of the birth of Jesus. Instead of pointing to the bad example of Europe as a continent unsure of everything but its profession of secularism, we might examine America's own superficial preoccupations and their impact on the feast that we call the Incarnation.

Incarnation means "to take on flesh," and it refers to the essence of the mystery at the core of Christmas itself. For the Christian God is not an icy and aloof deity who long ago looked away from the pool of stars we call our galaxy. Instead we recognize a God who made Himself recognizable by taking on our flesh, becoming human so that nothing of our experience is alien to him, from the exuberant feeling of setting out on a journey at dawn to the exuberance raised exponentially in the discovery of love and friendship.

Beneath the hum and glare of everyday life, most Americans have a feel for this wonder that is almost beyond imagining. There is, however, a fragile dynamic of narcissism in our national life that, like static on AM radio frequencies, interferes with the clear reception of the simple message about Christmas's meaning that God took on our flesh.

An obsession with the flesh, with taking on and remaking the body, dulls many people to the deeper meanings of this season. The *body* pervades our consciousness, from warnings about bodily distortions in an epidemic of obesity to reports that some women are so anxious to keep their bodies from taking on unflattering shapes that they diet and exercise in extreme ways, incidentally endangering the wonder of giving birth.

The *body* is everywhere in the bulky shapes of athletes who take steroids to achieve a massiveness that is alien to a natural physique in order to excel at athletics. *This is my body*, they proclaim over the altar of the gym bench, but, in fact, it is not their body but a grotesque costume that exacts a price from each organ and often brings premature death to the body that seemed so golden in a brief few moments of glory.

This is my body, proclaim the magazine covers of a dozen journals that whisper to uncertain men that their pages contain the secrets that will make them real men who will attract the admiring eyes of the culture. *Where your abs are*, these magazines promise, *there, too, will your heart be.*

An obsession with the body makes it very difficult for many people to achieve their real goal of becoming persons, that is, adult men and women whose identity does not depend on the appearance of their bodies nearly as much as on the reality of their inner selves.

People absorbed with incarnating themselves, with perfecting their own flesh, cannot look away from the mirror long enough to grasp the meaning of the feast of the Incarnation. Happy Winter Music Festival to them, but how sad these denatured carols and with what melancholy fittingness do they sing of the emptiness of such good but body-distracted people. They do not understand how their own human longings are met not in the exercising of their flesh to become like gods but in God's taking it on to become like us.

Biggest religion story of year: media's misunderstanding of religion

In discussing the headlines and stories about religion in 2004, a modified version of Winston Churchill's famous words applies: "Never in the history of reporting on religion has so large and consistent a distortion been imposed on so many by so few..."

Most religion writers are as seasoned to the human condition as old pastors. They have seen everything and, if they forget little, they forgive a lot. Because they understand the nature and subtleties of the experience of faith in the great religious institutions, they do not write the kind of shorthand and shortsighted accounts of belief that have appeared so often in a year in which faith was front and center in everything from politics to the movies.

This was the year in which Catholic candidate John Kerry was challenged by Catholic religious leaders over his pro-choice position on abortion. The bishops who raised questions made headlines, too, and were dismissed by pundits, many of them Catholic, for, imagine this, having the audacity to speak out on a religious issue.

This was the year Mel Gibson's *The Passion of the Christ* ignited a media uproar, led largely by the *New York Times's* Frank Rich, who condemned the film as anti-Semitic, a charge that even many rabbis thought unsustainable. But ordinary people flocked to see it as the kind of message for which they had been hungering. Yet, as in the pro-choice/pro-life debate, church authorities were almost uniformly presented as antediluvian oligarchs trying to force their own ideas onto everybody else.

But it was religion itself that suffered most. By year's end religion had been reduced to a vast right wing conspiracy bent on establishing a theocracy in America. Christianity, a broad, rich, and inclusive religious tradition, had been blurred in popular coverage into a dangerous fundamentalist sect, especially with a president who acknowledged the influence of Jesus in his life and the importance of his faith in his making difficult decisions. In short, Christianity has been reduced to the fascist fantasy of the narrow, uninformed, and prejudiced masses.

If this is all that some editors know about religion, about which they pontificate regularly, what do they really know about politics, terrorism, the energy crisis, global warming, or how you should vote, on which they also pontificate confidently every day?

While Christianity was being editorially distorted in some places, it was *Make Nice* time with the Muslim faith that is generally characterized as misunderstood, and, indeed, *Be Nice* time with those splinter Muslim terrorists who really believe in making a theocracy out of the world.

Immature religion deserves criticism, but mature religion at least deserves recognition as a powerful and positive force in the lives of individuals and the community. Mature religion was described as *intrinsic* by the late Harvard psychologist Gordon Allport who differentiated it from *extrinsic* religion.

Many in the media are covering the immature, or *extrinsic*, religion that people inherit along with the grandfather's clock and the worn-out Bible, which they never examine or internalize. *Extrinsic* religion, research shows, pretends to know all the answers and is compatible with prejudice. *Intrinsic* religion opens people to more questions and allows no place for prejudice of any kind.

Extrinsic religion is a superficial imitation of *intrinsic* religion, and some editors are therefore amazed when people say that, yes, my religion is important to me and I take its teachings to love my neighbor and to work for peace and justice seriously. Those who take religion seriously must be some kind of nuts, they suggest, dismissing them without making any distinctions about the substance of their faith.

That, of course, is why experts are still trying to explain the November elections so that they won't have to re-examine themselves and whether and in what they believe and what guides their own decisions. They are now reinterpreting the expressed concern of a majority of Americans for moral values so that it is not a function of religion.

This need to dilute the authority of intrinsic faith must be very stressful for some media pundits. The best resolution they can make is to learn something about religion so that they can stop embarrassing themselves in their coverage of it during the coming year.

The Seasons of 2005

The media, the tsunami, and real religion

The waters of the tsunami have washed across all of us and we cannot seem to break the surface of this overwhelming disaster...

What we look on as the waters recede—the clothing and the toys, the vacation baggage, the shaky visions from home videos—speak with the power that all mute objects acquire when they have belonged to people just like us. They whisper that these are deaths in our own family and that we are not yet able either to comprehend or to mourn them.

The media often cover the externals of supposedly "religious" news —appointing a gay Episcopal bishop, the sex abuse scandal's bankrupting Catholic dioceses, the flexed arm of conservative groups in politics—but cannot so easily perceive and report on the internalized religion that without fanfare binds together and inspires the lives of millions of believers.

But this past week, without explicitly knowing it, they covered internalized faith as they reported on the tsunami disaster. As when a photographer takes a picture of something in the foreground and catches a greater event in the background, the media have included the great background story to the horrific foreground devastation. It is that of religion as it functions when it is integrated into everyday life.

This is not infantile religion, which is not religion at all, but grown-up religion revealed at its un-self-conscious best: responding, without the pressures of political correctness or of heavy-footed moralizing, to people in need just-as-they-are in the world just-as-it-is. (see, for example, the *Washington Post,* "Worshipers Seek Comfort in Giving," by Debbi Wilgoren, January 3, 2005).

The great religions are giving without any questions or qualifications about the race, faith, politics, or gender identity of those whose lives have been devastated. Real religion—quite different from what is

practiced by religious extremists—sees through the surface character-
istics that seem to make us different to the human substrate that makes
us all the same.

Nor are the great religions using this terrible event as an example
of God's punishing sinners or as an occasion for seeking converts
among those they assist. While properly focusing on the *who*, *what*,
where, *when*, and *why* of the tragedy, reporters are doing the same for
faith woven into, rather than added onto, everyday life.

The small, cheap sidebar arguments about who gave how much
and when reveal that the Devil lives not in the details but in the politics
that does not know what authentic religion knows—that you must put
your own agenda aside when there is a disaster in the human family.

Unlike politics, internalized religion does not strive to be at the
foreground of the photograph. But it is everywhere in the background,
focusing, without worrying about itself or the advantage it may gain
from the moment, as it responds to the afflicted.

They may not know it, but the media are also reporting on the
Last Judgment, the event that shallow religion has turned into a disaster movie in which shame and humiliation shower down on all of us
sinners. But in the gospel accounts of this judgment, there is no mention of sin and God welcomes those who have fed Him in the hungry,
visited Him in prison, ministered to Him by clothing the naked.

The saved seem surprised that they have found God's favor. They
cannot remember when they did what merits eternal life. "When," they
ask, "did we see you hungry and feed you? When did we see you naked
and clothe you?"

These saved persons cannot remember the things they did that so
closely parallel the response of religious persons to the present disaster.
The spectacularly simple reason for this explains genuine religion. Truly
religious people cannot remember the good they do because, in giving
themselves un-self-consciously to human need, *they forget themselves.*

The big religious story this week is not about bankrupt dioceses or
James Dobson's threatening political reprisals on senators who don't
vote for pro-life judges. It is a simpler, everyday story about the internalized religion that inspires people to love others, to see them as relatives rather than as strangers, and to focus so much on helping them
that they have no time to think about themselves.

Religion's function: mystery rather than meaning

The tsunami had a peculiar impact in America. Many who had just celebrated Christmas demanding that religion keep silent in national life suddenly demanded that religion speak up to explain how the disaster fit into God's plan, if He exists, that is, and if He has a plan.

Even those supportive of religion have turned the tusnami into a test for faith itself. Thus, the *Wall Street Journal* (January 7, 2005), William Safire in the *New York Times* (January 10, 2005), and Rabbi Michael Lerner in *Tikkun* (January 12, 2005) call God into the dock for questioning: *Where do we find meaning in this terrible calamity?*

The presumption beneath these anguished cries is that religion's principal function is to give *meaning* to life by plucking some consoling theological rationale out of such whirlwinds to make them understandable and, therefore, more bearable by us humans.

This, of course, reduces religion to an instrument, a divining rod used to locate the deep spring of significance in the desert of our loss. As such, religion's utilitarian function is to make sense out of the sorrow that is directly deposited into everybody's account every day.

But the purpose of religion is not now, nor has it ever been, to explain life or death in simple, satisfying concepts. Expecting religion to explain life's meaning or to answer our deepest dread-filled questions transforms it into just another button to push on the American "quick fix" console.

"Get over it" is practically a slogan for the Prozac nation that does not want to contemplate problems as much as get rid of them and thereby achieve the illusory goal of *closure* and the uncertain glory of *moving on*.

A mass killing at a school? A coal mine collapse? A plane crash? Rush in the counselors along with the clean-up crews to tidy up the physical and emotional damage so that we need not look at it or medi-tate on either the first or the last things of our existence. When horrors occur, religion, in this distortion, should relieve us rather than chal-lenge us to plumb the depths of human existence.

You can tell immature religion because it views life as a disaster movie with salvation as a special effect. It gives ready answers and explanations for all its terrors. "God is punishing sinners," it claims, and "He'll get you, too," if you don't watch out. Sinfulness, it insists, explains everything from the tsunami to the AIDS epidemic, from the Democrats' election defeat to the devastating West Coast rains.

Mature religion does not offer the cheap grace of explaining or even interpreting what happens to us. Nor, despite fiery television preachers, many of whom have a better grasp of finance than of faith, is religion's principal function to scare us out of hell by scaring the hell out of us.

Religion is concerned with Mystery with a capital *M* that reaches beyond the galaxies, not to solve it, as Hercule Poirot does of mystery with a small letter *m* that is confined to the libraries of English country houses.

Religion's function is not to *explain* but to allow people to *experi-ence* the Mystery of being alive, the very thing they are prevented from doing by such all-purpose explanations as "God is chastising human-kind" offered by callow preachers who think that faith comes in pre-fabricated sections and that religion is the direction book on how to assemble it.

Religion does not give easy answers as much as it prompts us to ask ever more difficult questions. Far from completing the jigsaw puz-zle of life, religion invites us into the Mystery that is within and beyond all our experience. Beneath the rock and roll tumult of every day's misfortunes, religion bids us to recognize *our song* in what Wordsworth called "the still, sad music of humanity" ("Lines Com-posed a few Miles above Tintern Abbey").

Religion opens us, as Joseph Campbell expresses it, "just as we are" to the "world just as it is" rather than as it either could, should, or might be. Faith concerns itself with that which we cannot avoid, fully fathom, cure, or distract ourselves from—our own lives, for, when we taste even its dregs or feel its burning tears, we know at least that we are alive. The function of religion is to awaken us to what is taking place within us that takes us beyond ourselves—the *Mysterium tremendum et fascinans*, the tremendous and captivating Mystery of being, whose password of entry is always wonder rather than certainty, a question rather than an answer.

Abu Ghraib, the sex abuse scandal, and human nature

The New York Times Book Review *devotes its front page and almost three more inside pages to reviews of two books on the torture and sexual humiliation inflicted by some American soldiers on the captives in the now notorious Abu Ghraib prison.*

Abu Ghraib is being analyzed as if it were the first gusher of inhumanity ever to blow wild in plain sight. It is intimated that the investigative drill tapped into its sole source, the vast pool of American corruption welling out of Washington rather than in the proven reserves of inhuman crude that bubble beneath every continent on the globe.

Along with many other media outlets, this same newspaper has perennially celebrated what it terms "edginess" or "pushing the envelope" on sexual references in movies and television programming. These are code words for performance kinkiness in trivial settings that banner the oxymoron of the year in their disclaimer that they are *adult entertainment.*

Some over-celebrated series, such as HBO's *Sex in the City*, are more poignant than pornographic as they track the loneliness of those wounded by discovering that free sex is easy and committed relationships are hard. Other series feature humiliation as entertainment, such as Fox's *American Idol*, in which the apparent payoff is laughing at little people with big dreams who are literally exposed to ridicule on national television.

It isn't that this stuff is sinful, as some wild-eyed preachers might claim, but that it isn't sophisticated either. Still, can you give half a blessing to this immature separation of sex from human relationships or enjoy the ritualized humiliation of others and be surprised that more potent and degrading combinations of these may be found in places like Abu Grhaib?

If all Will Rogers knew was what he read in the newspapers, what would we learn the same way? The headline from a week earlier, "Ex-Priest's Trial Begins on Child Rape, Assault; Conviction May Be Difficult, Legal Experts Say" (*Los Angeles Times*, January 18, 2005, p. A02).

Or, a few weeks' earlier, "Sex Abuse by U.N. Troops Continues … World body is powerless to discipline offenders, and only a few have been punished since inquiry" (Maggie Farley, *Los Angeles Times*, January 8, 2005).

A short season before that, we learned that "British Boarding School Walls Hid Abuse" (Sarah Lyall, *New York Times*, October 11, 2004) and read that "at least half a dozen men … say that they were molested by teachers at the Caldicott School, in Buckhinghamshire between 1964 and 1970 … The common view, many former students say, is that if it happened, you are not expected to whine about it."

Then Superstation WGN reported (January 24, 2005) that an art teacher in suburban Chicago had been accused of molesting teenage students and that duct tape was involved.

Nothing is more Catholic than facing and accepting that the crack that runs across human nature was not discovered by television producers who think that they were the first ones to photograph or report it. And nothing is less Catholic than indulging in what old moral theology textbooks called "Pharisaic scandal," that is, the oohing and ahing by hypocrites whose moral outrage often masks their own secret tastes for the stimulation of such behavior.

We may blame some soldiers at Abu Ghraib but we cannot indict the whole army any more than we can indict all priests because of the sexual misdeeds of some of them. This behavior, whether at Abu Ghraib, the Caldicott School, or the occasional rectory, is execrable, a word whose origin comes from the Latin for *against the sacred* and whose meaning is "deserving of detestation." But the numerous reports of this behavior in a variety of settings suggest that it is not egregious, meaning "outrageous" but originating from the Latin for "standing out from the herd" (*American Heritage Dictionary of the English Language*).

Wherever they occur, these degrading violations are surely assaults on the sacredness of human personality but, instead of working up a fake furor, we might better identify the common denominator of this not-uncommon behavior. Those who indulge in it need no choreo-graphing by superiors because it so often represents their urgent if blind search for the growth that is missing inside them.

Those who humiliate others sexually to gratify themselves, whether guards, schoolmasters, or monks, are frequently found to have been denied, sometimes because of the conditions of their upbringing, the opportunity for full psycho-sexual development. Why and how this happens and what we can do about it—encouraging and supporting healthy family life being at the top of the list—is a far more important question to ask midst the trumped up moralizing and low down politicking that have so far surrounded this issue.

Freedom is more spiritual than political

Freedom is not just a political good but a spiritual value, something far more sacred than secular. Nor is it just a condition for a thriving democratic community. Freedom is a fundamental condition for the growth of human personality...

Our various usages of *freedom* bounce as numbered ping pong balls do in their miniature cages on lottery night. We are never quite sure what meaning will be plucked out by the ladies with fixed smiles who preside at such drawings.

Some usages, such as *freedom of speech*, might astound those who think that that freedom lets them spin words now this way and now that or to shock the innocence out of their audience. In return for its gift, freedom demands integrity, or wholeness, from all artists. As Justice Oliver Wendell Holmes famously said, freedom of speech "would not protect a man in falsely shouting fire in a theater and causing panic" (*Schenck v. United States*, 1919).

Freedom imposes a spiritual demand on artists because they work on the boundary between time and eternity every day. Ernest Hemingway felt that artists were free only in order "to put down what really happened...the real thing, the sequence of motion and fact which made the emotion and which would be as valid in a year or in ten years or, with luck and if you stated it purely enough, always" (*Death in the Afternoon*, 1932).

Freedom is therefore misunderstood and misused by those who think that they are rendering the truth by having characters use America's all-purpose verb and adjective in every other line of dialogue. Or that they are revealing some deep truth about America by featuring scenes of men having profound or mean conversations standing side by side at urinals. Such low exercises squander the high freedom of the artist not only because of their plumbing fixation but because the truth of such a scene would be a silent movie.

Another quicksilver American phrase is *the freedom to choose*. This classic phrase of the advertising/public relations complex pulls off the trifecta of cheapening art, freedom, and grammar. The meaning is vague because there is no object to the verb *to choose*. Freedom's inherent morality and spirituality are transferred to the act of choosing itself so that we need not, as in abortion, ponder the full complexity of the choice itself.

This soft focus on what we are actually doing is a favored American variant on freedom. So we demand *closure*, getting something over with, as in mourning that, in itself, is a sacred experience that cannot be hurried. Or in *Move On* without acknowledging where we have been, what we have done, or where we are going. Humans cannot *move on* freely from what they do, especially to each other, without becoming less free and less human at the same time.

Freedom's root is *pri*, which means "to love" and appears in the Germanic *frijaz*, "beloved, belonging to the loved ones." To be out of bondage means to be loved, as in the Old English *freo*, which survives in our word "friend." Freedom's sacredness is grasped in the condition that people seek to provide for those they love. In such safe environments humans need not be on guard and so can become their true selves.

Freedom is profoundly mysterious and genuinely sacred in its demands for a place in which it is safe to be human. Totalitarians use terror to deny people this sacred space for living. As historian Hannah Arendt notes, terror "destroys the one essential prerequisite of all freedom which is simply the capacity of motion which cannot exist without space" (*Origins of Totalitarianism*, 1951).

We may not then be engaged in a Holy War but, in engaging with terrorism, we are involved in the sacred work of protecting the space of true freedom that people need in order to become truly human. It is no easy task and the choices that leaders make are not small or easy ones but demand from them the same integrity that is demanded of the artist. This is a difficult time and freedom must be perceived not as part of a catch phrase for a cause but as a fundamentally spiritual experience.

"Freedom," Albert Camus wrote, "is not a reward or a decoration that is celebrated with champagne. Nor yet a gift, a box of dainties designed to make you lick your chops. Oh no! It's a choice...and a long distance race, quite solitary and very exhausting. No cheap champagne, no friends raising their glasses as they look at you affectionately. Alone in the prisoner's box before the judges, and to decide in face of oneself or in the face of others' judgment. At the end of all freedom is a court sentence; that's why it is too heavy to bear, especially when you're down with a fever, or are distressed, or love nobody" (*The Fall*, 1957).

Johnny Carson

Bereft parents an antidote
for Michael Jackson alive and Johnny Carson dead

Which is more poignant, the reported emptiness of Michael Jackson's Neverland existence or the loneliness of Johnny Carson's life? Both men rose to wealth, power, and fame by meeting the severe conditions imposed by America's entertainment culture that turns out to be— theologians take note—Purgatory itself...

And who would have expected that the antidote to the well-publicized emptiness of these men who had gained everything would come from an unknown couple who were filled with life even though they had lost everything?

Even Dante would not have suspected that the long red carpet on which celebrities tread into award shows leads directly into Purgatory West, a space that is actually brightly lighted and has central heating and air conditioning. As in many a house you could name, the surroundings are fine, it's the residents that, with only reruns of themselves on television to watch, are limping in place in unfinished lives—not totally unhappy but not happy, either—waiting to be cast in a sequel, with a better script, in which things will turn out better for them.

Both Jackson and Carson started serving time there in this life. That umbrella bobbing above Jackson's head does not shield him from the sun but from exposure to the half light of his own makeover. He is the nation's quintessential Purgatory figure, the middle-aged man who ends up with the most toys but few, if any, deep relationships with ordinary people.

Described as Johnny Carson's "longtime sidekick"—and how would you like that in your obituary?—Ed McMahon says that it is appropriate that the late comedian had no funeral because Carson believed that you did your thing, "put on your hat, and went out the door." Yes, Johnny liked to sail, he played cards, but he really wasn't close to anyone.

Without funeral rites, America does not know how to grieve for Mr. Carson and, without clear clues, does not know what to make of Mr. Jackson. But it knows that it received a blessing from out of the whirlwind of the Iraq War, from Bill and Janet Norwood whose Marine sergeant son was killed at Fallujah.

As guests at the State of the Union address, they rose before our eyes like a two-paned pietà, a sorrowing mother and father bearing their dead son in their arms, making forever sacred at least one moment of late night television, filling to overflowing the medium that runs on empty most of the day.

This was reality on television rather than reality TV. The latter entertains us with trifling mysteries of who will survive in artificial circumstances. Reality on television—Janet Norwood holding her dead son's dog tags and Bill Norwood tenderly holding her—reveals the mystery of life that is found in suffering as plain as the name of the Texas town, Pflugerville, from which they come.

Who would have guessed that Bill and Janet Norwood, who would blend into any check-out line in America, would take us with them into the deepest mystery of life—how love makes us inseparable while exposing us to the everyday risk of hurting and being hurt by life and by each other?

No doubt people will kindly remember and God will exempt from the real Purgatory entertainers who shared with us their clever gift of joking and singing to kill time. But Janet and Bill Norwood share with us their human gift of love and suffering that break open the eternal.

9/11, sacrament of love and loss

Grief arises at dawn as big and blinding as the sun itself, riding the symbol of the eternal that floods through the mystery of loving each other in time. So it did on the morning that New York City's medical examiner's office announced, that "it had exhausted all possible means of identifying human remains" from the 9/11 destruction of the Trade Towers (New York Times, *February 24, 2005*).

This story, a fragment in itself, was more revelation of mystery than reportage of fact, for the message to the families of the 1,161 victims that remain unidentified was addressed to everyone who has ever loved or wept for its loss, reminding us of how invested with the eternal are the flesh and bone of the persons we cherish in time.

Most of last week's news concerned invisible ink events that intrigue us briefly and disappear without a trace. They were well symbolized by the slug-like television trucks with divining rod antennae feeding off two events in that Valhalla of the ephemeral, California—the Academy Awards and the Michael Jackson's trial. These vehicle herds record America's one-night stands with celebrity that it can barely remember in the morning, much less a month later.

September 11 rises above these as great actors do above the awards because it remains the great sacramental event of our age whose mystery makes time holy even as it transcends it. In the heartbreak of its stricken families we recognize our own, so that we can see in each other's faces that we are all indeed within six degrees of separation.

The announcement dashed Kathy Bowden's hopes that "some part, any part, of her brother, Thomas H. Bowden, Jr., might be included in a burial...her family will probably go ahead with a burial this spring with only some personal effects and some dust from ground zero."

Matthew T. Sellitto wondered whether he would now get another phone call. After city officials had "informed the family three times that they had pieces of his son, Matthew C. Sellitto, he asked them not to call again until all the forensic work was completed. 'We knew the day was coming eventually, but it's still bittersweet,' he said."

And Meena Jerath stroked the razor-like double edge of loss when she spoke of Prem Nath Jerath: "...I am very sad and hurt that the identification process has ended without finding any trace of my husband...On the other side, part of me is relieved that no tiny fragment was found...If only a small piece were found, I would wonder what happened to the rest of him. What were his last moments like? Did he suffer a lot?"

All the heartache of all of time is found in these stories about people whose names may never appear in the newspapers again. They are Lenten acolytes bearing the invisible but searing mark of the ashes that they long only to bury tenderly, knowing that they contain the wholeness of the persons they loved so much. "These fragments," T. S. Eliot wrote, "I have shored against my ruins" (*The Waste Land*, "What the Thunder Said").

This is *our* mystery because there is no explanation for why it engulfs us except that if we are blessed with love that is eternal we must accept the losses, great and small, that come through experiencing it in time. A thousand small losses shower down on us in fragments, seeping into our days like time-released aspirins.

The mystery is that lovers live at such close range that they can hurt each other easily, thoughtlessly, forgetfully, without ever meaning to do so. Lovers grow closer together by collecting, mourning, and burying these little fragments all the time.

September 11 was not a triumph for terrorists but for these lovers who reveal the depths of the mystery of ordinary living in their simple yearning to touch again those taken up in the twinkling of an eye on that day. We read again in a different light (John 6) the instruction of Jesus after he broke the loaves to feed the people, "Gather up the fragments that remain that nothing be lost."

The widow and the Atlanta killer: An Easter story

Sometimes a story that seems a straightforward mystery solved, such as the brutal murders by a dangerous prisoner in Atlanta last week, contains within it an unanticipated mystery that turns it into two stories and makes it difficult for even veteran journalists to summarize and for us to comprehend fully...

This tragedy haunts us because we cannot easily grasp either mystery or see how they are connected with each other or with all of us. That means that we are dealing with a mythic story whose point is not violence, as it first seems, but spirituality, as it quickly becomes.

The narrative begins with the public murder of a just man and others in daylight by a man who quickly turns into a prince of darkness. At midnight, after killing again, he encounters a widow from whom he hears words so transforming that he can emerge from the darkness and enter the light again.

What happens between Ashley Smith, so like every biblical widow left with a child to raise, and Brian Nichols, who enters her apartment as the dangerous Barabbas freed from prison by the death of an innocent man and leaves it as Dismas, admitting his sin and seeking mercy?

The Mystery within the mystery of this bears truth deeper than those of Passion-time pageants. In it we experience the spiritual and mythical themes of faith and forgiveness, death and resurrection, darkness and light that fill the feasts of Passover and Easter that are set by the first full moon of the spring.

At spring's beginning, day and night are equal. The sun and the moon stare across the sky at each other. The moon that rises and dies and rises again is the symbol of time because all its light comes from the great sun that is the symbol of eternity.

The moon and the sun stare at each other across this story that so matches the season and matches all our stories as well. Within it, time and eternity, death and new life intermingle with each other as they do within all of us. We feel a deep longing and mark it down as "spring fever" when it is really the great human song of the season sounding within us, the pull of the eternal against the boundaries of time.

Meetings with women fill the scriptures, and these stories, whether at the side of wells or in the midst of weddings, often lead us to confront ourselves more truthfully. The escapee Brian Nichols does so after meeting Ashley Smith who, for him and for us, is not only the New Testament widow left with a child but the Old Testament valiant woman of considerable household skills. She is also, as it turns out, not without problems, for she has been accused of minor crimes over the years, making her even more like some of the women into whose eyes Jesus looked with understanding and forgiveness.

Would those who scoff at religious people be as self-possessed—as whole, we might say—as Ashley Smith as she speaks to Brian Nichols of her conviction that all things have a purpose and that there is a purpose in his coming to her house during the long hours of that night?

She does not condemn him or even preach to him but rather reads and speaks the word from the scripture and from Rick Warren's *The Purpose-Driven Life* (2002). Speak but the word, we recall, and my soul shall be healed. He confesses to her, saying that he deserves a bullet in the back for what he has done.

She accepts and does not soften his admission but joins herself in the risk that faith demands and accompanies him as he gets rid of the pick-up truck he has stolen after murdering another innocent man a few hours before. But first he put his guns safely away much as, during another long night, Peter lowered his weapon at Jesus' command, "Put up thy sword."

Some commentators have made low jokes about Nichols's taking a shower in Ashley Smith's apartment during that night even though he first sees that she covers her head with a towel, taking her, in a way, out of present time and place. This renders the night a timeless setting for washing himself clean in the waters, as a thousand seekers of wholeness have in biblical pools and torrents before him. He enters the waters a dead man and emerges with new life so that he surrenders in the day without the Bonnie and Clyde shootout many expected but with a peacefulness that many cannot understand.

It will be easy to report that Ashley Smith deserves the rewards she may receive for getting this killer to surrender. Perhaps we see how a man can be born again of water and the spirit. And perhaps she has worked a small Easter miracle that we did not expect when we first heard of this rampaging and monstrous killer—by bringing him out of the night and into the day so that we could see him as a human being.

Terri Schiavo

Why we cannot look away from Terri Schiavo's eyes

Terri Schivao is our spring moon, silent and pale, fragile but not barren, circling us as we circle around her bedside. Her eyes hold us even when we want to lower our heads and look away...

Do they disturb us because they are glossily vacant or do they arrest us as a light bobbing on the dark and distant sea does, sending a signal so unmistakably human that it breaks free of the entrapping television screen?

Terri does not allow us to change the subject even though many others are trying to do that very thing. A federal judge reduces the matter of continuing her feeding to the legal question of granting "injunctive relief," while lawyers define the issue as one of the conflicting rights of parents and a spouse over who makes the decision about a woman who is a daughter and a wife. And it is certainly easier to talk about our own need for living wills, to change the subject to the one we are really interested in, ourselves.

At the center of this noisy dispute we find the classic American impulse for pragmatic solutions built on certainty, on solving the problem in can-do fashion so that we can shake Terri's image out of our heads, reach *closure* and *move on*.

Perhaps we cannot look away from Terri's eyes because in their depths we glimpse a truth that makes us uneasy, that, as St. John of the Cross wrote on the Mount of Perfection, *there is no way here*, no certainty possible for us here either. We cannot finish this in time to watch Leno or Letterman and get a good night's sleep.

Terri speaks silently of the intrinsic uncertainty of the human condition, a notion that we resist even though it permeates every layer of this situation that overflows with so much of humanity's everyday sorrow. It is, after all, as much or more about the hazards of human love than about the conflict of legal rights. Has not everyone drunk from this cup of unexpected estrangement that is passed at one time or another around every family circle or handed, often inadvertently or carelessly, from one lover to another?

We cannot break away from Terri's eyes because their depths reflect the Mystery of being human, the Mystery that, by its very nature, cannot be solved but can only be entered and lived. The boundless Mystery of existence is the common ground of both religion and science.

In her classic study of medical students, sociologist Renee Fox discovered that as they advanced in their training they became *less* rather than *more* certain about events that they once presumed they could document without ambiguity. They might sign an hour on a chart but they found themselves incapable of scientific certitude about the exact moment of a patient's death.

They had encountered the same kind of uncertainty in science that Yale psychologist Paul Bloom recently described in the *New York Times* (September 10, 2004) about the moment when we become human: *The qualities we are most interested in from a moral standpoint—consciousness and the capacity to experience pain—result from brain processes that emerge gradually... There is no moment at which a soulless body becomes an ensouled one, and so scientific research cannot provide objective answers to the questions that matter most to us.*

Terri Schiavo has become a slim silver moon, reflecting, as that planet does, the light of eternity onto the plains of time. That is why we cannot easily look away from her eyes. We have come upon a mystery, *the* mystery, *our* mystery that defies anybody's claim to solve it quickly or certainly.

Terri's eyes reveal something about this *Mysterium tremendum et fascinans*, this overwhelming and gripping mystery that tells us that our lives are never measured with certainty or judged with finality. We cannot look away from this woman's eyes for we find our own image reflected in them, the mystery we share with her and with each other, the great spiritual mystery expressed in the Hindu phrase applied by Joseph Campbell to all religious insight, *Tat Tuam Asi*—This is you.

The end of the world happens every day

NBC-TV has combined two sure-fire concepts in popular culture—the mini-series and the end of the world—in a drama entitled Revelations *from the Bible book of the same name. We are told that it is "about a nun and a scientist's search for signs that Armageddon is at hand."*

The ads for this show even use a Latin phrase—*Finis omnium imminet,* roughly translated as "the end of everything is at hand"—to add a touch of solemnity to a drama that is further described as a "breakthrough faith-based thriller."

You can't make this stuff up except that somebody did make this stuff up. This kind of religious-tinged hokum suggests that, artistically speaking, the mini-series as a form is the end of the world.

Poet Robert Frost ("Fire and Ice," 1923) once famously posed the question—*How will the world end, in fire or ice?*—that still fascinates Americans who relish apocalyptic judgment in everything from the wildly popular "Left Behind" books to the scenarios—take your pick—of being found out and fried or frozen as a wrathful God lowers the curtain of the long running Earthbound Follies.

The end of the world is, of course, too important a subject to be treated in such a superficial manner. The spiritual meaning of this scriptural metaphor is not intended to set off our fears about losing everything but to awaken our wonder at all that we possess.

Despite high-level prophecies and low-grade entertainments, the end of the world is not even a future event. In fact, the world comes to an end for all of us every day in one way or another.

The world comes to an end whenever we see past its surfaces into its true depth. We read of *seers,* of those who claim to have *visions* and *messages from another world.* But *seers* are simply those *who are able to see* and *visions* are simply *what they see in this world spread out about them.*

These are not experiences reserved for the supposedly saintly who preach "Flee, the end is near." They are commonplace experiences for ordinary people who are not preoccupied with the *last things* but with the *next things*, people who look at life less as a farewell appearance than as a new creation that they want to hand on to their children and grandchildren.

The world came to an end on that hazy July night in 1969 when men first landed on the moon and we, in their company, thanks to television, were able to see earthrise for the first time.

An old world came to an end as we could see for ourselves that the earth is not *separate from* but *in* the heavens. Seeing the unity in the universe, we rediscovered the unity of human personality. What ended that night was an outdated world in which all creation—earth and heaven, body and soul—was divided and humans became whole again.

The old world comes to an end whenever we look into the eyes of the very old who have seen so much of love and loss or into the eyes of the very young who set out not knowing how much they will taste of both of these as they take their first steps into the profound mystery of life itself.

The old world ends whenever people fall in love. While it is said that love is blind, love actually allows us to see more of each other, transforming us and our sense of time and place.

An old world ends when a great pope dies and a whole configuration of power, influence, and purpose dissolves to make way for another. An old world also ends when we watch a middle-aged Prince of Wales receive a religious blessing with the middle-aged woman he has just married in a civil ceremony. It is the great symbol of *doing the best we can* and is as poignant as autumn in its revelation not of their *highness* but of their *ordinariness* and of how much they need good luck and fair weather just like the rest of us.

The mystical poet William Blake urges us to *cleanse the doors of perception and see the world as it is, Infinite*. We are not standing at Armageddon but at the entrance to the mystery of our existence. The "breakthrough faith based" *Revelations* can't teach ordinary people anything about the end of the world. They experience it with love rather than terror every day.

The real reason the world is fascinated by the pope

Why was it almost impossible for the world to look away from the death of Pope John Paul II and the election of Pope Benedict XVI?

The cynical might say that it gave Americans just what they love, power pitted against mortality in a reality show that trumped Donald Trump with a selection process that was far more suspenseful and far more consequential than his hammy television firing and hiring.

It is hard to improve on Monet-like sunsets behind St. Peter's and vast crowds that are real rather than digitized, not to mention settings by Michelangelo rather than by George Lucas's Industrial Light and Magic. Even commentators like Chris Matthews, who interpreted the papal transition in American political terms, could not diminish the aura of mystery that welled out of the ancient pageantry and solemn rites.

Irish bookie Paddy Powers offered odds on candidates as if the Papal Sweepstakes were being run in the Sistine Chapel. And some turned the late great pope into a kind of ecclesiastical Citizen Kane who, dying in a castle-like setting, murmured not "Rosebud" but "Ratzinger" as his last message to the world.

Don Imus, the radio and television host, may have spoken for us all when, noting that although he is not Catholic or closely associated with organized religion, he had found the event "fascinating," a word that means "to attract irresistibly."

We are fascinated because this transition was not about colorfully dressed strangers in a far country but about ourselves in our own clothes in our everyday lives. The event spoke to our deepest levels, telling us again one of the most important of all the great mythical— and therefore spiritual and religious—stories.

The death of one pope and the election of another became a common experience through the media coverage that, wanting to get the story right on the surface—*Who is this cardinal? What kind of wood is that in the dead pope's coffin? Where is the new pope from?*—transmitted its powerful depths without knowing it.

We experienced together the great theme of the search for the father, a journey that we must all make in one way or another. Understanding these dynamic mythic roots does not lessen but rather accents the religious significance of the event.

The word for pope is *papa*, a designation with powerful associations for everybody. The death of Pope John Paul II re-enacted the great mythic passage from Mother Earth back to the Father that is a central and compelling aspect of the mystery of our existence. We were stirred not only because of our esteem for the late pope but because the event presented us with our own inescapable human destiny.

The election of Pope Benedict XVI strikes the chord of another of our common stories, the search for the father, that is, an understanding of where we came from, a journey we all make in life.

This "father quest," as Joseph Campbell describes it, is a theme in James Joyce's novel *Ulysses*. The hero, Stephen Dedalus, knows who his earthly father is but must find his spiritual father, that is, the one who gave him his character, "the symbol of that ground or source of his being with which [he] . . . must put himself in relation."

Television was the principal medium by which we joined that spiritual search for the father that was the real spiritual magnet of the papal election. The world aches with the mystery of fatherhood, for its loss in those like actress Jane Fonda who poignantly details the unrelieved pain of those who vainly search through a lifetime for a relationship with their earthly fathers or for celebrating it as Tiger Woods did his winning the Master's Tournament by declaring, "That's for you, Pop." We all long for the kind of father that a good pope is, a *papa* who gives us the spiritual strength and comfort to live out the mystery of our lives.

We did not just watch something as bemused spectators on Vatican history. Something happened to us spiritually, something we did not expect and for which we could not have prepared ourselves. We may have tuned in to be entertained or informed about a contemporary story. Instead, we were drawn into and transformed by a story about ourselves and the great human quest for a spiritual father.

Ordinary people understand Ground Zero better than tycoons do

Within a few moments at Ground Zero on September 11 everything changed for all of us. In the long years since, however, so little has changed there that the Wall Street Journal *describes the site in lower Manhattan as "an empty canyon."*

The vast space has become poet Matthew Arnold's "darkling plain," not "where ignorant armies clash by night" but where money-obsessed tycoons battle by day. We are singed by what another poet describes as "fires in the burden'd air" ignited by the skirmishes between those who want to construct more retail stores and those who want offices instead.

Even Donald Trump, who will never be mistaken for a philosopher, much less a prophet, laments the failure in Old Testament tones. He describes the proposed designs as "a series of broken-down angles that don't match each other" that lack the majesty of the virtual duplicates of the original Trade Towers that he advocates.

And (surprised as I am to agree with the flamboyant entrepreneur), he has put his finger on why so little has been achieved in this place where so much happened. It is an example of the Fourth of July principle. The hot lava of politicians always flows into the vacuum left by religious leaders who even on subjects as noble as freedom often invoke clichés from quotation books rather than insights from their own experience.

That is less the fault of moguls than of monsignors, that is, the managerial class of religious leaders who are so preoccupied with building plans, parish boundaries, and bottom lines that their reactions are more like those of businessmen than of the pastors who wept with the grieving and buried the dead. Aside from expressing their usual pieties, they show little grasp of the great Mystery into which we were all taken up in the twinkling of an eye on that cruelly clear morning.

Ground Zero is suffering from what Joseph Campbell terms "mythic dissociation" (*Thou Art That*, 2001). When people are cut off from their deep spiritual roots they lose the sacramental sense of life. Campbell describes this isolation from one's spiritual roots as "the sense of desolation on two levels... the social, in a loss of identification with any spiritually compelling, structuring group; and... a loss of any sense of either identity or of relationship with a dimension of experience, being, and rapture any more awesome than that... held together only by lust or fear."

People then find themselves in what T. S. Eliot called the "Waste Land," exactly the description now given to Ground Zero that, laid waste, remains unrecognized by many so-called spiritual leaders as the site of the great sacramental experience of our time. Revealed in this staggering mystery of loss was the profound goodness of the men and women we mistakenly term "ordinary."

Only recently have poets and novelists and artists, following their calling, begun to explore the spiritual impact of 9/11, in Shakespeare's words, to "give sorrow words; the grief that does not speak whispers the o'er fraught heart and bids it break."

The wrangling interests think that their problems are commercial when they are fundamentally spiritual. They have had little help from the official spiritual leaders in naming correctly and dealing with the basic problem of identifying the right symbols to raise on sacred ground.

The *New York Times* (May 17, 2005) tells us, however, that the families of the 2,792 victims "feared that the events... were cooling into half-remembered, half-understood myths." They have erected three signs "that lay out the timeline of September 11, beginning at 6:32 AM, sunrise over New York City, and ending at 11:30 PM." After their unveiling, "a white-bearded man sat on the ground and played ...'Amazing Grace' on his flute. Couples hugged and parents held their children's hands as they read the Sept. 11 timeline."

These people are not as famous as Donald Trump or as rich as the deadlocked developers but they understand what has been missing and they have given sorrow words to heal the "mythic dissociation" that plagues reconstruction at Ground Zero. A sacrament is defined as an external sign of an inner grace. And that is what these people who never get their names in the paper have done for all those who do get their names in the paper but don't understand Ground Zero at all. The old man with the flute was right. It is an amazing grace for all of us.

Pols should heed traditional religion on saying they're sorry

Maybe the dumbest saying and surest marriage killer ever to come out of the movies is "Love means never having to say you're sorry." That saying, from the 1970s film Love Story, *has re-surfaced as "Politicians have to say they're sorry all the time."*

The most recent but by no means sole example of the politician getting tangled in public contrition is Illinois Senator Richard Durbin. After seeming to compare American military at the Guantanamo Detention Center to Nazis and such killers as Pol Pot, he first refused to apologize and then had a change of heart to rival St. Augustine's when Chicago's Mayor Richard M. Daley told him to do so.

The *Wall Street Journal*'s Donald Henninger (June 24, 2005) suggested that Durbin had missed his fifth grade nun's explanation of *analogy*. What the senator really missed was the good nun's explanation of the church's traditional position on contrition and confession.

Had he recalled the old church's common-sense teaching, he would not have slipped deeper into a, pardon the phrase, quagmire by following the trail blazed by the public relations/advertising complex that is much more dangerous to the nation than the military/industrial complex.

Traditional religion was very clear on the basics of human nature that public relations strives to eliminate altogether. For example, it recognized that we all sin, a concept stricken from the P.R. game book. The old church was not disturbed by sin or by sinners and saw itself, in the phrase of the late Albert Cardinal Meyer of Chicago, as the "home of sinners." It understood, as the current church does, that an important part of its mission is to condemn the sin and love the sinner.

First, of course, you must acknowledge the sin. Confession comes from the Latin for "to declare openly." That means to face the truth of what you have done and to admit it in simple, unambiguous language. In short, to tell the truth about yourself.

Public relations is so troubled by the concept of telling the truth in general and confessing sin in particular that it has no word to express this concept. It operates with a protoplasmic image of personality that is not capable of the passionate pursuit of good or evil, of great love, risk, or honor, or the betrayal of all of these.

People are capable only of wants and needs and the mission of the public relations/advertising complex is to manipulate these superficially. That, as Nobel laureate Saul Bellow once put it, is to give people the "plastic banana" in place of life.

Senator Durbin is a victim of a successful campaign to eliminate the human capacity to make mistakes or commit sins. Now public figures offer what psychiatrist Aaron Lazare describes in his book *On Apology* (2004) as "failed apologies." These include such vague and meaningless statements as "I apologize for whatever I may have done," which may fit in with no-fault insurance but not between people where real hurts must be acknowledged loud and true enough for others to hear.

Senator Durbin's first apology provides another example: "If you were hurt, I am sorry." Dr. Lazare observes that this is not only conditional, but "it even suggests that your sensitivity may be the problem."

This P.R. Apology Shuffle applies to all political parties and all public figures. Trent Lott suggested that his seeming endorsement a few years ago of Senator Strom Thurmond's past racial policies, "was a poor choice of words." Then he apologized four more times, even on Black Entertainment Television, making it clear that he was trying to save his image without scouring his soul.

P.R. is diametrically opposed to all religions in its operational assumptions that nothing significant ever occurs between human beings, that all the world's a stage and let us write lines for all the players. Real religion recognizes that everything of consequence in history takes place in that sacred space between human beings, that we can enlarge but also wound each other, and that we need to express what we do truthfully rather than obscure it with P.R. packaging. The truth will make us free, but failed apologies out of the P.R. factory only enslave us further. Ask Senators Durbin and Lott, they can tell you.

Saul Bellow

Saul Bellow's escape from time

One of my closest friends died in the first week of April called by
T. S. Eliot, "the cruelest month."

Brattleboro, VT. Saul Bellow liked the idea of getaways and would have smiled wryly at making his own under the cover of the deaths of the pope of Rome and the prince of Monaco and on the day that a big city con man was convicted of fraud in this small town that he loved so well. He spent long months at his nearby country home but he never lost his relish for the low side of cities with high minded ambitions like Chicago.

He was buried today in the small Jewish cemetery of Congregation Sher-he-harim. Great fir trees stand like temple elders near his grave in this quiet place on the south edge of this old mill town. But if Saul was born in Quebec, died in Boston, and rests now here, he remains a citizen of Chicago and to the end took in news about it as if it were a blood transfusion.

His weariness lifted away and he threw back his head in laughter when I told him of Mayor Richard M. Daley's midnight seizure of the small lakefront airport, Meigs Field, by having bulldozers put furrows in the runways. "He wants to give it back to the people," Saul said merrily from his sickbed, "before somebody else steals it away for good."

Saul's heart was with ordinary people and he sat, as Michelangelo and Da Vinci did centuries ago, at the town square observing the revelation of their faces with deep and sympathetic accuracy. He may have made fun of himself but he never made fun of the passing men and women bearing their burdens of love and work with minimal complaint throughout their lives.

He admired the first Mayor Daley and supported the second because he felt that they fundamentally had the good of these ordinary people

in mind. He chuckled often in telling of Richard J. Daley's once presenting him with an award for one of his books. "The reporters immediately started pressing him, 'Have you read it?' But old Daley was
smarter than anybody else in the room and he answered, 'I've looked
into it.'"

Saul was suspicious of reformers, those who thought that they
could perfect the human nature whose imperfections he chronicled in
his writing. He would discuss the collapse of some faltering reform
project like Campaign Financing with a sigh, "Another screw-up job
by the Good Intentions Paving Company."

We often explored Chicago together. "What larks we'll have," he
would say, quoting Joe Gargery to Pip in *Great Expectations* as he
picked me up outside our condo building. One morning a well-known
underworld figure who also lived there approached Saul's car as he
pulled up. Saul had fictionalized this man in *Humboldt's Gift* from
their experience of playing squash together at a downtown club. As in
real life, the novel depicted this man inspecting Saul's locker to find
out where he had his shirts and suits made. "Saul," he growled, "don't
put me in any more of your books!" Unfazed, Saul responded, "Not
until you give me the whole story of your life." The mobster, who was
to die in prison, waved his hand in resignation and walked away.

We made the rounds frequently, going from City Council meetings to numerous trials and visiting with city and state officials and
U.S. attorneys. He took no notes on these journeys but would later
reproduce them, catching their mood and detail with great accuracy.
"I'm a first-class noticer," he would explain with a disowning shrug.

He was delighted when the late mayor Harold Washington displayed a good reading knowledge of *The Adventures of Augie March*,
but felt more as if he were in the Chicago he knew when a state official
welcomed us by saying, "I am not used to having men of your statue
visit me."

In one of our last visits, he spoke of the tarnished paint on the
merry-go-round of public life in the city he had left in 1993 for a post
at Boston University. "Joliet prison," he said ruefully, "should really
build a special wing for former governors of Illinois."

During a morning of trials at 26th and California, Saul turned to me half in awe, half in confirmation of a suspicion, "In every one of these trials the wife has murdered the husband."

He was a philosopher about marriage, based on what he called his "deep experience" with it. He once advised a friend who was about to be married: "Just remember that women have more holds than a professional wrestler." But he often told me that I had won the first prize in marrying my wife, Sara, saying that he had not done so until he met and fell in love with Janis Freedman, who survives him.

When his last big novel, *Ravelstein*, appeared in 2000, he was taken to task for revealing the homosexuality of the main character based on his friend Allan Bloom. Bloom had actually asked Saul to tell his story after he died and Saul brought him to life vividly in the pages.

The second half of the story is that of his wife Janis's devoted care for him through many months of rehabilitation after he was poisoned by eating a white fish on a Caribbean island. He sent me the manuscript to read and called and asked what I thought of it. "It is really the story of your love for Janis," I told him. "I knew that you would understand," he replied.

Saul, like the Passover moon that filled the sky as he grew gravely ill, caught the eternal light of the sun to illuminate the human mystery of living in time. So, as the Passover moon disappeared, symbolizing death, and on the morning the new one was to rise, symbolizing renewed life, Saul, who had been sleeping, opened his eyes one last time and looked lovingly at Janis. He was escaping from time that he knew so well to enter the eternity that he knew even better.

The Supreme Court: America's College of Cardinals

America's Supreme Court has become the secularist equivalent of the College of Cardinals...

Men in the church and, until Sandra Day O'Connor in 1981, only men in America were considered for this lifelong appointment. This clothes them in special robes and media attention, deference and good seats at big dinners because of the presumption that they wield great power when, gathered in marbled palaces, they make decisions that shape the moral outlook and religious belief of millions of people.

Small wonder that storm warnings flutter across the political frontier and the media have gone into elliptical fits on the occasion of Justice O'Connor's retirement from the court.

Is the Supreme Court really our College of Cardinals or do we have a distorted sense of what both bodies actually do?

Membership in the College of Cardinals looks great on your resume, but what you actually do is quite limited. The principal activity of cardinals is to elect a new pope. Unless they have other positions, there is nothing much for cardinals to do except to look religious, as judges are meant to look judicious, in group pictures.

The cardinals, however, have a rule that would empty the chamber if the Supreme Court justices adopted it: after they turn eighty, they can no longer vote or go to the meeting, called a conclave, at which a new pope is elected.

That rule keeps this august group in better perspective than the Supreme Court. Catholics know that cardinals look nice but don't really do much. Americans don't much care how their Supreme Court justices look but they think that they do everything.

But Supreme Court justices do only one highly limited thing: make judgments on the *constitutionality* of various laws and legal actions. While the implications of these decisions may be very great, as in providing equal educational opportunities for African Americans after *Brown v. Board of Education*, the great campaign for desegregated schools was waged by African Americans themselves.

The Supreme Court was not the source of this moral insight; it merely passed on the constitutionality of a victory won at a far lower level by thousands of heroic but anonymous men and women. Good laws never precede but always follow moral movements that originate in the hearts of ordinary people. This impulse for justice, as in the drive against slavery and the whip of its evils that still cracks long after its abolition, has often been strongly supported by organized religion.

The Fourteenth Amendment granting voting rights to all did not inspire but followed the conversion of heart accomplished by the reformers whose names are lost to history. By design, the Supreme Court is not in the vanguard but at the end of the parade, never leading but always following to measure laws and cases not for their moral ambition or idealism but for their constitutionality.

The Supreme Court has not demanded this exalted position for itself. It has become the default source of judgment because of the collapse or misuse of authority in such other broadly construed institutions as big business, the media, higher education, organized religion, and even sports.

The Supreme Court fills an ethical and moral vacuum left by the collapse of leadership in and understanding of the true nature of authority in a wide range of venues. Courts are forced to decide matters that should be handled by common sense or by other institutions. Is it the court's real job to decide when the semester begins or when the World Series will be played or, indeed, whether abortion is a free moral choice?

The urgent moral issue is not who the next justice of the Supreme Court should be but why our vacuous institutions have lost so much of their own authority that the law and the courts have become their surrogates. Congress and lobbyists would serve the country better if they devoted a fraction of the energy and the money they are about to expend on choosing a new justice to discovering why authority has failed so disastrously in so many institutions that the law and the courts must do their work for them.

Stopping by a motel on a hazy morning

Stopping by the woods on a snowy and silent evening, poet Robert Frost suddenly saw right down to the bottom of the mystery of life. He tells us that the only sound came from his horse who "gave his harness bell a shake to see if there was some mistake."

I saw partway into that same mystery this week but it was a blistering summer morning outside a nondescript motel where the only sound rose like a howl off the nearby interstate.

A group of elderly travelers was assembled at the side of a tour bus as their driver heaved their bags into the luggage compartment as if he were tossing haunches to the lions at feeding time. These people waited in that undemanding and orderly way of the retired who, having survived such great public terrors as World War II and all the small private sorrows that time and chance deliver, betrayed none of the restlessness characteristic of so many crowds.

Because there was so little that they had not seen or felt, they were not worn out by the waiting that is such a big part of the mystery of existence. They will be just as patient on Judgment Day.

Except that this, as I soon learned, was Judgment Day. This early morning mustering, so like that of any gathering of men and women in airports, outside churches, or at any of the other intersections of American life, was for a pilgrimage to the quiet meadow in the Pennsylvania hills where Flight 93 had crashed on September 11, 2001.

These ordinary people were making their way to a place that is not advertised on billboards. You have to ask at the motel desk to get directions to find it, *That's right, you turn at that gas station down the hill...*

They were traveling unheralded to a place unheralded now because of the landslide of post–9/11 events. Like the arguments about how

286

much commercial space should be built at Manhattan's Ground Zero, these events have almost obscured the glade made sacred by the deaths of the brave men and women who wrested control away from the terrorists who wanted to crash the plane in Washington, DC.

These classic American midsummer travelers were turning the dawn into Judgment Day by seeking Shankhill, Pennsylvania, rather than Orlando or Hollywood, as their destination. They signaled that in this still place you could hear the sounds of everything of importance to humans—love, honor, and sacrifice.

What did these people bring with them to this site in the rolling hills? There were some flowers and messages, of course, but it was mostly that simple human gift of understanding sorrow so deep that nobody can name it.

It was as if these men and women brought their campaign ribbons and medals the way old soldiers do to place on the graves of their comrades not only to honor them but to drain off or lessen the grief that still stirs above their resting places.

These visitors brought the ribbons and medals earned in their own lives. They placed these invisible mementoes of living fully in time in this meadow that overflows with the simple mystery of being human and of the tenderness and love that finally conquer all the hurt and loss that are part of it. They were judging themselves, the dead, and us gently with these gifts as simple as those the Quakers sing about.

Poet Alice Duer Miller wrote during World War II of seeing English people plain "standing in a long / Line in the twilight and the misty rain / To pay their tax" ("The White Cliffs," 1941). Under the battered canopy of that motel on that hot morning watching these elderly travelers climbing on their bus to visit that place of mystery, you could see Americans plain as well.

What really happened to us as the shuttle came home

What really happened to us as the space shuttle Discovery *came streaking home on Tuesday? Most Americans were so relieved that it landed safely that they did not pay much attention to their other feelings—or even noticed if they had any—as the ship's light descended in the California darkness...*

So dominant was the anticipatory anxiety, according to the *New York Times* (August 7, 2005), that some Americans, having witnessed two shuttle disasters, planned not to let their children watch the event "to shield them from what could be a traumatic experience." They thereby deprived them of a true mystical experience.

As relief recedes perhaps we sense in a general way that we shared something greater than a dangerous adventure with a brave crew or a technological triumph with extraordinary scientists and engineers.

For this experience pulled us all into the story of creation in which we and the universe itself were born again. Measured by the finest of clocks and altimeters, the vessel's voyage was less about mathematics than it was about mystery.

Overheard on every radio as its images bloomed on every television screen, this expedition was far more than the background noise to our daily existences. Beneath the roar of the blastoff and the caressing silence of space it spoke not just to our eyes or to our intellects but to the deepest levels of our being.

Seldom have we shared an event that so mixed our human condition with our human destiny. The crew members revealed that we all belong to the same family, that in a real sense we were making the journey with them. They also reminded us of what the late Nobel laureate Saul Bellow called "Our universal eligibility to be noble."

A flag of our humanity fluttered from this sleekest of modern machines as bits of cloth flapped from the door the way they do from ill-packed vans on family vacations. This was the pennant of our glorious fallibility as it outwitted impersonal technology. The human hand that finally made a correction (looking like basic home repair—"Let's just see if tugging at this will work") revealed that a person as alive as us rather than a robot as inert as a parking meter was guiding the journey.

That subtle shifting within us during the long days from lift-off to touch-down was not from anxiety about the outcome as much as from hearing a song about our very beginnings and of the great elements of earth, air, fire, and water with which philosophers have always associated it.

Discovery's trajectory took the ship out of the hold of gravity and free of the grasp of time as we know it. Mythologically, its voyage was into the realm of the sun, the symbol of the eternal on which all the things of time depend for their light. The great drama took place at the border crossing between time and eternity.

We move back and forth across that border every time we forget ourselves to take care of somebody else, lose ourselves in our work, or fall in love. This journey was an epic re-enactment of this mystery of how we humans live both in time and eternity every day. This journey let us feel the mystery of living in these two realms that we catch only hurried glimpses of most of the time.

And as the vessel brooded over the void and then made its arc back from the eternal into the grip of time, its light shone in the darkness and the earth came into being. We were present at the creation and looking on the world and we could see that it was good. The space official said "Welcome home" to the spacecraft *Discovery*, but he was really talking to us.

Don Healey

God rest you, merry gentleman — Donald Healey

Teddy Roosevelt explained his post-presidential trip to Africa by saying that it was his "last chance to be a boy again." Becoming a friend of Don Healey's gave me that very same last chance...

At Gibeon the Lord appeared to Solomon in a dream by night; and God said, "Ask what I should give you." And Solomon said, "... give your servant therefore an understanding mind"... God said to him, "Because you have asked this, and have not asked for yourself long life or riches, or for the life of your enemies... I give you a wise and discerning mind; no one like you has been before you and no one like you shall arise after you." (1 Kings, 3:5–12)

If you know anything about Don Healey you know that he loved life in general and that he loved life at St. Maarten's Condominium in Naples, Florida, in particular. He and Maureen contributed greatly to its being a neighborhood more than a building. But he had a measure of Irish foreboding and preferred not to analyze the place's seeming wonder. He refused to talk about it, explaining his caution through telling how Marco Polo used to describe the wonders of Venice to Kublai Kahn. The entranced ruler demanded that the explorer tell him of Venice every evening. Finally, Marco Polo refused, saying, "I'm afraid if I tell you about Venice one more time it will disappear."

If you know anything about Don Healey, you know that he was so busy praying for others all the time that he didn't have much time to think about himself. He used the laps he swam at the pool at St. Maarten's as others do a rosary, melding with each stroke a prayer for somebody on his long list of those in need.

No wonder that the Lord said to him, "Because you have asked this, and have not asked for yourself long life or riches, or for the life of your enemies . . . I give you a wise and discerning heart."

If you know anything about Don Healey, you know how right it is that we gather today by the seaside. For Don so loved the sea and lived so close to it and in it for great parts of his life that it is impossible to think of him in the shadows. He appears to me crinkling his eyes in the full sunlight, just emerging from the deep, streaming with salt water.

If you know anything about Don Healey, you know that the sea twinkled in his pale blue eyes, the deep blue sea that he entered so confidently. The sun is the symbol of eternity and the waters are the symbol of our human depths. Few men lived their lives so fully in time and yet on such easy terms with the eternal; few have been as wise and knowing about our human depths as Don Healey.

If you know anything about Don Healey, you know that he had the gift of understanding others when they needed to say out loud something that they silently felt inside themselves. Don would nod like a wise confessor and absolve them of their concerns without imposing any penance on them. And he knew exactly how to ratify some feeling that we might express by saying gently, "Well, that's it . . ."

He said that one night when my wife and I were visiting the Healeys and I mentioned that marriage takes the restlessness out of one's life. "That's it," Don said, not as punctuation but in his gentle way of affirming something profoundly human. Understanding, this time Maureen's understanding of Don, was the point of the story he then told us of his first meeting her.

"I said my name was Healey—H-E-A-L-E-Y—and told her, 'Remember how to spell it because I intended to marry you and then it will be your name, too.'"

Maureen was already good at spelling and, lucky for Don, she understood this tall handsome suitor with the big city style right from the start and all through their adventurous life together.

We still feel the magnetic attraction of this love-at-first-sight story; we feel its gentle pull right now. You could never speak of Don *or* Maureen but only of Don *and* Maureen. They were married as the flavors in a salad are said to be married, intermingled so subtly that you cannot distinguish them one from the other.

If the mystery of a name began their relationship, we discover that Don's baptismal name not only describes him but carries within it, as a gene does our destiny, his own calling in life.

Don is the title that means *gentleman*. If you know anything about Don Healey, you know that he was a gentle man, a gentleman.

Don comes from *deme*, the root of both the Latin *Dominus* that means "Lord" and "Master" and of *domus* that means "home." And you know that this array describes a man comfortable at home, a husband, a father, a host, a *major domo* of hospitality, made so, of course by the understanding Maureen and her uncommon everyday magic. The understanding Maureen always made it look easy, as in taking care of Don, raising a family in Paris, Rome, and Hong Kong and, on short notice, graciously entertaining four or forty guests at sundown.

Don is also the title given to the "head, tutor, or fellow" at Oxford College. The Jesuits wanted Don to join their great teaching order. He felt a calling no less noble and took on teaching as part of his mission as a leader in the Central Intelligence Agency in which he served as head of station in such important places as Rome and Tokyo but also as a mentor and coach to generations of younger officers and staff members.

If you know anything about Don Healey, you know that he taught all his life. He did so in special classes at universities in Florida, in courses in which he shared his great knowledge of international matters, especially of the Far East. I recall his wry, life-is-like-this-smile when, after teaching one Florida winter for the extension division of a northern Catholic college, he held up the embossed T-shirt that they gave him as compensation. He was expert at transforming such low moments of comic opera into high moments of human comedy. His keen Irish wit made life easier to take, making the unbearable bearable for the rest of us.

You may not know that Don's vocation of service and patriotism is first described in the Old Testament Book of Numbers: "The Lord said to Moses, 'Send men to spy out the land of Canaan'... So Moses sent them... and said to them, 'Go up there into the Negeb, and go up into the hill country, and see what the land is like, and whether the people who live in it are strong or weak, whether they are few or many, and whether the land they live in is good or bad, and whether the towns that they live in are unwalled or fortified'" (13:1, 3, 17–19).

And Don reconnoitered the world and became an expert at subtly finding out what kind of land it was and whether the people living there were strong or weak, few or many, and whether the country in which they lived were good or bad, open or fortified. If because of his friendship we are all enriched, because of his service to the United States we are also all more secure.

He maintained his skills even after retirement and could relieve people of information as skillfully as a pickpocket could remove their wallets. They never felt a thing. A few years ago the Healeys and the Kennedys were in Key West gazing at a ten-story-tall cruise ship moored a hundred yards away, smugly keeping its secrets. Don sauntered over casually, chatted briefly with a ship's officer at the gangplank and returned in a few moments with the origin, destination, number of passengers, itinerary, and incidental cargo—everything from the officer but his gold watch. He never felt a thing.

He never used the word *spy*, preferring *agent*, which refers to somebody who gets things done. That describes Don, of course but he nonetheless did like to wear a black T-shirt that proclaimed in red letters, DENY EVERYTHING. And the word *spy* is not without relevance, for it comes from the old French word *spek* that means "to watch, to catch sight of, to observe." In the Latin, *spex* describes "one who sees," and in the Greek *scopus*, "one who watches." Don Healey was a true observer, a man who could not only see but could see into men and events not as a harsh judge but as that understanding man who did not miss anything but never used any of it against you.

We are happy to be here this morning to remember Don, who even in the full glory of the eternity is true to his calling and is not only watching but watching out for all of us. Of course, eternity began on that night half a century ago in time when he told Maureen how to spell his name. And it continues in their love for each other and for their children—Brian, Dan, Lisa, and John—and for *their* children as well. As a man of the sea and the sun, Don looked into the depths of creation and entered the eternal every day. He was waved across the border between time and eternity without any need to show his passport. St. Peter knew that Don had nothing to declare but his goodness and his loving and understanding heart.

If you know anything about Don Healey, you know that he is not at rest but, much as at the cruise ship, is subtly relieving many historical figures, including St. Peter, Marco Polo, and Kublai Kahn, of information he has always wanted to find out about them. They don't feel a thing.

Don, the gentleman, the leader, the master, the one sent out to reconnoiter for the rest of us, God rest you, merry gentleman.

And if you know anything about Don Healey, you know that he is here, standing right next to me, with one hand on my elbow and the other adroitly relieving me of my manuscript. Stop now, he whispers in my ear, stop now because if you tell any more about me, it may all disappear.

Leave the politicians in the mud as Katrina purifies us

Hurricane Katrina has been compared with 9/11 as a sudden unexpected disaster.

It resembles the latter alright, but for deeper reasons than the surface ones cited by reporters, pundits, and the politicians who circled and cawed as wildly as birds of prey over the wasted city.

While people debated shooting looters, they might better have winged a few of these politicians who, like the con men selling phony building supplies to the stricken, looted the shattered human experience of the thousands of sorrowing and the dispossessed in order to gain points for themselves and demerits for their opponents.

Some preachers quickly spoke of 9/11 and Hurricane Katrina as events of biblical proportion. They quoted the creation story in the first chapter of Genesis in which "the spirit of God moved upon the face of the waters" and quickly turned the pages to the story of the deluge and God's deal to spare Noah and his just followers. It is not only bad theology but also a sacrilege to imagine Katrina as a modern instrument of God's wrath against a wayward people.

The hurricane is an aspect of the overall mystery of existence and its revelation as simple and pure as most of its victims. Search their hearts and you won't find much sin. There is no room for it midst the woe packed so tightly there by life itself.

The central revelation of Katrina is exactly that of 9/11: it allows us to see what is obscured by the fluttering pennants of *People Magazine* covers. The latter give us peeks at celebrities but never at real persons. Katrina allows us to see the goodness of non-celebrities, of the real persons all around us whom we mistakenly describe as ordinary.

Against the background images of celebrities such as Sean Penn baling out his sinking relief boat with a red plastic cup we saw the thousands of men and women patiently bearing the deluge, saving their families and what they could of their possessions, most of them not feeling sorry for themselves or trying to make heroes of themselves. In short, we saw the way good people take on every day with its uncertain mixture of suffering and surprise, of sadness and love.

We also witnessed good being done by ordinary people, much of it through the churches that do not need permission and do not ask people to fill out bureaucratic forms before they feed and clothe them. Now we can all answer that Last Judgment question, "When did you see me thirsty and give me to drink, when did you see me hungry and give me to eat?" We saw it in New Orleans done by people too busy giving their attention to others to strike poses in search of any for themselves.

The waters of Katrina washed through all our neighborhoods because water is a fundamental sacramental symbol. We are all born in a burst of water and we are made members of the faith by the waters of baptism. Water is the great symbol of our inner lives, of our true depths, of the unconscious reservoir of all the experience of all human beings.

So water is found in the Old Testament, as Joseph Campbell has pointed out, as the means by which the Jewish people passed into Egypt and the way that they escaped from their sojourn there. They entered Egypt through Joseph's going into a well that, although dry, is a water source. And they left Egypt by passing through the waters of the Red Sea. Here we find the great New Testament themes of baptism and of the fish symbol of the followers of Jesus.

Campbell asks a question that after Katrina we may put to ourselves: "Who comes out of the water? And who went into the water?" He tells us that the patriarchs went into the water but the people came out. Moses is not the hero, the people are.

We went into the water as we entered the dust clouds of 9/11, as individuals focused on our daily cares and sometimes even distracted by the questions about Brad and Angelina asked by silly magazines.

We are coming out of these waters that have covered all of us as a people. We are aware that our neighbors are more like us than unlike us, no matter the sound of their voices or the color of their eyes or skin. The destructive waters bear the simplest but dearest of human possessions. We recognize that even the simplest possession, such as a picture of parents and children, breaks our hearts because it speaks of our common longings and of that unmistakable human resemblance of members of the same family.

The waters of Katrina are filled with mud, as Egypt was thought to be by the Jews. But out of that mud emerged a new people. It is no accident that politicians are often called mudslingers. Those who understand the revelation of the event know that we are called to leave them behind and emerge from these waters as a new people.

Why do people leave flowers on street corners?

There are shrine-seekers and shrine-makers. The first often see things that aren't there while the second look unblinkingly at the harshness and loss that is always there someplace in life...

The first quickly respond to such alleged sightings as the reports a few months ago of images of the Virgin materializing on the stained walls along underground highways in Chicago.

Prompt municipal powerwashing soon erased that, along with the messages of graffiti artists and the slush swipes of a million cars. Still, flocking pilgrims claimed that, yes, they could still see the Virgin there.

Is this mysticism or monkey business? Do people find faith in these questionable settings?

This brings us to the second group, composed of men and women intuitively guided to holy places that have not yet made the six o'clock news or the travel guides.

These people bring faith, tested in a thousand ways by loss and disappointment, with them. They bear the modern-day counterpart of the Bible's mustard seed of faith that moves mountains.

These are the Eucharists of Ordinary Time through which people who never get their names in the paper write large on the empty slates of everyday places, transforming them and making them sacred through the power of their honest hopes and prayers. Their pilgrimages are tributes to belief itself.

Flashy popular magazines document how the shallow of this world are drawn to the magnets of Nice, Malibu, and other places that are famous, as the old line goes, for being famous. These places are so infected by time—why do you think celebrities wear big watches?—that their spas don't spout healing waters and the management never mentions the eternal. The idea of the eternal may unsettle the famous but does not trouble ordinary people at all.

Ordinary people mark sacred places with clutches of flowers and wind-bent candles, proclaiming as explorers do new lands that these places belong to us, to the human family that may never sample sometime celebrity but drinks deeply every day from the cup of joy and sorrow.

Ordinary people speak to and for all of us when they spontaneously make a street corner sacred with their simple gifts of blossoms and flickering light. They place them at intersections where accidents have happened, on the sea after a ship has gone down, or everywhere in cities like hurricane-stricken New Orleans.

These are not tributes to death or to the evangelical terrorists who preach that the end is near. These gifts are not warnings that we should all repent in the hills.

These plain offerings certify these locations as sacred, not because death took place at them but because life filled them to overflowing, that here, in this place, men and women were alive enough to love each other and so break forever the chains with which time grappled them.

Only lovers brave enough to take on the hazards of time itself make places sacred. The floral pieces, often as homemade as real love itself, tell us that here, in this place, we are in touch with the eternal energy of love. It is outside time and, pausing to honor those who lived and died here, we find ourselves renewed instead.

The Seasons of 2006

Pope's encyclical helps heal sex abuse crisis

Blessed Pope John XXIII explained that he convened Vatican Council II in order to open some windows and let fresh air into a church long closed off from the world...

Through his first encyclical, "God is Love," Pope Benedict XVI does virtually the same thing. Writing about the mystery of God's love for us and our love for each other, he describes *eros* as a healthy component of human experience. He thereby opens a long-sealed window in official Catholicism in which anything concerning sex has been left to molder too long in the dark.

By letting in sunlight and fresh air he has also done more than all the resolutions, apologies, or even lawsuits have done to heal the wounds that Catholics have suffered in general because of distorted teachings on sexuality and those suffered in particular by victims of sex abuse by members of the clergy.

Unlike many church leaders who seem to blush and stammer when they speak of anything sexual, Benedict addresses the subject like a pastor who has heard the confessions of the whole world and never given a harsh penance to anybody.

The long-term rejection of the basic healthiness of eros and human sexuality by the official church led to an official embarrassment with these elements that had to be smuggled into human experience and made acceptable only for the purpose of continuing the human race.

This view also divided human personality into good and bad parts—the soul and the body, the spirit and the flesh—and made life into an unending border war between them. This corruption of the fundamental Christian outlook made human beings into an insoluble mystery to themselves, making them feel guilty for being healthy human beings with sexual feelings.

That tragic misreading of human nature contributed to an imbalance in certain Catholic environments that caused great suffering for many ordinary Catholics as they tried to understand their sexuality that had been made to seem out of synchronization with the pursuit of holiness.

Many good people experienced difficulty maturing in Catholic cultures that emphasized the negative nature of sexuality. We will one day understand better how they became victims of attitudes that compromised their growth and led them to choose lives of celibacy and complete chastity that they did not understand and whose pressures they could not endure.

Sexual abusers are not desperate fiends or calculating seducers but are often people who were first victims of a counterfeit of Catholicism whose institutions often unknowingly publicly rewarded them for rejecting sexual experience through promises that they could not privately sustain.

The sex abuse crisis is not caused, as some now say, solely by homosexuals. It is rather the bitter outcome of an era in which the healthy nature of sexuality was compromised by mistaken notions about human personality. People did not enter the priesthood or religious life to become sexual abusers; they found themselves confounded by a sexuality they did not understand and to which they gave stumbling and tragic expression.

The pope observes that "it is neither the spirit alone nor the body alone that loves: it is man, the person, a unified creature composed of body and soul, who loves. Only when both dimensions are truly united, does man attain his full stature. Only then is love—*eros*—able to mature and attain its authentic grandeur."

By the healthy way that Pope Benedict XVI discusses eros, sexuality, and human love in this encyclical he makes it possible for these sexual wounds to heal in the only way that they ever do, from the inside.

The Easter mystery, daylight saving time, spring fever, and spring training

Everybody knows the longing that comes with the returning light that we call spring fever. It fills us with a yearning that we cannot quite name and inspires daydreaming about destinations so vague that FedEx can't find them...

And we all know that last year Easter was celebrated a week before Daylight Saving Time arrived and this year it comes two weeks after we trade off an hour of shadowed sleep to gain an hour of extended light.

Spring fever has a long history, but Daylight Saving Time started only during World War I for a practical American reason—to save energy by reducing the need for artificial light. Now we claim to enjoy it for another trademark American purpose—to stretch the day for leisure activity.

These familiar rationales cannot, however, hide or explain away the Easter mystery of light and shadow that Daylight Saving Time symbolizes and that spring fever expresses. They are aspects of the same profound spiritual mystery of our existence, the religious mystery that we all experience even if we call it by another name or cannot name it at all.

Easter, like Passover, is set at the intersection of shadow and light that occurs at the vernal equinox when the hours of the day and the night are equal. At that moment the moon, which casts off its shadow as the symbol of rebirth, gazes across the heavens at the sun that is the source of its renewed light.

We feel the pull of life in the spring fever that rises in us as the sap in the reawakened trees does. We turn our faces as the flowers do theirs into nourishing sunlight. We respond to nature's rhythms, to this mystery of light and shadow that mantles all creation at this season.

On the conscious level, the first advocates of Daylight Saving Time thought they were resetting the clocks to accommodate commerce. On the unconscious level, however, they were acknowledging the mystery of the tension between the sun and the moon that invades our bones as silently as radiation. We feel it in our longing to break free of the frame of time and lay hold of eternity.

We are engaged with this mystery whenever we hurry our steps as we glance at our watches or whenever we feel the difference between playing or watching a basketball or football game dominated by the clock and a baseball game that is not. Football and basketball symbolize time's urgencies because they are played as the shadows of winter begin to gather and then overtake us. No wonder coaches emphasize the importance of "managing the clock," "time-outs," and the "sudden death" of "overtime." These games belong to the moon that symbolizes time and they recapitulate the mystery of time's inexorable demands on us.

Such phrases are unknown in baseball, whose players are called the boys of summer. It begins with spring training and, free of time's constraints, belongs to the sun that symbolizes eternity. It resists time as it is played past summer's peak and remains timeless. The mystery of the World Series is not found in who wins but in the lengthened shadows that the slanting sun casts across the playing field and us as well. "Wait until next year," that phrase that seems a muttered grumble after loss, is a cry of human longing for resurrection and new life after death.

We are engaged every day with symbols of the Easter mystery of throwing off the moon shadows of time to bathe in the sunlight of eternity. All time's burdens are reported every day. Our great losses and small misunderstandings cluster with every misery the world has ever known on the moon's cratered and shadowed surface. *When*, we ask in different ways, will the eternal sun break time's grip and flood us with the light of new life?

But fainter echoes of the Easter mystery, of the interplay of shadows and light, are easy to find. The *Wall Street Journal* tells of railroads adding 6 AM commuter trains because "more U.S. households are starting their days before dawn." Energy suppliers note that the greatest "uptick in usage is between the hours of 5 AM and 7 AM." CNN and CNBC respond by scheduling their morning shows an hour earlier. The *New York Times* tells of the Manhattan realtor who is trying to outwit time by showing properties and closing deals all night long.

That story has less to do with a midnight salesman than us and our daily Easter mystery of seeking the light of resurrection and new life every day of our lives.

Better to find its appeal than to ban Da Vinci Code

*Republican senators have now withdrawn their modified Tooth Fairy
Plan to leave a $100 gasoline allotment under every American's pillow.
That leaves organized religion, eager to ban, burn, or bankrupt the
soon-to-open movie of* The Da Vinci Code *in sole possession of the
dumbest idea of the season...*

It may be true to say that "you can't make up" the book's plot of Jesus'
fathering a child with Mary Magdalene and that the Holy Grail is not a
chalice but their bloodline—and their descendants now live—where
else?—in France and that the church has covered all this up along with
the female role in the origins of Christianity.

But, of course, novelist Dan Brown did make all this up. That is
what fiction writers do, as Andrew Greeley knows better than most
reviewers. He writes that the *Code* is "fast-paced, intricately plotted...
deserves to be...[a] bestseller...[and] practically all of it is fantasy"
(*National Catholic Reporter*, October 3, 2003).

Conservative religious groups, ever the avant garde in defending
the concrete and literal meaning of the scriptures, have published
books, set up web sites, and deployed designated heavy theological hit-
ters to decry the "errors" in Dan Brown's novel and to criticize Brown
himself as if he were an adjutant to the anti-Christ.

Now that the movie is opening, sonorous Catholic voices are being
raised, the loudest of which may be that of Tarcisio Cardinal Bertone,
the archbishop of Genoa, who claims that *The Da Vinci Code* is part of
a plot to build "a castle of lies" to negate the spiritual benefits of the
Vatican's Jubilee Year 2000 celebrations. "Don't read it," he urges "and
don't buy it."

Vatican-based Francis Cardinal Arinze urges people to sue those responsible for the book's attacks on Catholicism. Bertone's timing is bad, since twenty-five million copies of the *Code* have already been published in forty-two languages. Before filing a suit, Arinze should remember that the last people to take Dan Brown to court lost and must now pay $2.4 million of the publisher's legal bill.

That this frenzy of self-righteousness will sell more books and movie tickets may not discourage other church officials from condemning first and asking questions later. Thoughtful bishops, however, will worry less about the novel's inaccuracies and more about why it is that the book has touched a resonant chord in so many Catholic readers.

Great mythic themes cannot be fully disguised or blunted, no matter how they are appropriated or distended to serve the imaginative needs of any author. The best example may be a song whose words may be trite but whose melody transmits a message about love or loss that touches people deeply and sticks with them for life.

This explains why this book can be "beach reading" on the surface level and a story for all seasons on another. Indeed, Brown, throwing everything into boiling plot, may not have realized how some of his motifs would affect readers. We all respond when somebody—a writer, an artist, a filmmaker—expresses symbolically what we feel but have not been able to put into words for ourselves.

Perhaps *The Da Vinci Code*, like the songs of medieval troubadours that made people aware of romantic love, expresses out loud subjects that have roiled in the unconscious of good Catholics for a long time.

One of these is the subjugation that women have experienced in the practical order of authority and power in the bureaucratic display of the Catholic Church. That this bureaucracy supposedly covered up the love relationship of Jesus and Mary Magdalene is nonsense. Nonetheless it is a powerful device that expresses the control that church officials have exercised over the sexual lives of Catholics, making millions of them feel guilty just for being normal, healthy human beings.

The sex abuse crisis among church personnel exploded only after this book was published. That crisis should restrain high officials from condemning books with powerful themes dealing with sex and gender when these are the elements of this still unresolved and painful crisis that officials are still trying to control or cover up.

Good Catholics can be trusted to sift the gold from the sand in this much maligned book/movie. *The Da Vinci Code* reminds good Catholics that the Vatican bureaucracy is to the church, the mystery of the People of God, what the crumpled architect's drawings are to the glories of Chartres Cathedral.

Religious mystery not in 666 but in Whitney and Laura

The movie version of The Da Vinci Code *came in like a low tide of religiosity followed almost immediately by the low grade tsunami of mystical prediction that the biblical 666 beast was coming on 6/6/06. Both events proved too shallow for a hurried baptism, much less total immersion in genuine religious mystery...*

Indeed, neither the *Code* nor *666* has anything to do with religious mystery. That is found only in the Deep, in the waters that so tragically blurred the identities of two college students who were mistaken, one for the other even by their families, after a tragic Midwestern automobile accident at the end of April.

According to *USA Today* (June 2, 2006), Whitney Cerak, 19, and Laura VanRyn, 22, "looked remarkably alike," so that after a tractor trailer slammed into the car in which they were passengers, the coroner confused Laura who died with Whitney who lived, misinforming their families, plunging Whitney's into grieving and mourning and Laura's into waiting and praying for her recovery.

Only last week, while the synthetic mysteries of *The Da Vinci Code* and the biblical beast scuffed across our consciousness like paper scraps on a midnight street, the stark and unforgiving character of religious mystery challenged us to look it in the eye and not look away.

Only last week, after believing that they had buried her after a funeral attended by fourteen hundred friends and neighbors, the Ceraks learned that their daughter had lived and lay in a comatose state in a hospital. At the same moment the Van Ryns were told that the girl swathed in bandages with whom they had kept prayerful vigil since the end of April was not their daughter, Laura, but her friend Whitney.

The stories of this tragedy, one of crushing disappointment, the other of suddenly restored hope, are difficult to read. Everybody, from the coroner who resigned after learning of his error, to stunned family and friends ask why and how such a case of mistaken identity could have occurred. So great is the burden of these families that we feel it at a distance and feel, too, for these parents who seem to be laden like scapegoats with all the woes of our time and driven into a wilderness too bleak for us to contemplate.

Unlike cheap fiction and *faux* doomsday prophecy, this story is not about a secret code or an external personification of evil. This tragedy tells us there is no secret about religious mystery, that, in fact, it happens to ordinary people in broad daylight all the time. It also takes the ridiculous romance out of a creature arriving from the netherworld to force upon us the mistakes and bad choices that we make for ourselves all the time.

This is a harrowing narrative about ordinary people, typical Americans out of the heartland, suddenly swept up into pain that can barely be contemplated and never explained. Yet it carries echoes of biblical scenes in which a dead daughter is restored to her grieving mother, of another mother who witnesses the death of her only child, of the long-suffering and injustice that are the lot of good people, and of the depth of belief that they draw on when we do not know how to comfort them.

This tragedy carries within it all America's longing and confusion about identity, about who we are and what it means to be a person. In a year in which a number of writers, for example, have stolen their words from others and invented lives and identities to match the need for fame and power, this terrible mystery reminds us of the sacredness and singularity of our own personalities, of our calling to be ourselves even at the risk of being caught up in tragedies like this one.

This is religious mystery in its most profound sense, because it gives the lie to the panorama of phoniness known as reality television that has nothing to do with reality or genuine persons at all.

This is religious mystery that challenges the sadly ironic magazine titles *People* and *US*, for their pages have little to do with real people and those who gaze out of them are not like us. But being a person, a part of a real PEOPLE, being one of US, is beyond Britney, Angelina, and their clones. Reality and religious mystery are being lived out before our eyes by people we did not know at all until this week, the Cerak and VanRyn families. They are the real people, they are the ones like us.

The shuttle reveals more than TV Book of Revelation

Television topped itself this past weekend by an exposition of self-conscious and superficial religious mystery on Sunday night and a report of un-self-conscious and profound religious mystery on Monday morning...

The National Geographic Society, famous for its yellow covered magazine, veered perilously close to yellow journalism with its exploration of what it termed the "secrets" of the biblical Book of Revelation (*National Geographic*, May 2006). Any organization that features Tim LaHaye, author of an endless series of "Left Behind" books about an ever ending planet, as a commentator on humanity's chances for being saved is in the entertainment rather than the educational business.

The end of the world is foretold by the Book of Revelation, Mr. LaHaye believes, so we had better buy tickets from him for the last plane out, because he sees "no hope for the unsaved after this life." He, of course, is only one of the many salvation hucksters who believe that the Book of Revelation is a kind of theological Global Positioning System through which we locate ourselves in the battles, fires, and natural disasters that literally fulfill its presumed prophecies.

The Book of Revelation is also called the Book of the Apocalypse, accepted by many as a kind of divine dictation about the world's woes given to St. John who put it all down as a kind of coming attractions of the vengeance God would take on sinners before lowering the curtain on civilization.

Nobody would build roller coasters or make horror movies if Americans did not enjoy being scared in small doses, so there is no surprise in their enjoying a minor shiver at such distortions of the scriptures and the meaning of religion—especially when the television

314

program's digital wizardry dramatizes some of LaHaye's "whacko" scenarios about the disasters soon to be visited upon sinners, in short, us. This combination paint ball, wrestling, and video game rendition of the judgment already finalized on us trivializes both belief and believers.

The latter were better served by television's coverage of the return of the space shuttle less than twenty-four hours later. This voyage and return shifted our eyes from the earth so soon to be set afire by a judgmental God to the heavens and the wonder of our far-from-finished, much less finally judged, human journey.

Our true experience of religion involves mystery but not mystification. True religion does not solve or explain the mystery of our existence. It allows us to experience the mystery that is found, if it is to be found at all, when we enter everyday events rather than when we are ejected from them by a distant and easily displeased God.

The words *Mystery*, *Apocalypse*, and *Revelation* have a meaning in common. They refer to an "unveiling" rather than an indictment, an opening rather than access denied to the wonder of life, a way of entering our human sorrows rather than a punishment for our human shortfalls.

We can't get anywhere by the flight path of fear filed by Mr. LaHaye, who warns that if we don't get on board his Salvation Spaceship we will all be "left behind." We already had seats with the crew members of the shuttle, our surrogates in exploring the vastness of creation and of our calling to be at home in it.

The shuttle is the religious symbol of our century, for on its every venture it validates the truth that pseudo-prophets like LaHaye deny: The earth is not off course, a condemned star wobbling toward extinction. The blue and green earth is in the heavens, participating in the unity of the universe and reminding us of our own unity.

One astronaut was struck with wonder on our behalf when at one moment he could see the sun, the symbol of eternity, and the moon, the symbol of time. That revelation has to do not with the end of the world but with our discovery of the world where we may live on the often chilly plains of time but are warmed and nourished daily by the eternal sun.

Seminary guidelines emphasize celibacy over service

America's Catholic bishops have formally released their new guidelines for seminary training. The ninety-eight-page Program of Priestly Formation has been issued by the United States Conference of Catholic Bishops after being approved by the Vatican.

Do these regulations represent the bishops' perception of and solution to the sex abuse scandal that engulfed the church over five years ago? If so, church leaders apparently believe that a lack of celibacy caused the crisis and that more celibacy will cure it. Indeed, they give the impression that prime purpose of seminaries is to preserve celibacy and the chief work of the priest is to be celibate. What were they thinking?

The bishops now propose to ban any applicant who has been involved in the sexual abuse of a minor or shows evidence of sexual attraction to children. Since the first is a crime and the second is common sense, the question is, "Didn't you hierarchs know this before?"

Where, one wonders, did they decide that further sexual scandals will be averted if seminaries are made into training camps for the Celibacy Olympics in which priests fulfill themselves and find salvation by winning the gold medal?

The guidelines claim that "thresholds pertaining to sexuality serve as the foundation for living a lifelong commitment to healthy, chaste celibacy." Monsignor Edward J. Burns, executive director of the bishops' Secretariat for Vocations and Priestly Formation, notes that "this edition brings a higher level of integration of chaste, celibate living in all dimensions of priestly life."

Candidates must "give evidence that they have been celibate for at least two years." Exactly how would anybody ever do that anyway? Each seminary must now have a "coordinated and multifaceted program," including regular psychological evaluations, yearly conferences, and "clear and prudent guidelines." These are not to produce good pastors, which is why you might think seminaries exist. They are designed to help "seminarians adopt skills for celibate living." If celibate living is the goal, they should skip the theology and canon law and teach sewing, cooking, Homemaking 101, and survival skills.

The document also follows the Vatican guidelines to bar homosexuals from the priesthood. Let us skip the present tortured thinking on this subject because, in fact, we have many wonderful priests who are homosexual and who understand that the essence of pastoral work is to establish healthy and life-giving relationships with their people.

The best indicator of good seminary candidates is whether they can forge healthy relationships with other persons. This is not necessarily linked to celibacy yet remains the best test of a person's soundness to take on the demanding work of being a priest. Selection processes and seminary training should be ordered primarily to this goal.

A priest's ability to live a celibate life depends on and is expressed through the way he relates to those he serves. This document threatens to make more of celibacy than of the service for which it is supposedly designed. Celibacy is a not a sacrament but a "discipline" of the church. Making celibacy the center of seminary training seems to place that discipline above the first and greatest commandment of loving our neighbors.

To place celibacy, a subject about which church officials allow no discussion or research at this time, as the unquestioned prime virtue of the priesthood may serve not to prevent but rather unknowingly to invite future sexual abuse problems among the clergy. Approving men who can make healthy relationships of service and helping them to deepen their capacity for such intimacy is the best and probably the only guarantee against future sex abuse scandals.

Loaves and fishes gospel more about compassion than feeding

When the story of the miracle of the loaves and fishes is read in Catholic and many other Christian churches, earnest preachers emphasize the transformation of five loaves and a few fish into rations for five thousand with plenty of leftovers. But is there another story line here that explains why we sometimes experience this long ago miracle in our own lives?...

This reading is familiar not because, in different settings, we have all had the same experience. In this gospel story the problem is not that the crowd lacks food but that it is short on spiritual insight. The point of the story is less nutrition than compassion.

St. Matthew's Gospel makes Jesus' motivation clear. Looking at the hungry people who have followed him, Jesus says, "My heart is moved with pity for the crowd."

We can also wonder about the reaction of the crowd. Did they acclaim Jesus as the prophet for whom they had been waiting because he multiplied external food or because he enlarged their inner spiritual view of each other?

Did Jesus' compassion for them so move them that they experienced the change of heart essential to any spiritual growth so that, nourished by him, they were satisfied by just a taste of the tiny portions available?

Or did something else happen to them? Keeping to themselves even in a big group, had they also kept food for themselves, unwilling to share it with others until Jesus moved them to compassion so that they shared their supplies with each other?

By his manner and his words Jesus opened the eyes of the crowd before he filled their stomachs. What was the sudden spiritual insight

318

that enabled these men and women to look at each other in a new way? Feeling the compassion of Jesus, they felt compassion for one another. They grasped that just as they all felt the same hunger so they also felt the same sorrows.

We have all been in crowds whose members keep to themselves. Think of the last time you were at an airport. As travelers we all carry the same brand of sorrow in our baggage. It never sets off the metal detectors or arouses the suspicion of security guards.

You don't have to declare it to the customs agent.

Nobody, we think, even suspects the troubles we've had and we usually dread the possibility that, if we lower our guard, fellow passengers will tell us their troubles all the way to our destination. So we defend against that, as did the members of the crowd on that hillside, keen-eyed for their hidden food but blind to each other's woes.

Jesus understands that, like everyone in that crowd on the hillside, all of us in the security line or on the airplane carry exactly the same garden variety sorrows, of losses and misunderstandings, of broken hearts and longing for love. We conceal these as we superficially reveal ourselves at airports, removing our shoes and jackets, carelessly tossing the trinkets that whisper of somebody's love for us into an unloved tray, allowing a guard with a pirate's eye to paw through our bag as if it were a treasure chest, passing together through a miniature Last Judgment without noticing, except for an occasional shared smile, how much we are alike.

The gospel story resonates on the plane where there may be a few bags of peanuts but nothing like five barley loaves and a couple of fish to share with the crowd. We keep mostly to ourselves, following the pilot's instructions to fasten our seat belts and to stay in our own cabin. Most of the time we regard each other as fellow detainees or fellow oarsmen on the galleys and do not sense how much our battered hearts resemble each other.

The miracle of the loaves and fishes happens every time we see, better than the airport x-ray, the mixed inventory of grief and joy, discouragement and hope, that we are all carrying. It also occurs whenever we pause to look at the television images of people all over the world and realize that our common sorrow connects us all. The real reason why Jesus left the hillside was only in part to avoid the crowd's making him a king. He taught them, as he does us, how to work this miracle of multiplying nourishment by recognizing and bearing each other's sorrow and leaves us on our own to repeat it every day.